ORACLE SQL &
PL/SQL GOLDEN DIARY

ON

Refactoring, Interoperability of Versions

&

Integration of related concepts

for

High Performance

By

Asim Chowdhury, Technical Architect & Designer

Dedication

This book is dedicated to LORD Krishna and MAA Anandamayee for THE divine blessings

PREFACE

I have three intentions behind writing the book.
- ➤ Intention 1: Interoperability among database versions
- ➤ Intention 2: Integration of related concepts for performance
- ➤ Intention 3: Creation of Golden Diary in a nutshell by practical examples

These intentions have arisen based on the burning need of database users I have come across throughout my career with roles like PL/SQL developers , Database Administrators, Designers, Data analysts, Performance tuning analysts, Architects, Students, Professors, Interviewees and any DBMS enthusiast or aspirant for oracle certification. Some of these had extensive experience in what they do and have influenced me writing this book.

This book will act as a reference guide for learning some very complicated concepts in a simple but precise way which are discussed through various case studies. This will give food for thought while devising mechanism for best possible approach for a database solution given the circumstances.

You will learn

- Comparative analysis of database features and their usages across Oracle versions

- Learn to derive alternate approach for a functionality in different releases of database

- Learn related concepts associated with specific challenge

- Learn to choose the best approach from the set of related concepts to achieve best result

- Familiarize yourself with all concepts with real life example in a nutshell

- Learn how to be smart with database and surprise your colleague and boss by your solution

The audience of this book would like to cover multiple versions of Oracle and the features it offers. Seeking the best approach for a challenge has not been easy in past as it required a large investment of time and effort to go through the vast amount of documentation. This 270 pages book facilitates that investment, by exploring and churning the vast archives of oracle documentation and producing the output in a nutshell which otherwise readers would need to spend time on. Will appreciate if you can give your feedback in amazon, createspace or any online portal or reach me author.asim@gmail.com

-Author

ACKNOWLEDGEMENT

I would like to thank Stéphane Faroult (author of many Oracle books) who has been guiding me throughout the process. I am inspired by Tom Kyte (man behind asktom.com), Richard Foote (Oracle index specialist), Burleson consulting, Greg Doench (Pearson USA), Steven Feuerstein, I am indebted a lot to them.

My thanks go to Anish Joseph, Nagarjuna Kommineni, Amit Kumar, Abhisek Kumar, Shakti panday, Vishal Jain,Amit Joshi, Amit Chitnis, Avinash Chinchwadkar, Mohsin Hashmi, Venkat, Baskar, Ranjith, Pravin, Ashok, Vikas, Rashni, Swapan, Sumanta, Sunny, Bumba, Rusa, Swastik and all my colleagues, family and friends from for their encouraging words. Apologies for not being able to mention the many other names.

My thanks go to my Father Chittaranjan Chowdhury and mother Shephali Chowdhury who taught me how to be simple but think big.

Also my thanks go to my father in-law R.N. Bhui and mother in-law Jharna Bhui for their constant encouragement.

My thanks go to my uncle Ajoy Kar (Professor of Heriot Watt University, Edinburgh) for his encouragement of my work.

My thanks go to my wife Sutapa Chowdhury who sacrificed her successful career in IT industry to take care of our lovely Aditi and give me more space to concentrate on the work for this book. My wife is my guiding star.

My biggest thanks go to my little daughter Aditi Chowdhury who sacrificed her playtime with me because of my busy involvement with this book, she also constantly asked about the progress and her simple enquiries touched a chord in such a way that it gave me the boost I needed to finish the gigantic task of writing this book.

My deep gratitude to Maa Anandamayee for her divine blessings.

And finally my thanks go to GOD for His constant blessings without which it is impossible to pursue this task.

-Author

Table of Contents:

Chapter 1: Introduction with concepts (55 pages) --19

Create function based index on NVL function

Usage of Distinct to reduce processing time of a query
Column list ordering issue in a table and solution
What is Statistics?
Function statistics and use
Extended statistics and use
Explicitly generated extended statistics
Implicitly generated extended statistics
Ways to refactor code
Compress for OLTP
Space regained by compression
Index compression (Rebuild/Create)
Advanced Index compression in 12c
Database server
Normalization
1NF
2NF
3NF
Objective of normalization
Introduction of limited redundancy for performance
FOR UPDATE issue
FOR UPDATE SKIP LOCKED
DDL_LOCK_TIMEOUT
Definition
CONNECT BY PRIOR
START WITH
Sorting using "Order siblings by"
Break rows into column
Get last 7 days
New record generation using connect by
Example to find all possible bus routes to reach from point A to point E
CONNECT_BY_ROOT
SYS_CONNECT_BY_PATH
NOCYCLE
SGA
UGA
PGA
Calculate how much PGA and UGA memory is used

Convert number into words
Day of a month
First day of a month
Last day of a month
Working week dates for a week
Number of days between two dates
Get user db information of a system using sys_context?
Showing system privileges
Get the DDL for a table
Get object privileges
Setting the current schema
Resizing tablespace
Current size of database
Size occupied by data in the database
Space left in database
Size occupied by data by one schema
Definition of Cursor
Why Cursor should be closed
Solution for invalid cursor error
Solution for fetch out of sequence error
ROWID perform better than primary key in cursor "FOR LOOP" example
For update statement in Cursor select
Definition of Cursor variable
Strongly typed Cursor variable
Weakly typed Cursor variable
Built in cursor variable SYS_REFCURSOR
Restriction of using cursor variable in package spec
Few notable points about cursor variable
Definition of cursor expressions
How it works with and without cursor expression
Defining PL/SQL records
Referencing PL/SQL records
Few notable points about record
Defining PL/SQL INDEX BY table
Referencing PL/SQL index by table
Few notable points about index by tables
Defining Nested table
Referencing PL/SQL nested table
Difference between index by and nested table
Initialization and extension of nested table
Resolution of uninitialized collection error with and without bulk collect

Avoid sorting Using WHERE clause
Avoid sorting using oracle hints
Few notable points on elimination of sorting
Internal data type conversion and optimizer ignore index
Improper datatype and incorrect ordering
Correct order (Without order by clause) using proper datatype

Defining Index only scan
Few notable points on index only scan
Case study to improve performance manifold by index only scan and deterministic function
Primary key association with unique index
Primary key association with unique or non-unique index
Associate primary key with different index
Comparative analysis of primary key with UNIQUE index and NON-UNIQUE index
Rebuilding of index online and offline mode
When index is required
Avoidance of index

Chapter 3: Analytical query and Inter-row Pattern matching (28 pages) ------------------96

Defining Pattern
Examples of real life scenarios
Finding "W" shape pattern in stock price using 12c "MATCH_RECOGNISE" clause
Defining Pivot
Solution to convert rows into columns using PIVOT in 11g
Solution to convert rows into columns pre 11g
Solution to convert row into column in 11g without PIVOT keyword
String broken to display as multiple columns
String broken to display as multiple rows
Find colour pattern prior to 12c Solution
Find colour pattern in 12c Solution
Find same consecutive flag prior to 12c Solution
Find same consecutive flag in 12c Solution
Rank
Dense_rank
Row_number
Lead
Lag

"As of scn" approach

Start a group
Assigning table to the group
Enable flashback for the group
Disable flashback for the group
Remove certain table from the group
Drop the group from DB
Puzzle 1: AS OF TIMESTAMP clause it does not give data for the timestamp
Puzzle 2: AS OF SCN clause does not give data for the timestamp
Puzzle 3: AS OF TIMESTAMP clause get the column even if the column does not exist
Puzzle 4: flashback version query fail when it is run in different time

Chapter 5: Sub query factoring using WITH clause (12 pages)

Sub query factoring
Comparative analysis of WITH clause and conventional approach
All columns pivoting
Using Pivot
Using normal subquery:
Using multiple WITH clause
Inlining function/procedure from sql select
Inlining function/procedure from PL/SQL
"WITH_PLSQL" hint for select and update to eliminate error "unsupported use of WITH clause"
Restriction on using WITH clause from sqldeveloper
Comparative study of calling package constant from sql select in 12c and prior to 12c
Introduction of pragma UDF
Comparative study using "WITH CLAUSE", "PRAGMA UDF"
Restriction of Pragma UDF

Chapter 6: Integration of similar concepts (28 pages)

Caching/pinning object in general buffer cache
Caching/pinning object in keep buffer cache
Caching/pinning object in general buffer cache
Caching/pinning object in the In-memory Column-store
Example how to configure In-memory Column-store

Example how to use IM-COLUMN store
Scenario where IM column store is good or bad

Defining result-cached function
Defining deterministic function
Defining PL/SQL collection
Comparative analysis with examples
Restriction on using function result cache

Defining oracle user cache
Comparative analysis with example

Defining correlated update
Different approaches to update data
Correlated subquery
Example using correlated subquery
Example using LATERAL keyword in 12c
Example using inline view
Example using normal subquery
Case study with and without LATERAL keyword

Example using NOT IN method
Example using MINUS method
Example using JOIN method
Example using NOT EXISTS method
Few notable points about the usage

Example using nested loop join
Example using hash join
Example using parallelism
Example using multi-threading
Comparative analysis

Filtering data using "WHERE" clause
Filtering data using "HAVING" clause

Example using IN method
Example using EXISTS method
Example using DISTINCT method
How to avoid DISTINCT

Performance using IN method
Performance using INTERSECT method
Performance using JOIN method

Comparative analysis of Materialized view and Result cache

Chapter 8: Generic know how on Oracle PL/SQL for developer (27 Pages) ------219

Chapter 9: Generic know how on oracle administration for developer and dba (30 Pages) ---252

Setting sql trace
Finding trace file name
Convert trace file into txt file using TKPROF

Defining Case insensitive unique constraint
Solution 1: Using Virtual column
Solution 2: Using function based index
Defining ORA_ROWSCN
Ora_rowscn at **Block level (default)**
Ora_rowscn at **Row level**
Getting number of blocks occupied by a table
Getting number of rows associated with a block
Getting all the rows associated with a block
Use of ORA_ROWSCN on resolving LOST UPDATE

Chapter 1: Introduction with concepts (55 pages)

Here in this chapter we will discuss all the relevant concepts before we delve into practical example in subsequent chapters.

Concepts 1: SQL definition
Concepts 2: Oracle constraints
Concepts 3: SQL JOINS, Oracle JOIN methods and SET OPERATORS
Concepts 4: SQL Functions and regular expression
Concepts 5: Fast full index scan
Concepts 6: Index JOIN scan
Concepts 7: Indexing on null column rows
Concepts 8: Proper Usage of DISTINCT and column list ordering for insert
Concepts 9: SQL optimization and different type of Statistics
Concepts 10: Table compression/Index compression in 12c
Concepts 11: Partition pruning
Concepts 12: Context switch
Concepts 13: Database server and normalization
Concepts 14: Oracle SKIP LOCKED and DDL_LOCK_TIMEOUT in 11g
Concepts 15: Index usage with LIKE operator
Concepts 16: Materialized view
Concepts 17: Hierarchical Query
Concepts 18: SGA, UGA and PGA
Concepts 19: Useful queries
Concepts 20: PL/SQL Compiler
Concepts 21: PL/SQL optimizer
Concepts 22: PL/SQL Cursor
Concepts 23: Cursor variable
Concepts 24: Cursor expressions
Concepts 25: PL/SQL RECORD
Concepts 26: PL/SQL INDEX by Table
Concepts 27: PL/SQL nested Table
Concepts 28: VARRAY
Concepts 29: Exception handling
Concepts 30: Native dynamic SQL and Bulk binding
Concepts 31: STORED SUBPROGRAM
Concepts 32: DEFINER/INVOKER rights and remote dependencies
Concepts 33: Trigger
Concepts 34: Wrapping PL/SQL code, its limitation and solution to resolve in 11g
Concepts 35: PL/SQL WARNINGS
Concepts 36: CONDITIONAL COMPILATION and dynamic COMMIT

Concepts 1: SQL definition

Here we will discuss categorization of SQL.

SQL (Structured Query Language) is a means to communicate with a relational database by storing, modifying and retrieving data from RDBMS. It can be categorized as below:

DDL (Data Definition Language): This enables the user to create or restructure database objects like TABLE/INDEX/TYPE/VIEW etc. E.g. CREATE, ALTER, DROP, TRUNCATE

DML (Data Modification Language): This enables the user to manipulate data within the objects of a database. E.g. INSERT, UPDATE, DELETE, SELECT (as SELECT also generates redo). The "SELECT" statement is also known as DQL (Data Query Language) command.

DCL (Data Control Language): This enables the user to control access to data by means of privileges within a database. E.g. GRANT, REVOKE

TCL (Transaction Control Language): This enables the user to manage database transactions. E.g. COMMIT, ROLLBACK, SAVEPOINT, SET TRANSACTION. For example refer Chapter 7 Tips 17: Un-interrupted database testing using SET TRANSACTION

Note: SQL commands/keywords <u>are not case-sensitive</u>.

Concepts 2: Oracle constraints

Here we will discuss how to maintain data integrity in a database.

Constraints are the rules in a database to maintain relationships between tables and to maintain data integrity.

Different types of constraint are:

Primary Key: Uniquely identifies each row in a table. You can have just **one primary key** in a table and the <u>primary key column is NOT NULL</u>. Primary key can be created in column level or table level.
If you create column level primary key then the primary key can be on just single column, however in table level you can have primary key <u>on one column or set of columns</u> as shown:
Column level:
```
CREATE TABLE pri_key_col_t
  (empid NUMBER PRIMARY KEY,
   ename VARCHAR2(30)
  );
```
Table level: Here also you have just one primary key but the primary key is based on two columns. So in table level only you can create composite primary key.
```
CREATE TABLE pri_key_tab_t
  (empid NUMBER,
   ename VARCHAR2(30),
   sal number(10,4),
   PRIMARY KEY(empid,ename)
  );
```

Unique Key: Uniquely identifies each row in a table. You can have <u>any number of unique keys</u> in a table and the <u>unique key column can be NULL</u>.

20

```
CREATE TABLE uni_key_tab_t
  (empid NUMBER,
   ename VARCHAR2(30) UNIQUE,
   sal number(10,4)
  );
```

Foreign Key: This constraint creates a relationship <u>between child and parent table</u>. This constraint is created in the child table and points to the Primary Key of the parent table.

```
CREATE TABLE parent_tab_t
  (deptid NUMBER PRIMARY KEY,
   dname VARCHAR2(30)
  );
CREATE TABLE child_tab_t
  (empid NUMBER PRIMARY KEY,
   ename VARCHAR2(30),
   sal number(10,4),
   deptid number,
   FOREIGN KEY(deptid) REFERENCES parent_tab_t(deptid) ON DELETE CASCADE
  );
```

Parent and child tables are linked by this column deptid

Child and parent tables are linked

So once the relationship is established you cannot insert incorrect deptid in child_tab_t because it will validate that deptid must be present in parent_tab_t. This is how integrity of data is maintained.

Check constraint: This ensures that all values in a column <u>satisfy a certain condition</u>.

```
CREATE TABLE check_tab_t
  (empid NUMBER PRIMARY KEY,
   ename VARCHAR2(30),
   sal number(10,4),
   deptid number,
   CHECK(sal>0)
  );
```
So this CHECK constraint will ensure you must insert "sal" greater than zero.

NOT NULL constraint: This ensures a column cannot be null.

```
CREATE TABLE not_null_tab_t
  (empid NUMBER PRIMARY KEY,
   ename VARCHAR2(30),
   sal number(10,4) NOT NULL,
   deptid number,
   CHECK(sal>0)
  );
```
So NOT NULL constraint will ensure you must provide some value for "sal" and cannot keep it NULL.

DEFAULT constraint: This provides a <u>default value for a column</u> when nothing is provided.

```
CREATE TABLE default_tab_t
  (empid NUMBER PRIMARY KEY,
   ename VARCHAR2(30),
   sal number(10,4) DEFAULT 1000,
   deptid number
  );
```
The DEFAULT constraint will ensure sal is set as 1000 when you do not insert sal value for a record.

Refer to Chapter 7 Tips 5, Tips 6 and Tips 7 regarding default value enhancement in 12c

Concepts 3: SQL JOINS, Oracle JOIN methods and SET OPERATORS

Here we will discuss correlation among Joins, Joins methods and set operator to relate one or more tables.

Joins are used to relate one or more tables. Joins are fundamental in SQL and are the most used operation in a relational database. In SQL there are different types of joins (e.g. in ANSI standard)

INNER JOIN: Return rows when there is a match in both the tables.
E.g.
```
SELECT a.*,b.* FROM emp a
INNER JOIN dept b
ON a.deptid=b.deptid;
```

NATURAL JOIN: Return rows when there is a match in both the tables. It is similar to INNER JOIN, the only difference is that it does not use the ON clause, the join is on all same named columns from both tables. So you must be careful when you use this join as it may produce undesired result because it joins not only the foreign key column but all the columns from both the tables if they have same name.
E.g.
```
SELECT a.*,b.* FROM emp a
NATURAL JOIN dept b;
```

LEFT OUTER JOIN: Return all rows from left table (**EMP**) even if there is no matching row in right table (**DEPT**).
E.g.
```
SELECT a.*,b.* FROM emp a
LEFT OUTER JOIN dept b
ON a.deptid=b.deptid;
```

RIGHT OUTER JOIN: Return all rows from right table (**DEPT**) even if there is no matching row in left table (**EMP**).
E.g.
```
SELECT a.*,b.* FROM emp a
RIGHT OUTER JOIN dept b
ON a.deptid=b.deptid;
```

FULL OUTER JOIN: Return all rows from both tables joining when there is a match. It is basically UNION ALL of **LEFT OUTER JOIN** and **RIGHT OUTER JOIN** results.
E.g.
```
SELECT a.*,b.* FROM emp a
FULL OUTER JOIN dept b
ON a.deptid=b.deptid;
```

SELF JOIN: This joins the table with itself.
E.g.

```
SELECT a.ename
   ||' report to manager '
   ||b.ename "Emp reporting"
FROM emp a
JOIN emp b
ON a.mgr = b.empno;
```

CARTESIAN JOIN: Return Cartesian product based on joining every row of one table to every row of another table. This mainly happens when there is no join condition. If table "emp" has 100 rows and table "dept" has 10 rows then Cartesian join will return 10*100=1000 rows
E.g.
```
SELECT a.*,b.* FROM emp a
CROSS JOIN dept b;
```

You must use the appropriate join and be aware that the more data oracle fetches the more I/O is incurred. For example FULL outer join will return more rows than INNER join and so if a business requirement can be addressed with an INNER JOIN data then you should avoid using LEFT or RIGHT or FULL outer join.

Issue in LEFT, RIGHT and FULL outer join while using the filter criteria:
When you use INNER JOIN in ANSI standard it does not make any difference if the filter condition is in a "WHERE" or an "ON" clause.
However when you use OUTER JOIN there is significant difference in terms of output depending on whether the filter clause is in an "ON" or a "WHERE" clause.

ANSI INNER JOIN

```
SELECT *
FROM employees a
JOIN departments b
ON a.DEPARTMENT_ID=b.DEPARTMENT_ID
WHERE a.first_name LIKE 'M%';
```

```
SELECT *
FROM employees a
JOIN departments b
ON a.DEPARTMENT_ID=b.DEPARTMENT_ID
AND a.first_name LIKE 'M%';
```

The filter clause "a.first_name LIKE 'M%' " used in "WHERE" or "ON" clause produces the same result from both the queries above.

ANSI LEFT OUTER JOIN

```
SELECT *
FROM employees a
LEFT OUTER JOIN departments b
ON a.DEPARTMENT_ID=b.DEPARTMENT_ID
WHERE a.first_name LIKE 'M%';
```

The left outer join on department_id will return all the records from employee table even if that specific record is not there in departments table.

However the "WHERE" clause will filter out and give only all the employees whose first name starts with "M" from the result-set.

So if you have 100 people in employees table and 5 first name start with "M" then the final result-set will consist of only 5 rows.

However the following query will return a different result.

```
SELECT *
FROM employees a
LEFT OUTER JOIN departments b
ON a.DEPARTMENT_ID=b.DEPARTMENT_ID
AND a.first_name LIKE 'M%';
```

In this example the filter clause is included in the "ON" clause and hence it will behave like LEFT OUTER JOIN and return all the records from employee table even if that specific record is not there in departments table.

So if you have 100 people in employees table and 5 first names start with "M" still the final result-set will return 100 rows.

In fact irrespective of whichever predicate you use in the ON clause it will return all the rows from LEFT table (i.e. Employees)

So in the ON clause if you give "a.department_id **= -10** and b.department_id **= -2**0 "all rows will still be returned from employees table (note department_id **-10, -20** do not exist.)

So we can conclude that when you use any predicate (filter clause) as part of ON clause in an OUTER JOIN, it is ignored and it is <u>advisable not to use the filter clause as part of "ON" clause</u> but to use it in the "WHERE" clause.

You must follow this in all ANSI JOIN no matter if it is INNER or OUTER JOIN.

Also note Oracle will <u>internally translate</u> these various joins into different join methods like "Nested Loops join", "Hash Join", "Sort merge Join" etc. using its own discretion which is determined by the kind of optimizer, indexes and statistics present in the database.

Here are the Join methods Oracle internally use:

<u>Nested Loops join:</u>
In this type of join oracle will iterate over all the rows of outer table based on the joined index columns of the inner row source. This is ideal when driving table is small and joined column has highly selective non-unique index.

<u>Hash join:</u>
In this type of join oracle hashes the Join key of the driving row source (the smaller table) and then it runs through the probing row source (bigger table). This is ideal when driving table is small enough to fit into hash memory and does not have index on the joining column.

<u>Sort Merge join:</u>
In this type of join oracle sorts individually all the relevant rows of the first table and second table by the join key and then merges these sorted rows. This is done when JOIN conditions are inequalities.

Now let us discuss about SET OPERATORS:
You can join multiple queries using SET OPERATORS, Here is how it works:

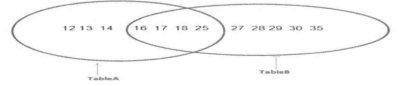

INTERSECT: Return rows when there is a match in both the tables, it is equivalent of <u>INNER JOIN</u>

```
SELECT empno FROM tableA
INTERSECT
SELECT empno FROM tableB
```
Will give: 16 17 18 25

Note: This operator will give the common column and common record only. However <u>JOIN</u> will give common column, common records and associated other column details from both the tables.

UNION: Return unique rows from both the tables

```
SELECT empno FROM tableA
UNION
SELECT empno FROM tableB
```
Will give: 12 13 14 16 17 18 25 27 28 29 30 35

UNION ALL: Return all rows from both the tables which contain the **duplicates**, it is similar to <u>FULL OUTER JOIN</u>

```
SELECT empno FROM tableA
UNION ALL
SELECT empno FROM tableB
```
Will give: 12 13 14 16 17 18 25 16 17 18 25 27 28 29 30 35

MINUS: Return all rows from first table after eliminating the common records

```
SELECT empno FROM tableA
MINUS
SELECT empno FROM tableB
```
Will give: 12 13 14
If you use tableB MINUS tableA will give: 27 28 29 30 35

Concepts 4: SQL Functions and regular expression

Here we will discuss inbuilt sql functions and regular expression functions for string pattern matching.

Some in-built <u>SQL functions</u> and <u>regular expressions</u>:
NVL2: This function is similar to NVL except that it accepts three parameters. First parameter is name of the column, second parameter is the customized value you want to return if the first column is NOT NULL and the third parameter is the customized value you want to return when the first column is NULL.
<u>Example shown as below:</u>

```
SELECT CUST_ID,ENTITLED_AMT,NVL2(ENTITLED,'CUSTOMER IS ENTITLED FOR PAYMENT',
    'CUSTOMER IS NOT ENTITLED FOR PAYMENT') ENTITLEMENT_STATUS
    FROM TABLE_NAME;
```

COALESCE: This function is similar to NVL, It accepts set of parameters and returns the first one which evaluates to NOT NULL value. It returns null when all values evaluate as null.
<u>Example shown as below:</u>

```
SELECT empid ,
  COALESCE(hire_date,join_date,admission_date) Emp_join_date
FROM EMP;
```

So in this example out of the 3 dates the first NOT NULL value is returned by the coalesce function.

25

You can **rewrite** COALESCE as below:

Option using NVL:

```
NVL (hire_date,NVL(join_date,admission_date))
```

Option using CASE:

```
CASE
WHEN hire_date IS NOT NULL THEN
  hire_date
WHEN join_date IS NOT NULL THEN
  join_date
ELSE
  admission_date
END
```

DECODE: This function evaluates a value conditionally. e.g. column is GENDER (which accepts M/F) You can use decode as below to return 'Male' when the value is 'M', 'Female' when the value is 'F' and 'Unknown' otherwise:

Example shown as below:

```
SELECT empid,
   DECODE(gender,'M','Male','F','Female','Unknown') AS gender
FROM EMP;
```

CASE: This is similar to **decode** and can be rewritten as below:

Example shown as below:

```
SELECT empid,
   CASE gender
     WHEN 'M'
     THEN 'Male'
     WHEN 'F'
     THEN 'Female'
     ELSE 'Unknown'
   END AS gender
FROM EMP;
```

Another example using CASE statement. The below scenario cannot be written using DECODE statement:

```
SELECT empid,
   CASE
     WHEN sal<7000
     THEN 'Low sal'
     WHEN sal=7000
     THEN 'medium sal'
     ELSE 'High sal'
   END
FROM EMP;
```

REGEXP_INSTR: This returns position of start or end of matching string.

Example shown as below:

```
SELECT REGEXP_INSTR ('Today IS sunny AND beautiful','sunny') FROM dual;
```

This will return: 10

```
SELECT REGEXP_INSTR ('Sunday 245', '[[:digit:]]') FROM dual;
```

This will return: 8

REGEXP_SUBSTR: This returns the part of the matching string
Example shown as below:

```
SELECT REGEXP_SUBSTR ('Today IS sunny AND beautiful','sunny') FROM dual;
```

This will return: sunny

```
SELECT REGEXP_SUBSTR ('Sunday 245', '[[:digit:]]+') FROM dual;
```
This will return: 245

REGEXP_REPLACE: This returns a string after replacing the text.
Example shown as below:

```
SELECT REGEXP_REPLACE ('Today IS sunny
AND beautiful','sunny','raining')
FROM dual;
```
This will return: Today is raining and beautiful

```
SELECT REGEXP_REPLACE ('Sunday 20 Mango and 43 orange', '[[:digit:]]', '$')
FROM dual;
```
This will return: Sunday $$ Mango and $$ orange

REGEXP_LIKE: This returns true if pattern is matched.
Example shown as below:

```
SELECT 1 FROM dual WHERE REGEXP_LIKE ('Sunday aaa', '[[:digit:]]');
```
This will return nothing as the string does not contain any digit

```
SELECT 1 FROM dual WHERE REGEXP_LIKE ('Sunday 245', '[[:digit:]]');
```
This will return: 1
Because the string does contain a digit

```
SELECT * FROM table_name WHERE REGEXP_LIKE (<column name>, '[a-z] [0-9]');
```
[A-z] [0-9] pattern means: data with lowercase and then a space then number.
[A-Z] [0-9] pattern means: data with uppercase and then a space then number.
[A-z]{3} pattern means: data with lowercase with any 3 consecutive small letter.

REGEXP_COUNT: This return the number of times a specific pattern is found.
Example shown as below:

```
SELECT REGEXP_COUNT ('Sunday 20345', '[[:digit:]]') FROM dual;
```

This will return: 5

EXTRACTVALUE: This returns the scalar value of an XML fragment, it operates on a single element.
Example shown as below:

```
CREATE TABLE test_xml
  ( a NUMBER, b XMLType
  );
INSERT
INTO test_xml VALUES
  (
    1,
    xmltype('
<levela>
<levelb><item>birds</item></levelb>
</levela>
')
  );
INSERT
INTO test_xml VALUES
  (
    2,
    xmltype('
<levela>
<levelb><item>animal</item></levelb>
</levela>
')
  );
```
Now you can select the xml fragment as below
```
SELECT a,extractValue(b,'/levela/levelb/item') "type_of_animal" FROM test_xml;
```

This will return:

A	type_of_animal
1	birds
2	animal

However if you have more than 1 element in the xml fragment then you must use [POSITION () =1 or 2 or 3] attribute to extract just only 1 element as below:
```
INSERT
INTO test_xml VALUES
  (
    3,
    xmltype('
<levela>
<levelb><item>species</item><item>insect</item></levelb>
</levela>
')
  );

SELECT a,
  extractValue(b,'/levela/levelb/item[position()=1]') "type_of_animal"
FROM test_xml;
```
The output:

A	type_of_animal
1	birds
2	animal
3	species

28

EXTRACT: This function extracts the date component from **datetime/interval** value.
Example shown as below for **datetime**:

```
SELECT extract(MONTH FROM sysdate) FROM dual;
```

If SYSDATE is 07-Aug-2016 it returns 8

Example shown as below using **interval** to derive number of years and months between 2 dates:

Without extract function:

```
SELECT TRUNC(months_between(sysdate,(sysdate-1250))/12)
  ||' years '
  ||TRUNC(mod(months_between(sysdate,(sysdate-1250)),12))
  ||' months'
FROM dual;
```

With extract function:

```
SELECT extract(YEAR FROM (sysdate-(sysdate-1250))YEAR TO MONTH)
  ||' Years '
  || extract(MONTH FROM (sysdate-(sysdate-1250))YEAR TO MONTH)
  ||' months'
FROM dual;
```

Here "**YEAR TO MONTH**" is the interval between 2 dates.
Similarly you can find the **age** or **no of year of experience** by just replacing the 2 dates.

Concepts 5: Fast full index scan

Here we will discuss mechanism to read index blocks instead of table blocks and different types of explain plan.

This kind of scan, reads all the index blocks instead of the table blocks. This fast full index scan happens only when you are accessing table columns which are part of a concatenated index.
This scan is useful for reducing the numbers of logical reads by not accessing the table at all and hence is also named "INDEX ONLY SCAN". To take advantage of this SCAN it is sometimes necessary to add an extra column to an existing index.
Using EXPLAIN PLAN command you can check whether <u>fast full index scan</u> happen.

```
Explain plan FOR SELECT * FROM (TABLE_NAME);
SELECT plan_table_output
FROM TABLE(dbms_xplan.display('plan_table',NULL,'serial'));
```

Note DBMS_XPLAN.DISPLAY function provides four levels of output based on the third parameter:

BASIC:

```
SELECT plan_table_output
FROM TABLE(dbms_xplan.display('plan_table',NULL,'BASIC'));

| Id | Operation      | Name      |
-------------------------------------------
```

TYPICAL (default):

```
SELECT plan_table_output
FROM TABLE(dbms_xplan.display('plan_table',NULL,'TYPICAL'));
```

```
-------------------------------------------------------------------------------
| Id  | Operation        | Name     | Rows  | Bytes | Cost (%CPU)| Time      |
-------------------------------------------------------------------------------
```

SERIAL:
```
SELECT plan_table_output
FROM TABLE(dbms_xplan.display('plan_table',NULL,'SERIAL'));
-------------------------------------------------------------------------------
| Id  | Operation        | Name     | Rows  | Bytes | Cost (%CPU)| Time      |
-------------------------------------------------------------------------------
```

ALL:
```
SELECT plan_table_output
FROM TABLE(dbms_xplan.display('plan_table',NULL,'ALL'));
-------------------------------------------------------------------------------
| Id  | Operation        | Name     | Rows  | Bytes | Cost (%CPU)| Time      |
-------------------------------------------------------------------------------


Query Block Name / Object Alias (identified by operation id):


Column Projection Information (identified by operation id):
```

Column Projection information contains which predicate is executed first and which order.

For complete example of index only scan refer to Chapter 2 Tips 11: Case study using "Index only scan" and DETERMINISTIC function for performance?

Concepts 6: Index JOIN scan

Here we will discuss mechanism how to read data from available indexes.

This kind of scan happens when <u>all the data retrieved</u> is from a combination of index columns. Here you can see all the data is present in an index columns and hence table access is avoided.
You can force an "index join" using hint /*+ INDEX_JOIN (table_name idx1 idx2) */

This kind of scan is very useful in high volume SQL where there is potential table lookup.
E.g.
```
CREATE TABLE apps_shop
  (
    app_id     NUMBER,
    shop_id    NUMBER,
    region     VARCHAR2(10),
    shop_desc  VARCHAR2(20),
    app_desc   VARCHAR2(20),
    status     VARCHAR2(1)
    );
CREATE INDEX apps_shop_idx on apps_shop(shop_id);
CREATE INDEX apps_region_idx on apps_shop(region);
```

Insert millions of records and then analyze the table/index.

Problem:

Now you have a query which takes huge time:

```
SELECT COUNT(*) FROM apps_shop WHERE shop_id=2345 and region='ASIA';
```

This takes huge time because oracle will have index range scan on "shop_id" and "region" individually and then merge the results from independent index scans.

However if you can scan the index together to get the required data it will be quick because both the filter criteria together return only handful of rows. So to achieve the fast response time we have 2 solutions:

Solution 1:

Drop the individual indexes and create a concatenated index as below:

```
CREATE INDEX apps_shop_region_idx on apps_shop(shop_id,region);
```

Solution 2:

Use INDEX_JOIN hints which will force the optimizer to use both the indexes together and thus avoid table access as all the information are available in the index columns "shop_id" and "region"

```
SELECT /*+ INDEX_JOIN(apps_shop apps_shop_idx apps_region_idx) */ COUNT(*)
FROM apps_shop WHERE shop_id=2345 and region='ASIA';
```

Concepts 7: Indexing on null column rows

Here we will discuss mechanism to store null values in a b-tree index.

Oracle does not store null value in B-tree index and hence when you query for null column values, an index is not used even if there is an index on that column.
There are two ways to store null in B-tree index:

Approach 1:

Create index on expression

```
CREATE INDEX idx1 ON table_name
  (null_column,-999
  );
```

Now if you have query as below the index will be used:

```
SELECT * FROM table_name WHERE null_column IS NULL;
```

Approach 2:

Create function based index on NVL function

```
CREATE INDEX idx2 ON table_name
  (NVL (null_column,-888)
  );
```

Now if you have query as below the index will be used:

```
SELECT * FROM table_name WHERE NVL (null_column,-888) =<SOME VALUE>;
```

Here we will discuss how to minimize processing time by using DISTINCT in appropriate place in a query and also discuss column list ordering issue and solution.

Usage of Distinct:

You can eliminate unnecessary processing time by using DISTINCT appropriately.

E.g. instead of using

```
SELECT DISTINCT user_def_fun (name) FROM TABLE_NAME;
```

Use below:

```
SELECT user_def_fun (name) FROM
  (SELECT DISTINCT name FROM TABLE_NAME
  );
```

In this approach you are applying **user_def_fun** function only on the distinct records and not on all the records and hence reducing the processing time and improving performance.

Column list ordering:

In the definition of a table the order of columns may not be in the same order when you **insert** or **select** from that table into another table with same structure. It may fail with error:

Setup:
Connect to U1 schema

```
CREATE TABLE emp_order
  (
    id        NUMBER,
    name      VARCHAR2(30),
    age       NUMBER,
    sal       NUMBER(10,4),
    hiredate  DATE
  );
INSERT INTO emp_order (id,name,age,sal,hiredate)
            VALUES(1,'Scott',34,234567.34,sysdate);
INSERT INTO emp_order (id,name,age,sal,hiredate)
            VALUES(2,'Rob',35,234567.34,sysdate);
INSERT INTO emp_order (id,name,age,sal,hiredate)
            VALUES(3,'Aditi',6,2367.34,sysdate);
INSERT INTO emp_order (id,name,age,sal,hiredate)
            VALUES(4,'Pat',34,23567.34,sysdate);
COMMIT;
```

Connect to U2 schema

```
CREATE TABLE emp_order
  (
    id        NUMBER,
    name      VARCHAR2(30),
    age       NUMBER,
    hiredate  DATE,
    sal       NUMBER(10,4)
  );
```

Problem:

Connect to u2 and run below:

```
INSERT INTO emp_order SELECT * FROM u1.emp_order;
SQL Error: ORA-00932: inconsistent datatypes: expected DATE got NUMBER
```

Solution:

As the column order can be different for the table **emp_order** in different schema you must explicitly refer to the column name.

This is how you can retrieve the column list from data dictionary and form the insert with ease.

```
SET SERVEROUTPUT ON
DECLARE
  ins_stmt VARCHAR2(10000);
BEGIN
  SELECT 'INSERT INTO '
    ||table_name
    ||'('
    ||LISTAGG(column_name,',') WITHIN GROUP (
  ORDER BY COLUMN_ID)
    ||')'
    || ' SELECT '
    ||LISTAGG(column_name,',') WITHIN GROUP (
  ORDER BY COLUMN_ID)
    ||' FROM U1.'
    ||table_name
    ||''
  INTO ins_stmt
  FROM all_tab_columns
  WHERE owner   ='U1'
  AND table_name='EMP_ORDER'
  GROUP BY table_name;
  DBMS_OUTPUT.PUT_LINE(ins_stmt);
  EXECUTE IMMEDIATE ins_stmt;
END;
/
```

Output:
```
anonymous block completed
INSERT INTO EMP_ORDER(ID,NAME,AGE,SAL,HIREDATE) SELECT ID,NAME,AGE,SAL,HIREDATE FROM U1.EMP_ORDER
```

With this tips in hand you can place the above INSERT statement inside a PL/SQL FOR LOOP and create a dynamic insert statement for many tables in your schema.

Note: You can form the dynamic sql using WM_CONCAT also which you will find in subsequent chapters however WM_CONCAT is unsupported in 11g and is <u>completely removed</u> in 12c and hence it is recommended to use LISTAGG.

Here we will discuss different approaches for improving the performance of SQL query and role of different statistics including function based statistics for enhanced performance.

There are two steps for optimizing SQL code

Step 1: Change the data model to have proper normalized structure with index, constraints and mview. You must analyze the structure to gather statistics (**Statistics** consist of row density, clustering factor, and number of distinct values, smallest, largest value, data distribution (column histogram) and presence of NULL etc. These statistics are used by optimizer to estimate the selectivity of WHERE clause predicates).

Also you must gather statistics for PL/SQL functions if they are used in SQL predicate. **Without function statistics** Oracle executes the query based on the order in which the predicate conditions appears in the "where" clause. So if you have less selective predicate function before the most selective predicate in your query then Oracle, in the absence of statistics, executes in the same order and hence performs slower. However if you gather statistics then Oracle will internally execute the most selective predicate before it executes the less selective predicates and this results in improved performance.

 Note statistics are used not only for deciding if Index/full table scan will be used but used for deciding selective predicate order in where clause, choosing appropriate JOIN methods.

Function statistics can be generated using command:

```
Associate statistics
WITH FUNCTIONS <FUNCTION name> DEFAULT selectivity 50;
```

Statistics generated using Associate statistics are "**default statistics**" and used only to help CBO to order the functions based on selectivity when used in SQL predicates.

To gather stats for table the command:

```
Analyze TABLE <TABLE name> compute statistics;
```

Again when you have multiple columns of the same table or you have expression (e.g. some oracle/user defined function) used in the predicate, then it is not possible for CBO to derive the selectivity of the column group or selectivity of the expression against another table column predicate using normal statistics. However using "**Extended Statistics**" it is possible to get the selectivity of group of columns and expressions. Also extended statistics has the added benefit that a function based index can be used not only in predicate clause but also in group by and having clause.

Extended statistics can be generated explicitly and implicitly as below:

Explicitly generated extended statistics:

```
DECLARE
  l_extend_stat VARCHAR2(30);
BEGIN
  l_extend_stat := DBMS_STATS.create_extended_stats
                   (ownname => 'HR',
                    tabname => 'EMPLOYEES',
                    extension => '(LOWER(first_name))'
                    );
  --For group of columns you can use extension=>'(column1,column2)'
END;
/
```

Implicitly generated extended statistics:

```
EXEC dbms_stats.gather_table_stats
            ('HR','EMPLOYEES',
              method_opt=>'for columns (UPPER(first_name))'
            );
```

Note extended stats are based on HASH function and hence they **work only with predicates based on equality** and do not work if you use <>, <, > and "BETWEEN" operators. Extended stats are used in DISTINCT operator also from 11gR2 onwards.

The difference between "Default statistics" and "Extended statistics" are
- o "Default Statistics" has fixed selectivity whereas for "Extended Statistics" selectivity is dynamic
- o "Default Statistics" is used only for predicate ordering of function in SQL "where" clause however "Extended Statistics" is used not only for predicate ordering but for making the function based index used in "Group by" and "Order by" clauses.

So if you have extended statistics you do not need default statistics.

You can view the column group or expression extended statistics has been generated for using the following query:

```
SELECT * FROM dba_stat_extensions WHERE owner='HR';
```

Step 2: Refactor the code
- ➤ Use WITH clause factoring
- ➤ Use Analytic function
- ➤ Use CASE/DECODE statement
- ➤ Use EXISTS instead of IN
- ➤ Avoid NOT IN as NOT IN does not allow an index to be used.
- ➤ Use join instead of subquery
- ➤ Use WHERE clause filtering before using HAVING clause filtering
- ➤ Use DISTINCT clause appropriately to reduce the work.
- ➤ Avoid implicit conversions of data type.
- ➤ Avoid applying function in the WHERE clause column or create function based index
- ➤ Use of Oracle hints (Hint is a suggestion to the optimizer)
  E.g.
  ```
  SELECT /*+ NL_SJ */   --Nested loop semi join
  SELECT /*+ HASH_SJ */ --Hash semi join
  SELECT /*+ FULL(e) CACHE(e) */ COUNT(*) FROM EMP e;
  --This puts the result of full table scan in the most recently used end of LRU
  ```

Concepts 10: Table compression/Index compression in 12c

Here we will look into saving space in database and improving performance by compression of table/index and also we will look into oracle 12c Advanced Index compression while rebuilding or creating an index.

Compression was introduced in Oracle 8i where you can compress only index keys. Oracle 9i added compression for Tables but it can only be done while creating via direct load or CTAS or Insert with Append. Oracle 11g introduced advanced compression where you can create a table with **COMPRESS FOR OLTP**.

```
CREATE TABLE tabl
  (
    a NUMBER,
    b VARCHAR2 (30),
    c VARCHAR2 (20)
  )
  COMPRESS FOR OLTP;
```

Also you can compress a table after creation using Alter command. `ALTER TABLE tabl move COMPRESS;`
Run the following query **before** the alter command and **after** the ALTER command to see how much space is regained by compression. Compression not only saves space but any query against the table after compression has <u>improved performance</u> as the number of BLOCKs scanned is reduced dramatically.

```
SELECT segment_name,
  segment_type,
  blocks
FROM dba_segments
WHERE segment_name IN ('TAB1');
```

Similarly while creating or rebuilding index you can use compression which allows us to store the index in fewer database blocks which not only save space but improve performance on large index range scan and index fast full scan.

```
ALTER INDEX index_name REBUILD ONLINE COMPRESS;
```

However one <u>must be careful</u> before compressing a particular index. If an index does not have lot of repeated data compression of index may <u>lead to increase in storage space</u> because of oracle internal mechanism of storing the index blocks.
You can see amount of space occupied by index (which can be run <u>before</u> and <u>after</u> compression):

```
SELECT index_name,
  leaf_blocks,--This will provide the storage space of index
  compression
FROM user_indexes
WHERE table_name='TABLE_NAME';
```

However from **Oracle 12c** onwards you need not worry whether compression will lead to increase in storage space because oracle 12c has introduced "**Advanced Index compression**" which will always decrease the storage space and improve performance for index range scan. This advanced feature is available only in enterprise edition.

In order to use "**Advanced Index compression**" just use the keyword "compress advanced low" while creating/rebuilding the index.

```
ALTER INDEX index_name REBUILD COMPRESS ADVANCED LOW;
```

After compressing an index using this option you can run the above "SELECT" query and will see that the leaf_blocks value is significantly lesser.
Note: "Advanced Index compression" does not work on <u>unique single-column indexes</u>.

Concepts 11: Partition pruning

Here we will define oracle internal mechanism to access the required partition from list of partitions.

Partition pruning is the mechanism which eliminates any unwanted partitions when accessing data from a large table. In other words this technique reduces the processing time by accessing only the portion of the table which holds the required data.

Concepts 12: Context switch

Here we will define the process involve in code execution from one engine to other engine.

When control is passed from one engine to another while executing code we call it "context switch". E.g. PL/SQL engine to SQL engine and vice versa.

Concepts 13: Database server and normalization

Here will define database instance and database OS files. Also will understand different level of normalizations.

Database server consists of a database and an instance. Database is a collection of OS files like data files, redo log files etc. Instance consists of SGA and background process like DBWn, LGWr, CKPt, SMOn, PMOn etc.

Normalization is a process of breaking a relation (table) into smaller relation (table) with a view to reduce redundant data and create appropriate structure. There are mainly 3 normal forms.

<u>1NF:</u> Here all the attributes (columns) values of a **table** are atomic (indivisible).
This normal form implements the following rules:
- Eliminate repeating groups in a table.
- For each set of related data create a table

The disadvantage of 1NF are:
- Redundant data
- You cannot remove a particular row as by deleting a row, you lose other important attribute values. E.g. if you remove employee rows from EMPLOYEE table (1NF) you lose department details.
- You cannot add a new department until an employee joins the department.

<u>2NF:</u> This means a table is in 1NF and additionally all the non-key attributes (columns) are dependent on the primary key column. However two non-key attributes (columns) **may be dependent** on each other

The disadvantage of 2NF are:
- Redundant data (less than 1NF)
- You cannot independently modify one non key attribute value as it may have dependencies with other non-key attributes. E.g. if the designation of an employee changes in EMPLOYEE table (2NF) you must change the dependent non key attribute (column) also.

<u>3NF:</u> This means a table is in 2NF and two non-key attributes (columns) **cannot be dependent** on each other. The objective of 3NF is to remove data from a table that is not dependent on primary key and place them in another table.

The **objective** of **normalization** are:
- To reduce redundant data.
- To maintain data consistency
- Flexible design to maintain the data
- To maintain data integrity
- To maintain database security

The redundant data causes the following problems:
- If same data is kept in more than one table unnecessary space is used

37

> With duplicate data present in different tables, there is a chance of making mistake by updating only one set of data from one table instead of all the tables where the same duplicate data exists. This increases the cost of maintenance and risk of failure as data can be inconsistent across the system.

However many times we **introduce redundancy** to a certain extent in a database to improve performance, in other words we de-normalize a table to reduce the cost of table JOINS to get data faster from a table without incurring the cost of JOINING multiple tables ("Joining" results in more I/O and CPU time). So there is a trade off in doing this. As a rule you normalize the data model however based on performance requirement you can sometime introduce limited redundancy to retrieve data faster and more efficiently.

One of the example of de-normalization is "Materialized view" which store redundant data but eliminates the need to join multiple tables and thus improve performance of materialized view. In fact we introduce limited redundancy in table level also to improve performance of critical queries.

Concepts 14: Oracle SKIP LOCKED and DDL_LOCK_TIMEOUT in 11g

Here we will discuss how to skip locked records and process the unlocked records.

In oracle when <u>FOR UPDATE</u> is used in one session for a set of rows then those rows are locked until a commit/rollback is issued. If another session uses FOR UPDATE clause for the same set of rows the session will wait for the rows to be unlocked.
If you use FOR UPDATE NOWAIT then a session wishing to update a locked row-set will come out with error:
ORA-00054: resource busy and acquire with NOWAIT specified or timeout expired

However in Oracle 11g using <u>FOR UPDATE SKIP LOCKED</u> clause you can query the records which are not locked by any other sessions.

Session 1:
```
SELECT * FROM test12 WHERE a = 1 FOR UPDATE NOWAIT;
```

Session 2:
```
SELECT * FROM test12 FOR UPDATE SKIP LOCKED;
```

This will return all the rows except a=1 which is locked by **session 1**.

DDL_LOCK_TIMEOUT:
In Oracle, running "ALTER" statement to add or modify table column causes below error
ORA-00054: resource busy and acquire with NOWAIT specified or timeout expired
So DBA has to try the "ALTER" command repeatedly <u>to get the exclusive **lock**</u>.

However in Oracle 11g you can set DDL_LOCK_TIMEOUT to certain value and hence the "ALTER" command will wait for that specified period (For this case 30 seconds) before it fails with ORA-00054
```
ALTER SESSION SET DDL_LOCK_TIMEOUT=30;
```

Concepts 15: Index usage with LIKE operator

Here we will discuss with a short example how to use "LIKE" operator so that index is used.

When using LIKE operator in a query and you want the index to be used then the wildcard (%) cannot be used as a predicate. The wildcard (%) can be used in the middle or end of the string.
e.g.

```
SELECT * FROM TABLE_NAME WHERE name LIKE '%FAR%'  --will NOT use an INDEX
SELECT * from TABLE_NAME where name like 'FAR%'   --will use INDEX
```

Concepts 16: Materialized view

Here we will discuss mechanism to store pre-computed data.

Materialized view is a database object that contain the results of a query. Unlike a standard view which does not store data, a materialized view stores data similar to physical tables. This provides a fast response by pre-computing and storing aggregated information. The only disadvantage is that a materialized view may be out of sync because of change in underlying data in the base tables. However using fast refresh you can keep mview always in sync with base tables.
E.g. syntax

```
CREATE MATERIALIZED VIEW Mview_name BUILD
IMMEDIATE | DEFFERED | ON PREBUILT TABLE REFRESH COMPLETE | FAST
| FORCE ON COMMIT | ON DEMAND | START WITH ENABLE QUERY REWRITE
AS
   (SELECT * FROM tab1 WHERE ....
   );
```

Concepts 17: Hierarchical Query

Here we will discuss how to retrieve tree like structure from relational data.

Relational database does not store data in a hierarchical way. Hierarchical query is a mechanism by which a tree like structure data can be formed/fetched from normal relational data.
This is implemented using

CONNECT BY PRIOR: This defines how a child row is related with a parent row recursively.
START WITH: This specifies the root node from which we will trace the tree either upward or downward based on how you are using PRIOR clause whether before the child column or parent column.

So if you have

```
SELECT * ......
START WITH empid=100
CONNECT BY PRIOR parent_column=child_column;--Bottom-UP approach
```

It will return rows start with empid=100 and recursively fetch all the records which are above empid=100;
You can read the above statement: "Give all the parent records starting with empid=100"

However if the child column come after the "PRIOR" clause as below

```
SELECT * ......
START WITH empid=100
CONNECT BY PRIOR child_column= parent_column; --TOP-DOWN approach
```

39

It will return rows start with empid=100 and recursively fetch all the records which are below empid=100;
You can read the above statement: "Give all the child records starting with empid=100"

So if you use prior empid= mgrid you will get all the child records starting with empid=101
You can use **SYS_CONNECT_BY_PATH (employee_name,'->')** in the select statement to print all the recursive child/parent records separated by "->".

```
SELECT level,
  empid,
  mgrid,
  substr(SYS_CONNECT_BY_PATH(employee_name,'->'),3) reporting_line
FROM EMP
  START WITH empid      =101
  CONNECT BY prior empid=mgrid
ORDER BY 1;
```

Output:

LEVEL	EMPID	MGRID	REPORTING_LINE
1	101	100	Kochhar
2	205	101	Kochhar->Higgins
2	204	101	Kochhar->Baer
2	203	101	Kochhar->Mavris
2	200	101	Kochhar->Whalen
2	108	101	Kochhar->Greenberg
3	113	108	Kochhar->Greenberg->Popp
3	206	205	Kochhar->Higgins->Gietz
3	111	108	Kochhar->Greenberg->Sciarra
3	110	108	Kochhar->Greenberg->Chen
3	109	108	Kochhar->Greenberg->Faviet

In this example you get all the recursive child record starting from empid=101.
Here "**LEVEL**" is pseudo column which indicates the level in a hierarchy as you can see from the output.
Note: To order/**sort** the siblings under a particular branch you can use order siblings by employee_name If you use this clause then under "Kochhar" all the child employees will be sorted in ascending order.

However if you use prior mgrid=empid you will get all the parent record starting with empid=101

```
SELECT level,
  empid,
  mgrid,
  substr(SYS_CONNECT_BY_PATH(employee_name,'->'),3) reporting_line
FROM EMP
  START WITH empid      =101
  CONNECT BY prior mgrid=empid
ORDER BY 1;
```

Output:

LEVEL	EMPID	MGRID	REPORTING_LINE
1	101	100	Kochhar
2	100	(null)	Kochhar->King

Example to **break rows into column**:

```
SELECT rownum,
   SUBSTR('unique',LEVEL,1) val
FROM dual
   CONNECT BY level < LENGTH ('unique');
```

This will give output:

ROWNUM	VAL
1	u
2	n
3	i
4	q
5	u

Note: you can use keyword "**ROWNUM**" instead of "**LEVEL**" keyword.

Get last 7 days:

```
SELECT sysdate-rownum FROM dual CONNECT BY rownum<8;
```

SYSDATE-ROWNUM
02-AUG-16
01-AUG-16
31-JUL-16
30-JUL-16
29-JUL-16
28-JUL-16
27-JUL-16

Similarly you can get next 100 days using connect by clause.

New record **generation using connect by**:

```
SELECT ROWNUM AS rn FROM dual CONNECT BY ROWNUM < 101;
```

This will generate 100 rows.

Example to find all possible bus routes to reach from point A to point E:

Let us say we want to find all the possible bus routes to reach from one place to other place. Here is the complete solution.

```
CREATE TABLE bus_route_path
  (
    route_id        NUMBER,
    start_bus_stop VARCHAR2(1),
    end_bus_stop   VARCHAR2(1)
  );
insert into bus_route_path values(1,'A','B');
insert into bus_route_path values(2,'A','D');
insert into bus_route_path values(3,'B','D');
insert into bus_route_path values(4,'D','E');
insert into bus_route_path values(5,'E','A');
insert into bus_route_path values(6,'B','E');
commit;

SELECT * FROM
(
SELECT      CONNECT_BY_ROOT start_bus_stop AS start_bus_stop,
            end_bus_stop,
            SUBSTR( SYS_CONNECT_BY_PATH ( start_bus_stop, ',' ), 2 ) || ',' || end_bus_stop AS route,
            SUBSTR( SYS_CONNECT_BY_PATH ( route_id, ',' ),2)                 AS route_num
  FROM      bus_route_path
  WHERE     CONNECT_BY_ROOT start_bus_stop <> end_bus_stop
  CONNECT BY NOCYCLE PRIOR end_bus_stop = start_bus_stop
  )
WHERE start_bus_stop = 'A' AND end_bus_stop = 'E';
```

The output:

START_BUS_STOP	END_BUS_STOP	ROUTE	ROUTE_NUM
A	E	A,B,D,E	1,3,4
A	E	A,B,E	1,6
A	E	A,D,E	2,4

CONNECT_BY_ROOT: This function returns the root node of hierarchical data in a row.

```
SELECT       CONNECT_BY_ROOT start_bus_stop
```

This clause will give the start bus stop for each possible hierarchical route.

```
WHERE        CONNECT_BY_ROOT start_bus_stop <> end_bus_stop
```

This clause will eliminate the path (generated by **SYS_CONNECT_BY_PATH**) where start and end bus stops have the same value. E.g. for this case **SYS_CONNECT_BY_PATH** can return the route as
"**A**, B, D, E, **A**".
This WHERE clause will remove this row from the result-set as Start and End **bus stops** are "A".

SYS_CONNECT_BY_PATH: This function returns the value starting with root node till the current node.

NOCYCLE: This is a keyword which instructs the hierarchical query to return data even if a "CONNECT BY" loop exists in the data. "CONNECT_BY_ISCYCLE" is used to detect which particular rows contain the loop.

 So in the above query if you remove "**NOCYCLE**" keyword then you will get error:
```
ORA-01436: CONNECT BY loop in user data
```

Concepts 18: SGA, UGA and PGA

Here we will discuss where to store data in different parts of database area.

- SGA is shared global area which forms part of system memory (RAM). SGA is used to store incoming data (data buffer) and internal control information. In other words this contains information which can be shared across connected sessions. PL/SQL package static constants are stored in SGA.
- UGA is user global area which forms part of system memory (RAM). UGA is the <u>supplement to PGA</u>. This contain <u>session specific data that persists across server call</u> boundaries. E.g. package level data.
- PGA is program Global Area which forms part of system memory (RAM). This contains session <u>specific data that persist only for the session</u> and gets released once the server call terminates. E.g. local data.
- You can calculate how much PGA and UGA memory is used:

  Step 1:
  ```
  SELECT *
  FROM v$mystat a ,
    v$statname b
  WHERE a.statistic#=b.statistic#
  AND b.name       IN ('session uga memory','session pga memory');
  ```

  Step 2: Run some code for which you want to calculate PGA/UGA memory used

  Step 3: Then rerun
  ```
  SELECT *
  FROM v$mystat a ,
    v$statname b
  WHERE a.statistic#=b.statistic#
  AND b.name       IN ('session uga memory','session pga memory');
  ```

  Now the difference between a.value from both query is the amount of PGA/UGA memory used.

Concepts 19: Useful queries

Here we will write some generic queries used by developer on a day to day basis.

- Convert number into words:
  ```
  SELECT TO_CHAR (TO_DATE (1567845, 'j'), 'jsp') FROM DUAL;
  ```
  ➔ One million five hundred sixty-seven thousand eight hundred forty-five

- Day of a month:
  ```
  SELECT TO_CHAR (to_date('06-may-2016','dd-mon-yyyy'), 'Day') "Day of a month"
  FROM DUAL;
  ```
  ➔ Friday

- First day of a month:
  ```
  SELECT TO_CHAR (TRUNC(to_date('06-may-2016','dd-mon-yyyy'),'MM'), 'Day') "First day of a month"
  FROM DUAL;
  ```
  ➔ Sunday

➤ Last day of a month:

```
SELECT TO_CHAR (last_day(to_date('06-may-2016','dd-mon-yyyy')), 'Day') "Last day of a month"
FROM DUAL;
```
→ Tuesday

➤ Working week dates for a week (i.e. Monday to Friday):

```
SELECT *
FROM
   (SELECT TRUNC(sysdate+7,'iw')-3-rownum+1 week_date
    FROM dual
      CONNECT BY rownum<=31
    )
WHERE week_date BETWEEN
    (SELECT TRUNC(sysdate,'iw') AS start_day_of_week FROM dual
    )
AND (SELECT TRUNC(sysdate+7,'iw')-3 AS end_day_of_week FROM dual) order by 1;
```

Note: **TRUNC** will remove the time portion from date variable.

→ If the SYSDATE is 04-AUG-2016 the output is:

WEEK_DATE
01-AUG-16
02-AUG-16
03-AUG-16
04-AUG-16
05-AUG-16

By replacing the SYSDATE by any other date you can get the week dates for that week.

➤ Number of days between two dates:

```
SELECT ROUND ( (MONTHS_BETWEEN ('01-May-2016', '01-Jan-2016') * 30), 0) num_of_days
FROM DUAL;
```
→ 120

➤ Get user db information of a system using sys_context:

```
SELECT sys_context('userenv', 'db_name') FROM dual;

SELECT sys_context('userenv', 'ip_address') FROM dual;

SELECT sys_context('userenv', 'db_domain') FROM dual;

SELECT sys_context('userenv', 'host') FROM dual;

SELECT sys_context('userenv','sid') FROM dual;

SELECT sys_context ('userenv', 'session_user') FROM dual;

SELECT sys_context ('userenv', 'current_schema') FROM dual;

SELECT sys_context ('userenv', 'instance_name') FROM dual;

SELECT sys_context('userenv','authentication_method') FROM dual;
```

You can get the above information using USERENV function also as below. E.g.

```
SELECT USERENV('SID') FROM dual; --This will give SID of your session. SID column of v$session
```

> ## Showing system privileges

1) To get what system privileges have been <u>assigned to a role</u> run:

```
SELECT * FROM role_sys_privs;
```

The output can be:

ROLE	PRIVILEGE	ADMIN_OPTION
CONNECT	CREATE SESSION	NO

2) To get what **system** privileges have been <u>assigned to a database user</u> run:

```
SELECT * FROM user_sys_privs;
```

Or you can run

```
SELECT dbms_metadata.get_granted_ddl ('SYSTEM_GRANT','U1') SYS_GRANTS
FROM dual;
```

The **output can be**:

```
GRANT FLASHBACK ARCHIVE ADMINISTER TO "U1"
GRANT CREATE TRIGGER TO "U1"
GRANT CREATE PROCEDURE TO "U1"
GRANT CREATE ROLE TO "U1"
GRANT CREATE SEQUENCE TO "U1"
GRANT CREATE VIEW TO "U1"
GRANT CREATE SYNONYM TO "U1"
GRANT CREATE TABLE TO "U1"
GRANT CREATE SESSION TO "U1"
```

To get the DDL for a table run:

```
SELECT dbms_metadata.get_ddl('TABLE','APP','U1') EMPLOYEE_DDL
FROM dual;
```

Here "APP" is table name and "U1" is the schema name.

3) To get what **object** privileges have been <u>assigned to a database user</u> run:

```
SELECT * FROM user_tab_privs;
```

The output can be:

GRANTEE	OWNER	TABLE_NAME	GRANTOR	PRIVILEGE	GRANTABLE	HIERARCHY
PROD	U1	APP	U1	insert	NO	NO
PROD	U1	LOC	U1	FLASHBACK	NO	NO

> ## Setting the current schema

```
ALTER SESSION SET CURRENT_SCHEMA = <schema name>;
```

Note: A <u>schema</u> is a collection of database objects whereas **schema owner** is called a <u>user</u>.

> ## Resizing tablespace

```
ALTER DATABASE DATAFILE '/usr/oradata/data_file1.dbf' resize 1G;
```

> ## Size of database (you must have access to the DBA tables)

Current size of database:
```
SELECT SUM (bytes) / 1024 / 1024 / 1024 AS db_size_in_GB FROM dba_data_files;
```

Size occupied by data in the database:
```
SELECT SUM (bytes) / 1024 / 1024 / 1024 AS size_occupied_in_GB
FROM dba_segments;
```

Space left in database can be calculated from the result of the above queries as:
Current size of database - Size occupied by data in the database

Size occupied by data by one schema:
```
SELECT SUM (bytes) / 1024 / 1024 / 1024 AS size_occupied_by_schema_in_GB
FROM dba_segments
WHERE owner = 'U1';
```

Note: You can use package to derive space usage using package DBMS_SPACE also.

Concepts 20: PL/SQL Compiler

Here we will discuss PL/SQL compilation steps.

PL/SQL compiler compiles code in the following sequence
  ➢ Parse the code (soft and hard parsing) which consists of syntax check like source code keyword, and semantic check like existence of the object, privilege, existence of the code in shared SQL Area, execution plan generation etc.
  ➢ The parsing creates unique hash code.
  ➢ From the unique hash code, PL/SQL compiler generates the binary i.e. executable form of the program (p-code).
  ➢ Now if the code is related with DDL then it is stored as metadata in oracle dictionary and gets executed as and when necessary. Since the PL/SQL code is stored in server side as metadata it enables transaction level security and you can view the source code using SQL query from the data dictionary.
  ➢ If it is not DDL then the source code is executed instantly.

Concepts 21: PL/SQL optimizer

Here we will discuss how to improve performance by setting higher value for PL/SQL optimizer level.

Since oracle 10g, PL/SQL code can be optimized during compilation time. This is done through optimizer setting PLSQL_OPTIMIZE_LEVEL to value 0, 1, 2 (2 is default) or 3.

The higher the value you set the more time it will take for the optimizer to compile the code but less time will be taken to execute the code.

PLSQL_OPTIMIZE_LEVEL =3 will enable PL/SQL inlining prior to compilation which is discussed in Chapter 8 Tips 3: PL/SQL code optimization by "inlining" in 11g

Concepts 22: PL/SQL Cursor

Here we will discuss how to define Cursor and use it for performance.

- ➤ A cursor is a pointer to a context area. Context area is an area of memory where result-set is stored. A cursor can hold more than one row but just one row can be processed at a time.

- ➤ Once processing is complete an open cursor should be closed for 2 reasons
  - Opening another cursor could get error "too many open cursors" if the limit of "open_cursors" default value 50 is exceeded.
  - If you try to reopen the same cursor an error "cursor already open" will be given.

- ➤ Cursor life cycle consists of **open cursor**, **fetch cursor** and **close cursor**.

- ➤ **Open cursor steps involved** : opening the context area where result set is stored, parsing the SQL statement, Binding the SQL and finally execute the SQL
  Fetch cursor: just fetch the resultset
  Close cursor: Just release the context area

- ➤ Cursor attributes are very useful and give useful information as shown using a simple example

```
set serveroutput on
DECLARE
  CURSOR c1 IS SELECT * FROM hr.employees;
  v_c1 C1%ROWTYPE;
BEGIN
  IF C1%ISOPEN THEN          ◄───────── This return Boolean true or false based
    CLOSE C1;                           on if cursor is open or not
  ELSE
    OPEN C1;
  END IF;
  LOOP
    FETCH C1 INTO v_c1;                 This return Boolean true or false based
    EXIT WHEN C1%NOTFOUND;  ◄────── on if cursor return one or more rows
    dbms_output.put_line('cnt is:'||C1%ROWCOUNT);  ◄─────────┐
    dbms_output.put_line('employee name:'||v_c1.last_name);  │
  END LOOP;                                                   │
END;                                                          │
/                                                             │
                              This return number of rows affected
```

- ➤ Do not fetch from already closed cursor as it will return error ORA-1002 "fetch out of sequence" and ORA-1001 "invalid cursor"
  E.g.

```
set serveroutput on
DECLARE
   CURSOR c1 IS SELECT * FROM t1;
   v_c1 c1%ROWTYPE;
BEGIN
   OPEN c1;
   LOOP
     FETCH c1 INTO v_c1;
     EXIT WHEN c1%NOTFOUND;
     CLOSE c1;
   END LOOP;
   dbms_output.put_line(v_c1.a);
END;
/
```

Output:

```
ORA-01001: invalid cursor
```

To resolve this, for this case "CLOSE c1" should be placed after "END LOOP" and then you will not receive the error.

➤ Inside the "cursor for loop" do not use COMMIT as it will invalidate the cursor and return error ORA-1002 "fetch out of sequence". Rather COMMIT outside the loop to avoid the error.
E.g.

```
DECLARE
   CURSOR c1 IS SELECT * FROM t1;
   v_c1 c1%ROWTYPE;
BEGIN
   OPEN c1;
   LOOP
     FETCH c1 INTO v_c1;
     EXIT WHEN c1%NOTFOUND;
     COMMIT;
   dbms_output.put_line(v_c1.a);
   END LOOP;
END;
/
```

Output:

```
ORA-01002: fetch out of sequence
```

➤ In the cursor for loop e.g. "FOR I IN CUR LOOP" "I" is declared internally as CUR%ROWTYPE

➤ "Cursor for loop" is recommended when you need to fetch all the data unconditionally
➤ When using "CURSOR FOR LOOP" or Normal cursor to update iteratively it is advisable to use ROWID instead of UNIQUE key column to update a record for better performance. To achieve this you add ROWID in the SELECT clause of the CURSOR or in a normal "FOR LOOP" and in the update statement use "ROWID" in the filter clause instead of using UNIQUE key column employee_id.
If you use "CURSOR LOOP" then instead of "WHERE ROWID=i.ROWID" you can also use "WHERE CURRENT OF <CURSOR_NAME>". "WHERE CURRENT OF" gives the current value of the cursor which eliminates the need of explicitly using unique/primary key to find out the current row. Both "ROWID" clause and "WHERE CURRENT OF" give almost the same performance benefit but note WHERE CURRENT OF <CURSOR_NAME> can be used with a "FOR UPDATE OF" cursor.
So in the above example you can use "WHERE CURRENT OF" if and only if you have cursor defined as below:

```
CURSOR c1 IS SELECT * FROM t1 FOR UPDATE OF sal,comm
```

<u>Example of using ROWID instead of UNIQUE KEY:</u>

```
BEGIN
  FOR i IN
  (SELECT employee_id,salary,job_id,rowid FROM employees
  )
  LOOP
    UPDATE employees
    SET salary =DECODE(i.job_id,'IT_PROG',i.salary*1.3,'IT_MGR',i.salary*1.2,i.salary*1.1)
    WHERE rowid=i.rowid;
  END LOOP;
END;
/
```

> In a cursor select statement
>> * If "FOR UPDATE of sal, comm" clause is used then in the "CURSOR FOR LOOP" you can update only the columns mentioned i.e. sal and comm.
>> * If "FOR UPDATE" clause is used, then in the "CURSOR FOR LOOP" you can update any column of the table.

Concepts 23: Cursor variable

Here we will define and discuss intricacies of using cursor variable.

> A cursor variable is a pointer to the work area where a cursor's result set is stored. It can be associated with different query at runtime dynamically. It is similar to pointer in C.
> When you use REF cursor in that you can COMMIT inside the LOOP and will not get invalid cursor or fetch out of sequence error.
> E.g.

```
CREATE TABLE t1(a NUMBER, b NUMBER);
CREATE TABLE t2(a NUMBER, b NUMBER,c NUMBER);
INSERT INTO t1 VALUES(1,2);
INSERT INTO t2 VALUES(1,2,3);
COMMIT;


  set serveroutput on
  DECLARE
    TYPE rc is REF CURSOR;
    v_rc rc;
    v_c1 t1%ROWTYPE;
    v_c2 t2%ROWTYPE;
  BEGIN
    OPEN v_rc FOR SELECT * FROM t1;
    LOOP
      FETCH v_rc INTO v_c1;
      EXIT WHEN v_rc%NOTFOUND;
      COMMIT;
    dbms_output.put_line(v_c1.a);
    END LOOP;
    OPEN v_rc FOR SELECT * FROM t2;
    LOOP
      FETCH v_rc INTO v_c2;
      EXIT WHEN v_rc%NOTFOUND;
      COMMIT;
```

49

```
        dbms_output.put_line(v_c2.a);
      END LOOP;
    END;
    /
```

- A cursor variable can be created using a previously defined cursor variable type or the pre-defined oracle built-in cursor variable "SYS_REFCURSOR". This built-in cursor variable is of type "WEAK" means it does not have return type. If it is of type "STRONG" then there is a fixed return type.
  This is **strong cursor variable type as it has return type**

  ```
  TYPE rc IS  REF CURSOR of EMP%ROWTYPE;
  ```

  So if you use built-in cursor variable then **instead of**
  ```
  DECLARE
  TYPE rc IS  REF CURSOR;
  v_rc rc;
  ```

  You can use as below:
  ```
  DECLARE
  v_rc SYS_REFCURSOR;
  ```

- A cursor variable type can be strong (with a return type) or weak (no return type)

- Only a "cursor variable type" can be declared in a package however "cursor variable" cannot be declared in a package as the cursor variable does not have persistence state.
  e.g.
  ```
  CREATE or REPLACE package pl is
        TYPE cv is ref cursor; --This is "cursor variable type". This is allowed here
        V_cv cv;              -- This is "cursor variable" and hence not allowed here
        V_cv1 sys_refcursor;  -- This is "cursor variable" and hence not allowed here
  ```

- A cursor variable cannot be used over a database link and hence you cannot pass a cursor variable to a procedure when you have remote procedure call.
- A cursor variable cannot be used in comparison operator like equality, inequality or nullity.
- Database table column can be a nested table type but database table column cannot be a cursor variable type.
- A cursor variable and "explicit cursor" cannot always be used interchangeably e.g. a cursor variable cannot be used in a "cursor for loop".
- A null value cannot be assigned to a cursor variable.
- A host variable can be declared as a cursor variable but remember the cursor variable must be of weak type (no return type)
- One of the difference between Ref cursor and normal cursor is: SELECT query is determined at run time for <u>ref cursor</u> but for <u>normal cursor</u> it is determined during compilation.

Concepts 24: Cursor expressions

Here we will discuss how to reduce I/O by returning nested cursor from within a query.

Cursor expressions return nested cursor from within a query. The nested cursor is implicitly opened when the <u>cursor expression is fetched</u> from within a query. So using cursor expression you can return normal data as well as complex parent-child data in a single query which results in reduced I/O and improved performance.
Let us take one example as to how it works without cursor expression:

```
SET serveroutput ON
BEGIN
  FOR i IN
  ( SELECT p.cust_id FROM dc_cust
  )
  LOOP
    dbms_output.put_line('parent is:'||i.cust_id);
    FOR j IN
    ( SELECT c.location_id FROM cust_loc c WHERE cust_id = i.cust_id
    )
    LOOP
      dbms_output.put_line('child is:'||j.location_id);
    END LOOP;
  END LOOP;
END;
/
```

This query is executed for each cust_id

The output:

```
anonymous block completed
parent is:110529
child is:22318
child is:36907
child is:54240
parent is:110606
child is:24
child is:2683
```

Child for the parent 110529

Child for the parent 110606

Note there is huge I/O involved to achieve this as in the second loop you execute the query for each record of first loop. However using cursor expression you can do this with single query executed only once and produce the same result:

```
SET serveroutput ON
DECLARE
  l_dc_cust_id dc_cust.cust_id%TYPE;
  l_children SYS_REFCURSOR;
  l_loc_id dc_loc.location_id%TYPE;
  CURSOR c_cust_id_loc IS
    SELECT p.cust_id,CURSOR(SELECT c.location_id FROM dc_loc c WHERE c.cust_id = p.cust_id) occu_loc
    FROM dc_cust p;
BEGIN
  OPEN c_cust_id_loc;
  LOOP
    FETCH c_cust_id_loc INTO l_dc_cust_id,l_children;
    EXIT WHEN c_cust_id_loc%NOTFOUND;
    DBMS_OUTPUT.put_line('Parent is: ' || l_parent);
    LOOP
      FETCH l_children INTO l_loc_id;
      EXIT WHEN l_children%NOTFOUND;
      DBMS_OUTPUT.put_line('Child is: ' || l_loc_id);
    END LOOP;
    CLOSE l_children;
  END LOOP;
  CLOSE c_cust_id_loc;
END;
/
```

This is cursor expression

The cursor expression result is fetched into this nested cursor
And this open the REF cursor implicitly

Concepts 25: PL/SQL RECORD

Here we will discuss how to define a PL/SQL record.

- A PL/SQL record consists of different elements similar to a database table which has different columns. In other words it is analogous to "C language structure"
  e.g.

```
TYPE l_rec IS RECORD (name varchar2 (30), age number); -- L_rec is "record type"
      V_rec l_rec;                                      -- V_rec is the name of the "record"
```

- Reference of record type element value: **v_rec.name and v_rec.age**
- We cannot compare 2 "records" directly, we have to compare individual elements of the record.
- We can assign a record to another if they have the same type.
- We cannot check the NULLITY on the record directly using "IS NULL". We have to check individual elements of the record.
  So "IF v_rec IS NULL;" is incorrect,
  "IF v_rec.name IS NULL OR v_rec.age is null;" is correct

Concepts 26: PL/SQL INDEX by Table

Here we will discuss how to defining PL/SQL INDEX BY table.

- INDEX BY TABLE consist of homogeneous elements, elements can be scalar type or record type. It is analogous to "C language array of structure" but sparse in nature. PL/SQL table stores multiple values in memory and hence PL/SQL block does not need to go to database every time. This results in better performance.
  E.g.

```
DECLARE
        TYPE l_r IS RECORD (name varchar2 (30), age number);--L_r is "record type"
                                               --This is like structure in C
        TYPE l_IBT_typ IS TABLE OF l_r INDEX BY BINARY_INTEGER;
                                               --l_IBT_typ is "index by table type"
                                               --This is like array of structure in C
        V_IBT_typ l_IBT_typ;                   --V_IBT_typ is the name of "index by table"
BEGIN
        NULL;
END;
/
```

- Reference of PL/SQL index by table's 1st array element value:
  V_IBT_TYP (1).name
  V_IBT_TYP (1).age

- To make index by table NOT NULLABLE use this:
```
TYPE l_IBT_typ IS TABLE OF l_r NOT NULL INDEX BY BINARY_INTEGER;
```

Concepts 27: PL/SQL nested Table

Here we will discuss how to define a Nested table compare it with PL/SQL index by table also will discuss how to resolve uninitialized collection error by means of BULK binding.

- NESTED TABLE consist of homogeneous elements, elements can be scalar type or record type. It is analogous to "C language array of structure"
  E.g.

```
DECLARE
        TYPE l_r IS RECORD (name varchar2 (30), age number);--L_r is "record type"
                                                    --This is like structure in C
        TYPE l_NST_typ IS TABLE OF l_r;            --l_NST_typ is "nested table type"
                                                    --This is like array of structure in C
        V_NST_TYP l_NST_typ    := l_NST_typ();     --This initialize the nested table
   BEGIN
        V_NST_TYP.extend;                          --This will create one null element
   END;
   /
```

> Reference of PL/SQL nested table's 1st array element value:
> **V_NST_TYP (1).name**
> **V_NST_TYP (1).age**

> It differs from INDEX BY table as follows:
>   -- NESTED table can be stored inside database but INDEX BY table cannot be stored
>   -- NESTED table must be initialized and extended but <u>INDEX BY table need not</u>.
>   -- Both NESTED TABLE and INDEX BY table data is stored in PGA memory, however only
>   NESTED TABLE type can be created in database and stored as a table column data.

> **Note:** For NESTED table/Varray if you use bulk collect then you need not initialize or extend
>   the collection. If you do not use BULK COLLECT then initialize/extend is a must for
>   nested table and varray.

Example:

```
CREATE OR REPLACE PACKAGE collection_pkg
IS
TYPE plsql_tab IS TABLE OF NUMBER INDEX BY PLS_INTEGER;
TYPE nest_tab IS  TABLE OF   NUMBER;
TYPE varr IS VARRAY (10) OF NUMBER;
END collection_pkg;
/
```

Now if you use the "PL/SQL table **plsql_tab**" collection it works fine with no error:

```
SET serveroutput ON
DECLARE
  v_collection collection_pkg.plsql_tab;
BEGIN
  v_collection(1) :=100;
  dbms_output.put_line( 'First val is = '||v_collection (v_collection.FIRST));
END;
/
```

However if you use "nested table collection **nest_tab** or varray collection **varr**" it will fail with error.

```
SET serveroutput ON
DECLARE
  v_collection collection_pkg.nest_tab;
BEGIN
  v_collection(1) :=100;
  dbms_output.put_line( 'First val is = '||v_collection (v_collection.FIRST));
END;
/
```

This will error out:

```
ORA-06531: Reference to uninitialized collection
```

To resolve this we have 2 solutions (This solutions are same for **both nested tables and varray** collection and can be used interchangeably by just replacing **nest_tab** to **varr**)

Solution 1:
Initialize the nested table and extend the nested table as highlighted below:

```
SET serveroutput ON
DECLARE
  v_collection collection_pkg.nest_tab :=collection_pkg.nest_tab();
BEGIN
  v_collection.extend;
  v_collection(1) :=100;
  dbms_output.put_line( 'First val is = '||v_collection (v_collection.FIRST));
END;
/
```

Solution 2:
Use bulk collect, which eliminates the need of initialization as well as the need to extend a collection.

```
SET serveroutput ON
DECLARE
  v_collection collection_pkg.nest_tab ;
BEGIN
  SELECT 100 bulk collect INTO v_collection FROM dual;
  dbms_output.put_line( 'First val is = '||v_collection (v_collection.FIRST));
END;
/
```

Note: To get more details about bulk collect refer to Concepts 30: **Native dynamic SQL and Bulk binding**

Concepts 28: VARRAY

Here we will discuss how to define a varray and compare it with PL/SQL nested and index by table.

> VARRAY consist of homogeneous elements, elements can be scalar type or record type. It is analogous to "C language array of structure"
> E.g.

```
DECLARE
    TYPE l_r IS RECORD (name varchar2 (30), age number);--L_r is "record type"
                                              --This is like structure in C
    TYPE l_VARR_typ IS VARRAY(10) OF l_r;     --l_VARR_typ is "varray type"
                                              --This is like fixed array of structure in C
    V_VARR_TYP l_VARR_typ   := l_VARR_typ();  --This initialize the nested table
BEGIN
    V_VARR_TYP.extend;                        --This will create one null element
END;
/
```

> Reference of PL/SQL varray's 1st array element value:
> **V_VARR_TYP (1).name**
> **V_VARR_TYP (1).age**

- It differs from INDEX BY table as follows:
    - Varray must be initialized and extended but index by table need not.
    - Varray data is sequential but index by table data is not sequential.
    - Varray has upper bound on number of element but index by table do not have

- It differs from NESTED table as follows:
    - Varray data is sequential but nested table data is not sequential.
    - Varray has upper bound on number of element but nested table do not have
    - Using varray we cannot do SQL operation but using nested table we can do that.

- BULK COLLECT is used generally to populate a collection (PL/SQL table, nested table and Varray) in one go.

- All type of collection (INDEX BY table, NESTED table, VARRAY) have the following collection methods:
    EXISTS, COUNT, DELETE, FIRST, NEXT, LAST, PRIOR

- In addition to the above methods, NESTED tables and VARRAY have the following 3 collection methods:
    TRIM, EXTEND, LIMIT
    The following example shows how to use collection methods

```
SET serveroutput ON
DECLARE
type test_coll_t IS TABLE OF NUMBER;
  v_test_coll_t test_coll_t :=test_coll_t(100);--initialize and create 1st element with value 100
BEGIN
  v_test_coll_t.extend(3);--Create 3 null elements i.e. 2nd, 3rd and 4th
  v_test_coll_t.delete(2); --Delete the 2nd element
  v_test_coll_t.trim(1); --Delete the element from end of the collection, i.e delete 4th element
  dbms_output.put_line('first element is:'||v_test_coll_t.first); --Provide the 1st element
  dbms_output.put_line('next element is:'||v_test_coll_t.next(v_test_coll_t.first)); --Provide the next element
  dbms_output.put_line('last element is:'||v_test_coll_t.last);--Provide last element
  dbms_output.put_line('value of first element is:'||v_test_coll_t(v_test_coll_t.first)); --Provide the value of 1st element
  dbms_output.put_line('value of last element is:'||v_test_coll_t(v_test_coll_t.last)); --Provide the value of last element
  dbms_output.put_line('count of element is:'||v_test_coll_t.count); --Provide the count of element in the collection
  dbms_output.put_line('limit of element is:'||v_test_coll_t.limit);--for nested tab it is null, varray can have max value
  IF v_test_coll_t.exists(2) THEN --This check the existence of a element in a collection
    dbms_output.put_line('2nd element exists');
  ELSE
    dbms_output.put_line('2nd element deleted');
  END IF;
END;
/
```

The output:
```
PL/SQL procedure successfully completed.

first element is:1
next element is:3
last element is:3
value of first element is:100
value of last element is:
count of element is:2
limit of element is:
2nd element deleted
```

Concepts 29: Exception handling

Here we will discuss mechanism to capture different kinds of error in PL/SQL.

Any error (<u>oracle error</u> or <u>user defined error</u> or <u>business error</u>) detected while executing a PL/SQL code can be captured using EXCEPTION block. This is very important in any programming to make sure all kinds of errors are handled appropriately by adopting appropriate approach and report them.
E.g. <u>Pre-defined Oracle exceptions:</u> (these predefined exceptions are stored in STANDARD package)

```
DECLARE
  V_col Tab.column%TYPE;
BEGIN
  SELECT column INTO v_col FROM Tab;
EXCEPTION
WHEN no_data_found THEN
  dbms_output.put_line('no data IN TABLE TAB');
WHEN OTHERS THEN
  Raise_application_error(-20001,'Error IS:'||sqlerrm);
END;
/
```

To know how to systematically display error content in the exception block refer to Chapter 8 Tips 8: **Restructuring error stack in 12c**
To know how to systematically display backtrace content in the exception block refer to Chapter 8 Tips 9: **Restructuring backtrace in 12c**

<u>User defined oracle exception:</u>

Use PRAGMA EXCEPTION_INIT pragma to associate user defined exception with an Oracle error number
E.g.

```
DECLARE
  deadlock_ex EXCEPTION;
  PRAGMA EXCEPTION_INIT (deadlock_ex,-00060);
  V_col Tab.column%TYPE;
BEGIN
  SELECT column INTO v_col FROM Tab;
EXCEPTION
WHEN deadlock_ex THEN
  dbms_output.put_line('deadlock detected, error is:'||sqlerrm);
WHEN OTHERS THEN
  Raise_application_error(-20001,'Error IS:'||sqlerrm);
END;
/
```

Business exceptions:
E.g. here the exception is raised against any business error

```
SET serveroutput ON
DECLARE
  sales_ex EXCEPTION;
  V_col Tab.column%TYPE;
BEGIN
  SELECT column INTO v_col FROM Tab;
  IF v_col =0 THEN
    raise sales_ex;
  END IF;
EXCEPTION
WHEN sales_ex THEN
  dbms_output.put_line('business error, v_col value is zero');
WHEN OTHERS THEN
  Raise_application_error(-20001,'Error IS:'||sqlerrm);
END;
/
```

Concepts 30: Native dynamic SQL and Bulk binding

Here we will discuss dynamic execution of SQL and processing records in bulk.

- ➤ Native dynamic sql is implemented using 2 constructs
  - 1. Execute immediate
  - 2. Open <cursor name> for

- ➤ Native dynamic sql will make a code to run from direct SQL. So functionality like "CREATE table/ALTER table/or any new SQL syntax" can be executed from PL/SQL using NDS execute immediate construct.

- ➤ Database object name or column name cannot be passed as bind variable otherwise we will receive invalid identifier error. This is because during "parsing of SQL statement" ORACLE check the syntax and semantic of statement, however parsing step happens before "binding" any variables to the dynamic statement which result into invalid identifier error.
  E.g.

```
DECLARE
   column_name VARCHAR2(30) :='a';
   v_a          NUMBER;
BEGIN
   EXECUTE immediate 'CREATE TABLE Test123(:1 NUMBER)' USING column_name;
END;
/
```

Output:

```
ORA-00904: : invalid identifier
```

However you can use the identifier as normal variable as shown in the below example:

```
DECLARE
   column_name VARCHAR2(30) :='a';
   v_a          NUMBER;
BEGIN
   EXECUTE immediate 'CREATE TABLE Test123('||column_name||' NUMBER)';
END;
/
```

Note: For real life example of binding collection using EXECUTE IMMEDIATE (NDS) refer to Chapter 4 Tips 7: **Move all versions of flashback data dynamically**
Chapter 8 Tips 17: **Improve performance by incorporating one parse and multiple execute use of BIND variable**

➢ Using construct "Open <cursor name> for" we can implement NDS as shown below:

```
SET serveroutput ON
DECLARE
   v_cv SYS_REFCURSOR;
   v_stmt VARCHAR2(2000);
   v_job  VARCHAR2(20) :='IT_PROG';
type emp_rec_tab
IS
   TABLE OF hr.employees%rowtype INDEX BY binary_integer;
   v_emp_rec_tab emp_rec_tab;
BEGIN
   v_stmt :='select * from hr.employees where JOB_ID=:b';
   OPEN v_cv FOR v_stmt USING v_job;
   FETCH v_cv bulk collect INTO v_emp_rec_tab;
   FOR j IN 1..v_emp_rec_tab.count
   LOOP
     dbms_output.put_line('first_name :'||v_emp_rec_tab(j).first_name||' sal is:'||v_emp_rec_tab(j).salary);
   END LOOP;
   CLOSE v_cv;
END;
/
```

The output:
```
PL/SQL procedure successfully completed.

first_name :Alexander sal is:9000
first_name :Bruce sal is:6000
first_name :David sal is:4800
first_name :Valli sal is:4800
first_name :Diana sal is:4200
```

➢ Bulk binding is a way of processing more than 1 record in a single call by eliminating context switch between SQL and PL/SQL engine
   1. For DML use FORALL construct
   2. For select use BULK COLLECT construct

➢ SAVE EXCEPTIONS construct saves all the error records in SQL%BULK_EXCEPTIONS PL/SQL table and continue processing all the DML statements.
   E.g.
```
FORALL I IN 1..V_NST_TYP.COUNT SAVE EXCEPTIONS --This will save the exception records
--INSERT INTO some_tab values(V_NST_TYP(I));--This will insert only the proper records
EXCEPTION
FOR J in 1..SQL%BULK_EXCEPTIONS.COUNT LOOP
  DBMS_OUTPUT.put_line('Error: ' || I ||
  ' Array Index: ' || SQL%BULK_EXCEPTIONS(i).error_index ||
  ' Message: ' || SQLERRM(SQL%BULK_EXCEPTIONS(i).ERROR_CODE));
END LOOP;
```

   SQL%BULK_EXCEPTIONS PL/SQL table has 2 elements error_index and error_code.

➢ SQL%BULK_ROWCOUNT (i) stores number of row impacted at i[th] iteration. This is used with FORALL statement.
   E.g.
```
CREATE TABLE t1  (a NUMBER, b NUMBER);
INSERT INTO t1 VALUES  (1,2);  ⎤
INSERT INTO t1 VALUES  (1,2);  ⎬ ←——————— 3 records for key a=1
INSERT INTO t1 VALUES  (1,9);  ⎦
INSERT INTO t1 VALUES  (2,2);  ⎤
INSERT INTO t1 VALUES  (2,5);  ⎬ ←——————— 3 records for key a=2
INSERT INTO t1 VALUES  (2,8);  ⎦
INSERT INTO t1 VALUES  (3,20); ⎤
INSERT INTO t1 VALUES  (3,25); ⎦ ←——————— 2 records for key a=3
COMMIT;
```

```
SET serveroutput ON
DECLARE
type tl IS TABLE OF NUMBER INDEX BY binary_integer;
  v_tl tl;
  k NUMBER :=1;
BEGIN
  SELECT DISTINCT a bulk collect INTO v_tl FROM tl;
  FORALL I IN 1..v_tl.count
  UPDATE tl SET b=b*10 WHERE a=v_tl(I);
  FOR I IN 1..v_tl.count LOOP
    dbms_output.put_line('Number of record updated at iteration:'||k||' for column a='||v_tl(I)||' is:'||SQL%BULK_ROWCOUNT(I));
    k :=k+1;
  END LOOP;
END;
/
```

Output:
```
anonymous block completed
Number of record updated at iteration:1 for column a=1 is:3
Number of record updated at iteration:2 for column a=2 is:3
Number of record updated at iteration:3 for column a=3 is:2
```

➤ "INDICES OF" clause let us iterate over <u>non-consecutive sparse collection</u> (which has got some deleted element in between) in a FORALL statement.
E.g.
```
CREATE TABLE t2   (a NUMBER);

DECLARE
type tl IS TABLE OF NUMBER INDEX BY binary_integer;
  v_tl tl;
BEGIN
  SELECT DISTINCT a bulk collect INTO v_tl FROM tl;
  v_tl.delete(2);--This removes the 2nd element
  FORALL I IN 1..v_tl.count
INSERT INTO t2 values (v_tl(I));
END;
/
```
This will fail because you have deleted 2nd element from the collection and then trying to INSERT into table t2 rest of the element.
```
ORA-22160: element at index [2] does not exist
ORA-06512: at line 7
22160. 00000 -  "element at index [%s] does not exist"
*Cause:    Collection element at the given index does not exist.
*Action:   Specify the index of an element which exists.
```

To resolve this you can use INDICES OF clause as below:

```
DECLARE
type tl IS TABLE OF NUMBER INDEX BY binary_integer;
  v_tl tl;
BEGIN
  SELECT DISTINCT a bulk collect INTO v_tl FROM tl;
  v_tl.delete(2);--This removes the 2nd element
  FORALL I IN INDICES OF v_tl
INSERT INTO t2 values (v_tl(I));
END;
/
```

Note: Bulk collect does not restrict the size of a collection and hence if the SELECT return large amount of data it is advisable to limit the resultset. To see how to LIMIT the resultset Refer **to** Chapter 8 Tips 18: **BULK OPERATION hinders performance and the solution**

➢ Execute immediate construct make the code to evaluate at run time not in compile time.

➢ NDS is faster than static sql if it is executed less number of time because it remove the context switching between SQL and PL/SQL engine as it executes the code natively.

➢ We cannot use FORALL and "SELECT BULK COLLECT" together as below
   E.g.
```
FORALL I IN 1..<nested table>.COUNT
SELECT * BULK COLLECT INTO <other nested table>;
```

➢ We can use FORALL and "BULK COLLECT" together in the returning clause as below
   E.g.
```
FORALL I IN 1..<nested table>.COUNT
INSERT INTO <table name> values ... RETURNING * BULK COLLECT
INTO <other nested table>;
```

Concepts 31: STORED SUBPROGRAM

Here we will define stored subprogram and will discuss all the concepts associated with it.

➢ Stored subprograms are actually named PL/SQL blocks which are stored inside database.
➢ We can pass a function or procedure name as an argument to any stored subprogram. To do this you must use NDS execute immediate construct.
   E.g.
```
CREATE OR REPLACE
PROCEDURE proc_test(
    func_name VARCHAR2,
    ret_val OUT VARCHAR2)
IS
BEGIN
  EXECUTE IMMEDIATE 'BEGIN :v :='||func_name||'; END;' USING OUT ret_val;
END;
/
```

➢ To execute a stored program from other schema we have to provide
```
GRANT EXECUTE ON <stored program name> TO <schema name>;
```

61

- ➤ Example of autonomous_transaction:

```
CREATE OR REPLACE PROCEDURE autonomous_progress_proc(msg VARCHAR2)
IS
  PRAGMA AUTONOMOUS_TRANSACTION;
BEGIN
  INSERT INTO LOG_UNIT(log_date,MESSAGE)
  VALUES(sysdate,msg);
  COMMIT;
END autonomous_progress_proc;
/
```

Pragma is compiler directive. Pragma autonomous_transaction instructs PL/SQL compiler to start a new independent transaction inside the main transaction.

```
BEGIN
  INSERT INTO log_unit(log_date,message) VALUES(sysdate-2,'This is a test');
  autonomous_progress_proc('This is genuine message');
  ROLLBACK;
END;
/
```

- ➤ So even if there is "ROLLBACK" still "This is genuine message" is inserted in the table. Only the message "This is a test" is rollback.
- ➤ **Note:** When you have autonomous procedure/function you <u>must commit/rollback</u> inside that procedure (as shown in **autonomous_progress_proc**). If inside the procedure you do not use "COMMIT/ROLLBACK" then if you execute that autonomous procedure it will fail with error:

```
ORA-06519: active autonomous transaction detected and rolled back
```

- ➤ Pipelining <u>table function</u> works similar to FIRST_ROW hint i.e. it does not wait for entire result-set to be constructed before returning the result. It returns the result of the pipelining table function using PIPE ROW command.

  e.g.

```
CREATE OR REPLACE type n_typ IS TABLE OF NUMBER;
/
CREATE OR REPLACE FUNCTION pipe_fl(a NUMBER)
 RETURN n_typ PIPELINED
  IS
  BEGIN
    FOR I IN 1..a
    LOOP
      PIPE ROW (i);
    END LOOP;
    RETURN;
END pipe_fl;
/
```

Now if you run:

```
SELECT * FROM TABLE (pipe_fl (5000)) WHERE rownum<10;
```

Will return promptly.

It is observed that pipelined function works faster than non-pipelined function for 1st few rows. However if you want all the 5000 records then PIPELINED does not work fast.

Note: Using "<u>TABLE operator</u>" and "<u>ORDER BY</u>" you can convert any collection and rearrange the content sorted. E.g.

Select COLUMN_VALUE FROM **TABLE** (pipe_f1 (500)) order by COLUMN_VALUE;

➤ DETERMINISTIC is optimizer hint which informs the query optimizer if the function should be called redundantly or use the pre-computed result.
E.g.

```
CREATE OR REPLACE FUNCTION upper_name_f(ename VARCHAR2)
    RETURN VARCHAR2 DETERMINISTIC
  IS
  BEGIN
    RETURN UPPER(ename);
  END upper_name_f;
/
```

Now let's say you have 1000 distinct employee name in product_sale table but there are 1 million records in that case if upper_name_f is called millions of time it will re-use pre computed value of ename.

Let us take one more example where factorial value need to be derived for millions of records in a table but number of values for which factorial need to be derived is only few thousand then the use of "DETERMINISTIC" keyword gives manifold performance improvement by re-using the pre-computed factorial value:

```
CREATE OR REPLACE FUNCTION fact(num NUMBER) RETURN NUMBER DETERMINISTIC
IS
  fac_val NUMBER := 1;
BEGIN
  FOR i IN 1..num LOOP
    fac_val := fac_val*i;
  END LOOP;
RETURN fac_val;
END fact;
/
```

Note: DETERMINISTIC function operate only for a session level. However if you want to get the advantage across all the sessions then just replace "DETERMINISTIC" by "RESULT_CACHE". Since "RESULT_CACHE" is cross-session specific the performance is realized if the same query is executed from different sessions. You can use "RESULT_CACHE" from 11g onward. For in-depth analysis refer to Chapter 6 Tips 2: Result cache function **or** deterministic function **or** PL/SQL collection

➤ AUTHID clause determines if a subprogram is created with DEFINER or INVOKER right model. The default is definer right. If you use AUTHID CURRENT_USER then the subprogram will be invoker right.

➤ NOCOPY is compiler hint which passes IN OUT parameter by means of reference instead of value. For normal IN OUT parameter, actual and formal parameter refer to different memory location whereas when you use IN OUT NOCOPY then actual and formal parameter refer to same memory location.
IN OUT NOCOPY performs faster because it does not copy actual parameter into formal parameter, instead it refers to the memory location of the actual parameter.
In order to use NOCOPY just replace
"IN OUT" by "IN OUT NOCOPY"
"OUT" by "OUT NOCOPY"
In your subprogram where you pass parameters/arguments.

➤ If a function has DML inside it then we cannot call the function from SQL SELECT statement, if you try you will get error "**ORA-14551: cannot perform DML operation inside a query**".
Here is the workaround to call the function from SELECT statement by means of AUTONOMOUS_TRANSACTION.

```
CREATE OR REPLACE    FUNCTION f1
    RETURN NUMBER
  IS
    PRAGMA AUTONOMOUS_TRANSACTION;
  BEGIN
    UPDATE tab1 SET cola=120;
    COMMIT;
END f1;
/
SELECT f1 FROM dual;
```
This will run successfully and update the table.

➤ If a function **return datatype** is Boolean, binary_integer, associative array then you cannot call the function from SQL select because these datatype are not supported in SQL.

➤ Overloading is the process of declaring procedure/function inside a package with same name more than once but having different parameters in terms of datatype, number of parameter, different argument name etc.

So if two overloaded procedure are having same type of argument but with different argument name, then in order to call the overloaded procedure you must use named notation.

Creation of overloaded function:
```
CREATE OR REPLACE PACKAGE reg_cntry_pkg
IS
  FUNCTION overload_func(region_name VARCHAR2) RETURN NUMBER;
  FUNCTION overload_func(country_name VARCHAR2) RETURN NUMBER;
END reg_cntry_pkg;
/
CREATE OR REPLACE PACKAGE BODY reg_cntry_pkg
IS
  FUNCTION overload_func(region_name VARCHAR2) RETURN NUMBER
  IS
  BEGIN
   RETURN 1;
  END overload_func;
  FUNCTION overload_func(country_name VARCHAR2) RETURN NUMBER
  IS
  BEGIN
   RETURN 2;
  END overload_func;
END reg_cntry_pkg;
/
```
Execute the overloaded function:
```
DECLARE
  region_id  NUMBER;
  country_id NUMBER;
BEGIN
  region_id  :=reg_cntry_pkg.overload_func(region_name=>'ASIA');
  country_id :=reg_cntry_pkg.overload_func(country_name=>'INDIA');
END;
/
```
This PL/SQL block will work fine prior to 11g and from 11g.

However <u>named notation</u> cannot be used from SQL SELECT statement **prior to 11g**.

```
SELECT reg_cntry_pkg.overload_func(region_name=>'ASIA') FROM dual;
```

Prior to 11g this statement will fail. In 11g and above this will work fine as named notation can be used both in PL/SQL call and SQL SELECT call.

Note: You cannot use positional notation as below for this example

```
DECLARE
  region_id  NUMBER;
BEGIN
  region_id  :=reg_cntry_pkg.overload_func('ASIA');
END;
/
```

It will fail with error:

```
PLS-00307: too many declarations of 'OVERLOAD_FUNC' match this call
```

Because oracle will not be able to find out which overloaded function it will execute as both the overloaded function in the package has parameter which is of type VARCHAR2. This is why we used named notation for this case.

If you have more than 1 argument in your package (E.g. **Package1.overload_func**) function then you can use <u>mixed notation</u> (i.e. positional **plus** named notation) as below:

```
A :=Package1.overload_func(1,region_name=>'Asia');
```

Positional notation

Named notation

> Positional notation: Here argument value is passed in the same order as they exist in the subprogram
> Named notation: Here argument value is passed in any order as we associate the argument value to the actual parameter name.
> Mixed notation: Here we mix positional and named notation. Note in this case positional notation must be preceding the named notation.

> Package public variables persist for the duration of a session and hence all the subprograms executed from the same session will share the value set in that specific session. <u>Other sessions will see the actual value</u>.
> This is how you can see <u>different versions of the package variable</u> from different sessions.
> e.g.

```
CREATE OR REPLACE PACKAGE persist_pkg
IS
  A NUMBER :=100;
END persist_pkg;
/
```

Session 1

```
SET serveroutput ON
BEGIN
  Persist_pkg.a :=1500;
END;
/
```

This value 1500 of the package variable (a) will persist in the "session 1" no matter how this variable is called from any sub program or anonymous block.

Session 2

```
SET serveroutput ON
BEGIN
  Dbms_output.put_line(persist_pkg.a);
END;
/
```
This will return: 100

- ➢ **Package cursor** and **package variable** state persisted throughout the session is the <u>default behaviour</u>. Using **pragma** serially_reusable we can change the behaviour so that the cursor and variable state is <u>persisted only for the duration of the **call/execution**</u> (Not throughout the session). If there is next call to the package then the package is again re instantiated.
  e.g.

```
CREATE OR REPLACE PACKAGE time_pkg
IS
  PRAGMA SERIALLY_REUSABLE;
  X VARCHAR2(30) :=TO_CHAR(sysdate,'dd-mm-yyyy hh24:mi:ss');
END time_pkg;
/


  SET serveroutput ON
  BEGIN
    dbms_output.put_line(time_pkg.X);
  END;
  /
```

This return exact time in seconds when it is executed each time as below.

Anonymous block completed
26-04-2016 18:05:06

Anonymous block completed
26-04-2016 18:05:07

Using this PRAGMA, a cursor declared in package specification need not be closed as it is open only for the duration of the execution.

Using <u>PRAGMA serially_reusable can reduce the load</u> on PGA by not storing any value throughout the session. This feature is in contrast of package initialization which load the package in memory and persists across the session. Package initialization is discussed in chapter 8 Tips 15: **Improve performance using Oracle package initialization**

Note: If you do not use the pragma the output will always be same, as long as the session persist because by default the package variable value persists throughout the session. This kind of pragma is used in package when you are short of PGA memory and your program refer to cursor <u>which holds large amount of data</u> and may potentially cause PGA swapping issue. When you refer this PRAGMA in your package then the package cannot be called from "**SQL select**" and **TRIGGER** and gives error:

```
06534. 00000 - "Cannot access Serially Reusable package %s"
*Cause:   The program attempted to access a Serially Reusable package in
     PL/SQL called from SQL context (trigger or otherwise). Such an
     access is currently unsupported.
```

Here we will discuss different model (Definer and Invoker) and will discuss handling of dependencies for subprograms

➤ In definer rights model a program is executed based on the privilege of the creator/definer.
E.g.
Connect to U1:

```
CREATE OR REPLACE
PROCEDURE proc_def
IS
BEGIN
  EXECUTE immediate 'CREATE TABLE T_DEF(a number)';
END proc_def;
/

GRANT EXECUTE ON proc_def TO u2;
```

Connect to U2
Exec U1.proc_def
This will create the TABLE "**T_DEF**" in "U1" schema <u>which is definer</u> of "proc_def" procedure.

➤ In invoker rights model a program is executed based on the privilege of the caller/invoker of the program.
E.g.

```
CREATE OR REPLACE
PROCEDURE proc_inv AUTHID CURRENT_USER
IS
BEGIN
  EXECUTE immediate 'CREATE TABLE T_INV(a number)';
END proc_inv;
/

GRANT EXECUTE ON proc_inv TO u2;
```

Connect to U2
Exec U1.proc_inv
This will create the TABLE "T_INV" in "U2" schema <u>which invokes</u> procedure "proc_inv".

➤ Both definer right and invoker right model roles are disabled inside stored program for compilation.

```
CREATE OR REPLACE
PROCEDURE proc_def_in_u2
IS
  v_a NUMBER;
BEGIN
  SELECT a INTO v_a FROM u1.T_DEF ;
END proc_def_in_u2;
/
```

```
CREATE OR REPLACE
PROCEDURE proc_inv_in_u2 AUTHID CURRENT_USER
IS
  v_a NUMBER;
BEGIN
  SELECT a INTO v_a FROM u1.T_DEF ;
END proc_inv_in_u2;
/
```
Both will fail with error

`PL/SQL: ORA-00942: table or view does not exist`

To resolve this solution is:
Connect to u1

`GRANT SELECT ON t_def TO u2;` --This provides explicit grant (not via role)

➢ Definer right model <u>roles are disabled</u> inside stored program <u>at runtime</u> also.
Connect to u1:

```
CREATE role select_role;
GRANT SELECT ON T_DEF TO select_role;
GRANT select_role TO U2;
```

Connect to u2:

```
CREATE OR REPLACE
PROCEDURE proc_def_in_u2
IS
  v_a NUMBER;
BEGIN
  EXECUTE IMMEDIATE 'SELECT a FROM u1.T_DEF' INTO v_a ;
END proc_def_in_u2;
/
```
This compile fine as it is NDS
But in **runtime** it fails with error <u>table or view does not exist</u>

➢ Invoker right model <u>roles are enabled</u> inside stored program <u>at runtime only</u>
Connect to u1:

```
CREATE role select_role;
GRANT SELECT ON T_DEF TO select_role;
GRANT select_role TO U2;
```

Connect to u2:

```
CREATE OR REPLACE
PROCEDURE proc_inv_in_u2 AUTHID CURRENT_USER
IS
  v_a NUMBER;
BEGIN
  EXECUTE IMMEDIATE 'SELECT a FROM u1.T_DEF' INTO v_a;
END proc_inv_in_u2;
/
```
This compiles fine as it is NDS
Also at **runtime** it does not give any error as roles are enabled for invoker right code at runtime.

➢ When an invoker right code is called from definer right code (e.g. any definer right stored Procedure, Trigger, DBMS_JOB etc.) then it is executed under the authority of the definer i.e. creator.

68

E.g. the invoker right code is called from DBMS_JOB.

```
VARIABLE jobno NUMBER;
BEGIN
  DBMS_JOB.SUBMIT(:jobno;
  'proc_inv_in_u2;';
  SYSDATE+1);
  COMMIT;
END;
/
```

This will <u>fail because</u> the invoker right code proc_inv_in_u2 will act like DEFINER when it is called from DEFINER RIGHT program DBMS_JOB.

➤ Using parameter "REMOTE_DEPENDENCIES_MODE" you can set the remote dependency as TIMESTAMP or SIGNATURE. <u>Default is TIMESTAMP model</u>. In this model oracle compares **LAST_DDL_TIME** of an object before invalidating the dependent object.
In SIGNATURE model oracle compare the interface i.e. procedure name, arguments etc. before invalidating the dependent object.

Concepts 33: Trigger

Here will define and mention few notable points about usage of trigger.

➤ Trigger is a stored object which fires implicitly (unlike stored procedure/function which need to be execute explicitly) when a triggering event like DML/DDL/system event occurs. The way constraints are used to automatically enforce data integrity similarly trigger can be used to enforce data integrity as well as enforce business validation.

E.g. Using CHECK constraint we implement data integrity as below:

```
CREATE TABLE check_tab_t
  (empid NUMBER PRIMARY KEY,
   ename VARCHAR2(30),
   sal number(10,4),
   deptid number,
   CHECK(sal>0)
  );
```

Instead of using CHECK constraint we can maintain data integrity using trigger also:

```
DROP TABLE check_tab_t;
CREATE TABLE check_tab_t
  (empid NUMBER PRIMARY KEY,
   ename VARCHAR2(30),
   sal number(10,4),
   deptid number
  );
```

```
CREATE OR REPLACE TRIGGER trig_check_tab_t before
  INSERT OR UPDATE ON check_tab_t FOR EACH row
BEGIN
 IF INSERTING OR UPDATING THEN
  IF :new.sal=0 THEN raise_application_error('-20001','Sal must be greater than zero');
  END IF;
 END IF;
END trig_check_tab_t;
/
```

So now if you try to insert the below it will give error:

```
INSERT INTO check_tab_t VALUES(3,'Asim',0,10);
SQL Error: ORA-20001: Sal must be greater than zero
ORA-06512: at "U2.TRIG_CHECK_TAB_T", line 4
ORA-04088: error during execution of trigger 'U2.TRIG_CHECK_TAB_T'
```

➤ In the above example if you use "**after insert**" instead of "**before insert**" then it will not give the above error. However the error is expected and correct one and hence you must use "**before insert**" trigger for this case.

Also note if you use "**after insert**" type of trigger you cannot modify the inserted value
E.g. inside the trigger you <u>cannot set</u>
:NEW.Sal:=1000;
However if you use "**before insert**" type of trigger you can do the above. This is because "**after insert**" type of trigger is executed after the DML (insert/update/delete) and hence you cannot modify already inserted value.

➤ **NEW** and **OLD** are pseudo records and the data structure is similar to PL/SQL record which contains the value for the updated/inserted rows. These 2 pseudo columns are only available in the row level trigger.

➤ **NEW** pseudo record is not available for deleted rows and **OLD** is not available for inserted rows

➤ "WHEN" clause used in a trigger restricts the trigger execution based on the condition mentioned in the "WHEN" clause. Note do not use ":" before **NEW/OLD** pseudo column in the "**WHEN**" clause. E.g. in the above example if you want to use "WHEN" clause:

```
CREATE OR REPLACE TRIGGER trig_check_tab_t before
  INSERT OR UPDATE ON check_tab_t FOR EACH row WHEN NEW.sal>10000
```

➤ "**_SYSTEM_TRIG_ENABLED**" parameter must be set to **true** in order to fire system event trigger (e.g. startup, shutdown, servererror etc.) and user event trigger (logon, logoff, DDL etc.).

➤ Cannot commit inside DML trigger but using PRAGMA autonomus_transaction you can commit inside the trigger.

➤ Trigger helps to maintain data integrity and helps to implement complex business rules.

➤ Helps gather session and system level statistics on logon/logoff/shutdown.

➤ For some advanced example on trigger refer to Chapter 6 Tips 13: **Mutating trigger resolution using collection or Global temporary table**

Here we will discuss how to protect PL/SQL source code efficiently.

Wrap is an oracle utility which will protect the PL/SQL source code. Wrap is a one way encryption process for your file and there is no way you can un-wrap the function, so make sure your original file is backed up. The objective of wrap functionality is to make sure that someone who is having access to DBA_SOURCE cannot see the original source code. Conventional way of using WRAP utility from OS prompt:

```
Wrap iname=[pl/SQL file name.sql] oname=[output file.plb]
```

Limitations of WRAP utility:
  ➤ You cannot wrap the source code of a trigger (you can only wrap procedure/function/package)
  ➤ Wrap does not detect syntax or semantic error and hence the wrapped code compiles fine even if there is missing object or incorrect syntax
  ➤ Wrapped code is forward compatible for import into database i.e. you can import 10g wrapped module into 11g but not vice versa.

To resolve the first limitation it is advisable to keep the code of trigger body in function/procedure and wrap the function/procedure and call that from trigger body.

To resolve last two limitations, oracle 11g has introduced WRAP function and CREATE_WRAPPED procedure in DBMS_DDL package.

E.g. of using DBMS_DDL.WRAP function.

```
SET SERVEROUTPUT ON 10000000000
DECLARE
  l_source  VARCHAR2(32767);
  l_wrap    VARCHAR2(32767);
BEGIN
  l_source := 'CREATE OR REPLACE PACKAGE body white_pkg AS' ||
              'PROCEDURE pl is ' ||
              'BEGIN ' ||
              'protected_pkg.protected_pl;'||
              'END;'||
              'END;';

  l_wrap := SYS.DBMS_DDL.WRAP(ddl => l_source);
  DBMS_OUTPUT.put_line(l_wrap);
END;
/
```

Here we will discuss how to identify potential performance issues and presence of unwanted code during compilation.

  ➤ From oracle 10g onward we can identify potential performance issues and presence of unnecessary code through warning messages during compilation and accordingly modify or repair your code to make it more robust in terms of performance and scalability.

  ➤ Example 1 performance issue:
```
ALTER SESSION SET PLSQL_WARNINGS='ENABLE:ALL';
```

```
CREATE TABLE num_tab   (a NUMBER);

CREATE OR REPLACE PROCEDURE proc_pref_warn
AUTHID DEFINER
AS
   x varchar2(10):='11';
BEGIN
    INSERT INTO num_tab VALUES(x);
END proc_pref_warn;
/
```
This procedure will give the following warning during compilation

⚠ Warning(6,30): PLW-07202: bind type would result in conversion away from column type

Because in table "**num_tab**" the column is of data type number however the variable "x" used in the procedure is varchar2 and hence it will force internal data type conversion from char to number which results in bad performance.

For **implicit data type conversion** refer to chapter 2 Tips 10: **Ordering table rows without using ORDER BY clause of indexed column and steps to eliminate SORTING**

➤ Example 2 unnecessary code identification:
```
CREATE OR REPLACE PROCEDURE proc_warning
IS
   x NUMBER :=12;
   PROCEDURE junk_code
   IS
   BEGIN
     NULL;
   END junk_code;
BEGIN
   DBMS_OUTPUT.put_line ('value of x is:'||x);
END proc_warning;
/
```
This procedure will give the following warning during compilation

⚠ Warning(1,1): PLW-05018: unit PROC_WARNING omitted optional AUTHID clause; default value DEFINER used

⚠ Warning(6,4): PLW-06006: uncalled procedure "JUNK_CODE" is removed.

Because in the procedure <u>we have **not**</u> used "AUTHID DEFINER" and "JUNK_CODE" is <u>unnecessary</u> and hence needs to be removed otherwise this will add to the maintenance cost.

Note the procedure does not contain any error and hence when you fire
```
SHOW ERRORS PROCEDURE proc_warning
```
It will return no error and hence you can use your code as it is.

➤ To check whether the warning flag is set in your database, use the following command:
```
SET serveroutput ON
BEGIN
   dbms_output.put_line('PLSQL warning is:'||$$PLSQL_WARNINGS);
END;
/
```
This will output:
```
PLSQL warning is:ENABLE:ALL
```

Here we will define conditional compilation and explore different dimension of conditional compilation to have version independent code, control on choosing different approaches without touching the code, conditional control on commit/rollback etc.

> "**CONDITIONAL COMPILATION**" is introduced in Oracle 10gR2. This process excludes or includes <u>certain portions of code</u> at the time of compilation.

> This means an API can contain both OLD and NEW versions of code, in other words this lets you create version independent code. Pre-12c environment you can compile the code which contains 12c related new features. This is possible because $IF/$ELSE are pre-processor **selection directives** which will selectively exclude certain portions of code during compilation.
> E.g.

```
ALTER session SET PLSQL_CCFLAGS='version_12c: true';


CREATE OR REPLACE
PROCEDURE version_independent_p
IS
BEGIN
  $IF $$version_12c $then
  --Use code related WITH 12c NEW feature LIKE match_recognize clause;
$ELSE
--Use code prior TO 12c feature;
  $END
END;
/
```

This will compile fine in 11g also even though **match_recognize** clause <u>is undefined in</u> Oracle 11g as it was introduced in 12c (in 11g you must set **version_12c :false**).

> "**Version_12c**" is a <u>user defined inquiry directive</u>. This is set using **PLSQL_CCFLAGS initialization parameter** (This parameter allow PL/SQL programmer to control conditional compilation of each PL/SQL unit).
> We have <u>predefined inquiry directives</u> like PLSQL_LINE, PLSQL_UNIT, PLSQL_DEBUG, PLSQL_WARNINGS etc. All the inquiry directives **are prefixed by $$** as shown in the example above.

> Similarly you can use user defined inquiry directive to declare a variable suitable to an environment. Also you can keep dynamic and static code together in the same application. In fact you can keep different approaches for a particular design in the same code and use different approach based on feasibility by setting the user defined directive to point to a certain approach.
> E.g.

```
SET serveroutput ON
ALTER session SET PLSQL_CCFLAGS='Approach:2';
BEGIN
  $IF $$Approach   =1 $THEN dbms_output.put_line('Inside Approach 1');
  $ELSIF $$Approach=2 $THEN dbms_output.put_line('Inside Approach 2');
  $ELSE dbms_output.put_line('Inside Approach 3');
  $END
END;
/
```

For this case we have set Approach to 2 and hence Approach 2 will be used. Note without touching the code we are able to control the code as to which approach to use.

➤ Do not put "COMMIT" directly in your code, rather conditionally put "COMMIT" so that you can control from outside the code when to "COMMIT" by user defined inquiry directive.
This way you can disable "COMMIT" in your code and run the program. After you analyze the result you can "ROLLBACK" the change and test again.
E.g.

```
ALTER session SET PLSQL_CCFLAGS='IS_COMMIT:FALSE';


CREATE OR REPLACE
PROCEDURE proc_flexible_commit
IS
BEGIN
  INSERT INTO t1 VALUES
    (12,999
    );
  UPDATE t1 SET b=599 WHERE a=1;
  $IF $$IS_COMMIT $THEN
  COMMIT;
  $ELSE NULL;
  $END
END;
/
```

```
EXEC proc_flexible_commit
```
This will perform all the activity and you can "ROLLBACK" the change as the records are not committed.

You can change the setting to enable COMMIT using:
```
ALTER PROCEDURE proc_flexible_commit COMPILE PLSQL_CCFLAGS='IS_COMMIT:TRUE
REUSE SETTINGS;
```

You can see the current setting for procedure either TRUE or FALSE:
```
SELECT name,
  plsql_ccflags
FROM user_plsql_object_settings
WHERE upper(NAME)='PROC_FLEXIBLE_COMMIT';
```
Output:

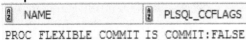

NAME	PLSQL_CCFLAGS
PROC_FLEXIBLE_COMMIT	IS_COMMIT:FALSE

Similarly you can use "IS_DEBUG" user defined directive if you want to see debug information.
Note "IS_DEBUG" coupled with "IS_COMMIT" user defined directive will make your application robust in terms of instrumentation and helps resolving/testing any issues in smartest possible way.

Chapter 2: Different viewpoint of Index for developer and dba (22 pages)

An index is a database object which points to the data in a table. It creates an entry for each value that appears in the table's indexed column, it provides fast access to tables' rows.

Here in this chapter we will not discuss creation of different types of index rather we will discuss the practical usability of this index from the viewpoints of the developer and the dba.
You will be thrilled to know that intricate functionality can be implemented using this structure with ease.

Tips 1 : Function Based Index or Indexed Virtual column in 11g?
Tips 2 : Invisible index and usage?
Tips 3 : Multiple indexes on same column in Oracle 12c?
Tips 4 : INDEX order in composite index or INDEX only access?
Tips 5 : Table lock on parent table for missing index on foreign key column
Tips 6 : virtual indexes- INDEXES WITH NO SEGMENTS Benefits
Tips 7 : Oracle index skip scan case study run time drop from 4 hr. to 10 sec?
Tips 8 : How to force optimizer to use or not use index?
Tips 9 : Non Unique index with null values or not null value for the column?
Tips 10: Ordering table rows without using ORDER BY clause and steps to eliminate SORTING?
Tips 11: Case study using "Index only scan" and DETERMINISTIC function for performance?
Tips 12: Primary key with UNIQUE index or NON-UNIQUE index?
Tips 13: When to use index and when not to use index

Tips 1: Function Based Index or Indexed Virtual column in 11g?

Here we will discuss how to create Index on a function/expression. Also we will explore how to create index on a column which is derived and virtual in nature. Then we will have comparative analysis between FBI (Function Based Index) and VI (Virtual Index).

Function based index was introduced in Oracle 8i, it is an index which is created on the function of a table column. So instead of indexing a column we are indexing the result of a function on the column.
The function can be an oracle function or a user defined function.

Note that to create a <u>function based index</u> on a user defined function you need to make sure the *user define function* is deterministic, otherwise <u>function based index</u> will not work.

You can query DBA_IND_EXPRESSIONS table to see the details of the expression in a function based index. Note the indexed expression (like UPPER (name)) is stored as hidden virtual column for the table being indexed.

Oracle Virtual Column was introduced in Oracle 11g, it is a derived/pre-computed value using either oracle function or user defined function or an expression.

Note that to create a <u>virtual column</u> in a table based on a user defined function, you need to make sure the *user define function* is deterministic, otherwise <u>virtual column</u> creation will not work using that function.

Let us take a simple example

This function will find the occurrence of a string in the main string:

```
CREATE OR REPLACE
  FUNCTION f_Count_occurrences(
      p_string    IN CLOB,
      p_substring IN VARCHAR2)
    RETURN NUMBER
    deterministic <------------------------     This clause is mandatory here
                                                For the function to be indexed
  IS
    l_occurrences NUMBER;
  BEGIN
    IF ( p_string   IS NOT NULL AND p_substring IS NOT NULL ) THEN
      l_occurrences := ( LENGTH(p_string) - ( NVL(LENGTH(REPLACE(p_string, p_substring)), 0) ) ) / LENGTH(p_substring) ;
    END IF;
    RETURN ( l_occurrences );
  END f_count_occurrences;

drop table testll;
Create table testll(class_processed varchar2(34));
insert into testll values('123/456');
insert into testll values('123/456/44');
insert into testll values('123/456/2/3/4/5');
insert into testll values('123/456/6/7/78/899#88#56');
```

Function used for <u>function based index</u>:

```
create index testll_f_Count_occurrences_idx on testll(f_Count_occurrences(class_processed,'/'));

select f_Count_occurrences(class_processed,'/') from  testll;
select f_Count_occurrences(class_processed,'#') from  testll;
```

Function used for <u>oracle virtual column</u>:

```
alter table testll add(class_proc_count2 generated always as (f_Count_occurrences(class_processed,'#')) virtual);
```

Alternatively, to create a table with a virtual column and "index on that virtual column":

Virtual column

```
Create table testll2(class_processed varchar2(34),class_proc_cnt as (f_Count_occurrences(class_processed,'/')));
insert into testll2(class_processed) values('123/456');
insert into testll2(class_processed) values('123/456/44');
insert into testll2(class_processed) values('123/456/2/3/4/5');
insert into testll2(class_processed) values('123/456/6/7/78/899#88#56');
commit;
create index testll2_cnt_idx on testll2(class_proc_cnt);
select * from testll2;
```

User defined Function

Some observations:

1. You cannot create a <u>function based index</u> and <u>virtual column</u> on the same expression, so for understanding we cannot create both for expression
   ```
   f_Count_occurrences(class_processed,'/')
   ```

2. When you use <u>virtual column</u> based on normal computation like commission as **salary/100** or **salary*10/bonus** then <u>virtual column</u> usage is better than <u>function based index</u> because we have to create the function and need to index it against the column.

3. When you use <u>virtual column</u> you need to maintain the DDL required to create the <u>virtual column</u> but <u>function based index</u> can be independently added/altered/dropped.

4. <u>Virtual column</u> can be indexed like a normal column. We have seen many cases the performance gain by using **indexed virtual column** is more than using <u>function based index</u>. However often both perform equally. So you need to test both the concepts for your scenario before deciding which one performs better.

5. <u>Virtual column</u> can refer to column from the same table where it is defined.

6. Need to **analyze** the index and table after it is created to collect **statistics**

   ```
   Analyze TABLE Test11 compute statistics;

   Analyze INDEX test11_f_count_occurances_idx compute statistics;
   ```

   Analyze command is supported for backward compatibility, you can instead use DBMS_STATS:

```
EXEC DBMS_STATS.gather_table_stats('U1', 'TEST11');
EXEC DBMS_STATS.gather_index_stats('U1', 'TEST11_F_COUNT_OCCURANCES_IDX');
```

If you would like to delete the stats use:
```
EXEC DBMS_STATS.delete_table_stats('U1', 'TEST11');
```

Tips 2: Invisible index and usage

Here we will explore how to make an index not used in an application and subsequently used without the need to rebuild the index.

Invisible index was introduced in Oracle 11gR1. It is an index which is maintained by the database, however it is ignored by the optimizer with its default setting.
If the **OPTIMIZER_USE_INVISIBLE_INDEXES** parameter is set to **FALSE** (which is the default setting) then the invisible index is not used unless you use oracle hint.

To create an invisible index the syntax is
```
CREATE INDEX index_inv ON table_name  (column_name) INVISIBLE;
```
You can view if an index is visible or invisible using:
```
SELECT index_name, visibility FROM dba_indexes WHERE index_name='INDEX_INV';
```

In order to use the Invisible index you need to do <u>one of the following</u> activities

- ➤ Setting using parameter:
    ```
    ALTER SESSION SET OPTIMIZER_USE_INVISIBLE_INDEXES=TRUE; --Session level

    ALTER SYSTEM SET OPTIMIZER_USE_INVISIBLE_INDEXES =TRUE; --System level
    ```

- ➤ Use hint **USE_INVISIBLE_INDEXES** in select statement from 11gR2 onward

    ```
    SELECT /*+ USE_INVISIBLE_INDEXES */
      ...from table_name;
    ```

    If you use the <u>index hint</u> as below in 11gR1 (only), invisible index will be used.
    ```
    SELECT /*+ INDEX(table_name index_inv) */
      ...FROM table_name;
    ```
    However the above <u>index hints</u> will be ignored for invisible index from 11gR2 onward and hence you have to use hint **USE_INVISIBLE_INDEXES** if you want to use the invisible index.

- ➤ Invisible index if present will be automatically invoked and help resolve table lock on parent table for missing index on foreign key column as shown in this chapter Tips 5

- ➤ Altering the index:
    ```
    ALTER INDEX index_inv VISIBLE;
    ```

Invisible index is used in the following situations:

➢ There are situations where we need to test if a particular index is impacting an application positively or negatively. Before 11g we need to drop the index or make the index unusable to test that. After the test we need to make it usable and rebuild the index which is a very costly operation.

However in 11g you can do that by using invisible index. Once it is invisible you can check how your query performs without the index and accordingly you can decide if you can either drop the index or make it visible for regular usage by all the applications and thus avoid a costly rebuild operation.
We just make an index visible/invisible using simple command

```
ALTER INDEX index_name INVISIBLE;
```
And after the test we can make it visible
```
ALTER INDEX index_name VISIBLE;
```

Later we can drop the index if the index is not required

➢ The underline index is used when a certain module in an application requires a specific index whereas another module of the application must not use that index. So using hints as shown above we are able to selectively use the index without impacting the whole application in terms of response time (only select operation). However you must check the impact **on the throughput** of the application as Oracle will continue to store all the details in terms of cardinality, uniqueness, space usage and all other metadata related attributes

➢ Invisible index is used to associate primary key with unique index to non-unique index and vice versa as shown in this chapter Tips 12

Tips 3: Multiple indexes on same column in Oracle 12c?

Here we will understand how to reduce database downtime and avoid subsequent issues (whilst a new type of index is created after old index is dropped) by maintaining different kinds of index on the same column.

Having **multiple indexes** on same set of columns allows you to switch between indexes based on situation and application requirement and also lets you quickly see the impact of various types of index on the same set of columns in the application. Multiple indexes will be useful when you want to convert from one type of index to other type of index with a minimal downtime. However only one of the indexes on the column will be visible at single point of time.

Also note we can create more than 1 index on 1 column or set of columns only if index type **is different and one of the index is visible at single point of time**.

Pre **12c** we could never create more than 1 index on 1 column or set of columns. In **12c only** we can do that.

Note in Oracle 11gR1 **invisible index** was introduced as shown in previous tips. Now we have to use the invisible index concept to create multiple indexes on same column.
E.g.
```
CREATE TABLE EMP(EMPNO NUMBER,ENAME VARCHAR2(30),SAL NUMBER,HIRE_DATE DATE);
INSERT INTO EMP VALUES(1,'STEVE',2546,SYSDATE-100);
INSERT INTO EMP VALUES(2,'JOHN',2547,SYSDATE-140);
INSERT INTO EMP VALUES(1,'ALEEN',2548,SYSDATE-160);
COMMIT;
```

```
CREATE INDEX emp_idx_1 ON EMP
  (empno,ename
  );

CREATE Bitmap INDEX emp_idx_2 ON EMP
  (
    empno,ename
  )
INVISIBLE;
```

Note one of the indexes is invisible and both indexes are of **different type**. You can change this anytime as below:

```
ALTER INDEX emp_idx_1 INVISIBLE;
ALTER INDEX emp_idx_2 VISIBLE;
```

You can even create **unique** and **non-unique** index on the same set of columns.

```
CREATE UNIQUE INDEX E_U_IDX ON EMP(ENAME);
ALTER INDEX E_U_IDX INVISIBLE;
CREATE INDEX E_NU_IDX ON EMP(ENAME);
```

Tips 4: INDEX order in composite index or INDEX only access?

Here we will discuss how important it is to order properly the indexed columns in an index and access data from only the index.

When creating index make sure you understand the application well. If the frequent business requirement on a certain table (let us say the table has got more than 30 columns) can be fulfilled by querying 4 columns of that table it is suggested to create a composite index on these 4 columns so that all the necessary details can be fetched with index access only and thus by eliminating table access, performance can be enhanced greatly.

Many time DBA creates composite index on 3 columns and hence just to retrieve the 4th column oracle has to access the table for each required row. This simple understanding saves time in many nightly jobs which are inherently complex and very slow in response time.

There is another simple concept one must remember. You have composite index, however your application mostly uses the 2nd column of the index instead of 1st column of the index as a predicate, this results in the index not being used and suboptimal performance is encountered.
In this kind of situation it is highly advisable to order the composite index based on how frequently each column is used as the predicate in your application.

Tips 5: Table lock on parent table for missing index on foreign key column

Here we will find out why parent table get locked for the duration of child table modification which degrade performance in terms of response time and throughput. Will discuss possible solution for this.

Oracle places an exclusive lock on a child table if you do not index the foreign key constraint in that child table and you are trying to modify the corresponding child and parent table.

This will show in **v$session** wait event: **"enq: TM – contention"** this indicates there are un-indexed foreign key constraints.

Take the **example** below

```
CREATE TABLE emp   (empid NUMBER PRIMARY KEY, deptid NUMBER  );
CREATE TABLE dept   (deptid NUMBER PRIMARY KEY  );
ALTER TABLE emp ADD CONSTRAINT emp_fk FOREIGN KEY(  deptid) REFERENCES dept
(deptid);

INSERT INTO dept VALUES (10 );
INSERT INTO dept VALUES (20 );
INSERT INTO emp VALUES (1,10 );
INSERT INTO emp VALUES (2,20 );
COMMIT;
```

Now open 2 Oracle sql **sessions:**

Session 1

Modify any record from child table EMP.
e.g.
```
DELETE FROM emp WHERE deptid = 10;
```

Do not commit

Session 2
Try to modify any record of parent table DEPT, it will simply hang
e.g.
```
DELETE FROM dept WHERE deptid = 20;
```

Please note Oracle will place an exclusive lock on the whole table even if you are modifying a single record and the **record is different** from the <u>one you are updating</u> in **Session 1**

You can see from v$session, the TM lock by running the query:
```
SELECT l.sid,
  s.blocking_session blocker_session,
  s.event,
  l.type,
  l.lmode,
  l.request,
  o.object_name,
  o.object_type
FROM v$lock l,
  dba_objects o,
  v$session s
WHERE UPPER (s.username) = UPPER ('U1')
AND l.idl              = o.object_id (+)
AND l.sid              = s.sid;
```

The output look as below:

SID	BLOCKER_SESSION	EVENT	TYPE	LMODE	REQUEST	OBJECT_NAME	OBJECT_TYPE
10	(null)	SQL*Net message from client	AE	4	0	ORA$BASE	EDITION
10	(null)	SQL*Net message from client	TM	3	0	EMP	TABLE
10	(null)	SQL*Net message from client	TM	2	0	DEPT	TABLE
10	(null)	SQL*Net message from client	TX	6	0	(null)	(null)
247	10	enq: TM - contention	AE	4	0	ORA$BASE	EDITION
247	10	enq: TM - contention	TM	0	4	EMP	TABLE

To resolve the lock you must have an index on the foreign key column of the child table as below

```
CREATE INDEX emp_fk ON emp
  (deptid
  );
```

Note: Even if you create invisible index (instead of default visible index), still it will resolve the table lock issue.
Also you must make sure there is no child record present when you will attempt to delete from parent table.

The following query identifies which tables are affected because of not having an index on the foreign key column of the child table

```
SELECT *
FROM
  (SELECT a.constraint_name cons_name ,
    a.table_name tab_name ,
    b.column_name cons_column ,
    NVL(c.column_name,'***No foreign key Index***') ind_column
  FROM dba_constraints a
  JOIN all_cons_columns b
  ON a.constraint_name = b.constraint_name
  LEFT OUTER JOIN all_ind_columns c
  ON b.column_name      = c.column_name
  AND b.table_name      = c.table_name
  WHERE a.owner         ='SCHEMA_NAME'
  AND a.constraint_type = 'R'
  )
WHERE ind_column='***No foreign key Index***';
```

This will list out all the foreign key columns which do not have an associated index for that foreign key column in the child table.

Another **disadvantage of missing foreign key index** is as below:
When parent and child tables are joined on the foreign key column then the absence of foreign key index will **result into sort merge join** or **full table scan instead of nested loop join** and this in turn increase the response time and degrade performance of your application.

Tips 6: virtual indexes- INDEXES WITH NO SEGMENTS Benefits

Here we will explore how to check if certain index could be useful if it really existed in the database without creating a real index.

Virtual indexes is an object which helps us simulate the existence of an index - without actually building a full index.
So if you have a very large index that you want to create without allocating space and to determine if the index would be used by the optimizer then create one virtual index.

This virtual index is nothing but an index created with NOSEGMENT. This allows you to test and tune your application. Sometime this virtual index is called "**fake index**" because they do not really exists. When you are using the virtual index it will tell in the **execution plan** if the index will be used potentially however in **execution time** oracle may prefer not to use the index. The "virtual index" is meant for only checking if the index could be useful <u>if it really existed</u> in the database.

First, note that virtual indexes are only enabled for a session that sets a certain parameter as below:

```
ALTER Session SET "_use_nosegment_indexes" = TRUE;
```

Now, create the virtual index, using the special keyword **NOSEGMENT**:

```
CREATE INDEX Index_V ON TABLE_NAME   (Column_name)
NOSEGMENT compute statistics;
```

With the index in place, simply use explain plan as usual to see if the index is used as below:

```
Explain plan FOR SELECT * FROM (TABLE_NAME);
SELECT plan_table_output
FROM TABLE(dbms_xplan.display('plan_table',NULL,'serial'));
```

To find if there is any virtual index present in the database just run:

```
SELECT index_owner,
   index_name
FROM dba_ind_columns
WHERE index_name NOT LIKE 'BIN$%'
MINUS
SELECT owner, index_name FROM dba_indexes;
```

Note: Don't forget to drop the index when your testing is complete!

```
DROP INDEX Index_V;
```

Tips 7: Oracle index skip scan case study run time drop from 4 hr. to 10 sec

Here we will explore how to let a concatenated index be used in a query even if leading edge predicate is skipped in multi-column index. We will discuss tactical solution to convert index skip scan to index range scan.

We have table "XXX" with millions of records. In this table columns "exact_date","pnr" and "svcno" has a <u>unique index</u>.

Also this table has concatenated <u>non unique index</u> "idx_mon_date" on the set of columns [month_date (This store only mmyyyy), Tno, amt]

month_date(This store only mmyyyy), Tno,amt

Non unique index idx_mon_date

Now we have the requirement to get the report for a period **1/4/2012** to **15/4/2012**
This is the query:

```
SELECT pnr,
   Drum,
   Tno,
   amt
FROM xxx
WHERE Tno IN ('3234', '5678', '9786', '4567')
AND exact_date BETWEEN '20120401' AND '20120415'
AND amt  = '0'
AND Drum = '0';
```

This query takes more than 4 hours to execute, when the period is increased so too does the execution time.
Table is analyzed and data is structured properly. All indexes are in proper place and rebuilt and analyzed. There is no **distinct cause** for the **slowness** of the query. But it is a very critical report and needs to be published soon.

What is the solution?
The **explain plan** for the query is as below:

```
---------------------------------------------------------------------------------------------------
| Id | Operation                           | Name        | Rows | Bytes | Cost (%CPU)| Time     | Pstart| Pstop |
---------------------------------------------------------------------------------------------------
|  0 | SELECT STATEMENT                    |             |    1 |   41  |  376K  (1)| 01:27:57 |       |       |
|  1 |  PARTITION RANGE ALL                |             |    1 |   41  |  376K  (1)| 01:27:57 |    1  | 3422  |
|* 2 |   TABLE ACCESS BY LOCAL INDEX ROWID | xxx         |    1 |   41  |  376K  (1)| 01:27:57 |    1  | 3422  |
|* 3 |    INDEX SKIP SCAN                  | idx_mon_date| 6629K|       | 30471  (1)| 00:07:07 |    1  | 3422  |
---------------------------------------------------------------------------------------------------
```

A close look shows **distinctly** there is an **index skip scan** on "idx_mon_date".
Actually the **index skip scan** was introduced to allow Oracle to "skip" leading-edge predicates in a multi-column index so that our concatenated index can be used in the query.

Oracle state that the **index skip scan** is not as fast as **a direct index lookup**, but states that the **index skip scan** is faster than a **full-table scan**. So large tables with concatenated indexes, the index skip-scan feature can provide quick access even when the leading column of the index is not used in a limiting condition and hence give better performance as against full table scan.

However for this case if we introduce "**month_date**" column in the query "where" clause we get **INDEX RANGE SCAN** as the predicate (leading edge column is present for index idx_mon_date)

```
SELECT pnr,
   Drum,
   Tno,
   amt
FROM xxx
WHERE Tno IN ('3234', '5678', '9786', '4567')
AND exact_date BETWEEN '20120401' AND '20120415'
AND month_date='042012'
AND amt      = '0'
AND Drum     = '0';
```

And here is the execution plan

```
---------------------------------------------------------------------------------------------------
| Id | Operation                           | Name        | Rows | Bytes | Cost (%CPU)| Time     | Pstart| Pstop |
---------------------------------------------------------------------------------------------------
|  0 | SELECT STATEMENT                    |             |    1 |   48  | 10130  (1)| 00:02:22 |       |       |
|  1 |  PARTITION RANGE ALL                |             |    1 |   48  | 10130  (1)| 00:02:22 |    1  | 3422  |
|* 2 |   TABLE ACCESS BY LOCAL INDEX ROWID | xxx         |    1 |   48  | 10130  (1)| 00:02:22 |    1  | 3422  |
|* 3 |    INDEX RANGE SCAN                 | idx_mon_date| 62185|       |  6881  (1)| 00:01:37 |    1  | 3422  |
---------------------------------------------------------------------------------------------------
```

The execution time drop to **10 seconds** (it was taking **more than 4 hrs.** before the change)

Note: If **Exact_date** is DATE column then you can store time portion (HH24:MI:SS) of the date. However if you store the time portion (default behavior of DATE datatype) then in order to get the result correctly you need to use TRUNC (Exact_date). But this approach will make the index ignored, so you have 2 options to use index:

Option 1: Create function based index on TRUNC (Exact_date) and change the query filter criteria as below:

```
TRUNC(Exact_date)=to_date('20120401','YYYYMMDD')
```

Option 2: Instead of the below filter clause

```
Exact_date=to_date('20120401','YYYYMMDD')
```

Use the following filter criteria:

```
Exact_date>=  to_date('20120401','YYYYMMDD') AND
Exact_date<  to_date('20120401','YYYYMMDD')+1
```

This way you are able to use the index on "Exact_date" and you are able to cover all the 24 hrs.
period for the particular date.

Tips 8: How to force optimizer to use or not use index?

Here we will discuss different ways to force optimizer to use or ignore an index.
We can force optimizer to use an index or not to use an index by embedding an oracle hint in the sql query.
Example 1:

```
SELECT /*+ INDEX(tab1 idx1) */ * FROM tab1 a,tab2 b WHERE a.id=b.id;
```

Here you not only force the table to use index but you can force the optimizer to use a specific index of the table.

Example 2:

```
SELECT /*+ NO_INDEX(tab1 idx1) */ * FROM tab1 a,tab2 b WHERE a.id=b.id;
```

Here you force optimizer not to use index tab1. Idx1

Example 3:

```
SELECT /*+ ORDERED */ * FROM tab1 a,tab2 b WHERE a.id=b.id;
```

This hint is used when you as a dba know the optimal order of joining multiple tables instead of Oracle trying all possible execution plans and making a decision.

You can use /*+ **INDEX_JOIN** (tab1 index1 index2) */ when two or more indexed columns can be joined.

Note: without **INDEX_JOIN** hints optimizer will join only single column indexes. Please refer to Chapter 1 Concepts 6: **Index JOIN scan** for example with case study.

These simple example show how you can use index hints.

There is another way to force optimizer to use index:

By adjusting **optimizer_index_cost_adj** initialization parameter for that **session** or **system** as a whole.
In the **session level** you can set:

```
ALTER session SET optimizer_index_cost_adj=60;
```

The **optimizer_index_cost_adj** parameter defaults to a value of **100**, but it can range in value from 1 to 10,000. A value of 100 means that equal weight is given to index versus multi block reads.

This parameter dictates how much optimizer like full-table scans or index scan.

With a value of 100, the CBO likes full-table scans and index scans equally, and a number lower than 100 tells the CBO index scans are faster than full-table scans.

So by setting the parameter with a value close to 1000 you can tell optimizer not to use the index and by setting the parameter with a value lower than 100 you can tell optimizer to use the index.

It is recommended to set this parameter in SESSION level only as this will impact all tables in the system if it is set at SYSTEM level.

Tips 9: Non Unique index with null values or not null value for the column?

Here we will explore non-unique index with null values vs. non unique index on not null values.

A non-unique index may be created on any column that is widely used in an application.
As per the table definition the non-unique column can be nullable or not nullable.

If the column is defined as nullable and you query the table for the null value then there will be full table scan as Oracle does not index a null value.
However if you define the column as NOT NULL and when there is no value for the column then you can store a default value say "unknown", then when you query the table for the default value "unknown" Oracle will use the index and full table scan is eliminated

So as a general rule any column that always contain data should be declared as not null and there should be some default value, This will allow efficient index search instead of full table scan for null values.

Note: You can create index on null values refer to Chapter 1, Concepts 7 "**Indexing on null column rows**"

Tips 10: Ordering table rows without using ORDER BY clause and steps to eliminate SORTING

Here we will discuss different ways of ordering resultset without the costly internal sorting operation.

Sorting is the process by which all the data returned by a query is arranged in certain order for you to analyse the data effectively. Sorting is a very costly operation and requires a lot of work to be done by the Oracle engine. In oracle using "ORDER BY column-name ASC" and "ORDER BY column-name DESC" allows you to sort the result-set in ascending or descending order respectively.

Since sorting is very costly operation its avoidance is one of the challenges for the **dba/developer**.

Here are the steps to **avoid sorting:**

Approach 1: Create an index on the ordering columns. In this case even if you use order by in your query it does not use sorting. Note the "ORDER BY" clause uses the index.

Approach 2: A common mistake an oracle developer makes is to specify the ORDER BY clause in a query even if the query is inherently sorted.
For example if you have a query with "WHERE" clause criteria and the "WHERE" clause column has index then the result-set will be returned as per the indexed column. So when you write a query which does not have any "WHERE" clause

86

which needs to be sorted/ordered by certain column, in that case use a dummy "WHERE" clause like "empno>0" which will inherently use the index and <u>sorting is avoided</u>.

Approach 3: If you do not want to use a dummy where clause you can still order the data using hint as below:
Select /*+ INDEX_ASC (table_name specific index) */.....

If you want to sort the rows in descending order
Select /*+ INDEX_DESC (table_name specific index) */.....

Sample example to show how to avoid sorting:

```sql
CREATE TABLE batch_log
  (
    p_grp     VARCHAR2(30),
    batch_id  NUMBER,
    unit_nm   VARCHAR2(30),
    tot_cnt   NUMBER
  );
ALTER TABLE batch_log ADD CONSTRAINT pk_batch_log PRIMARY KEY
(
  p_grp,batch_id,unit_nm
)
;
```

Now insert a set of records:

```sql
INSERT INTO batch_log VALUES
  ('grp1',1,'ul',100
  );
INSERT INTO batch_log VALUES
  ('grp1',3,'ul',200
  );
INSERT INTO batch_log VALUES
  ('grp1',2,'ul',300
  );
INSERT INTO batch_log VALUES
  ('grp1',4,'ul',400
  );
INSERT INTO batch_log VALUES
  ('grp2',4,'ul',500
  );
INSERT INTO batch_log VALUES
  ('grp1',6,'ul',600
  );
INSERT INTO batch_log VALUES
  ('grp1',5,'ul',400
  );


SET DEFINE OFF;
INSERT INTO batch_log VALUES
  ('grp1',7,'u&v',700
  );
```

Note "**SET DEFINE OFF**" is required to let you insert "u&v" in the table, otherwise it will prompt for your input and will insert wrong data.

Substitution variable: These are special type of variables that enable oracle to accept input from user at run time. When these variables are prefixed by single ampersand (&) then it asks for user input for each reference, E.g.

```
SELECT * FROM test1 WHERE cst_id=&cst_id;
SELECT * FROM test2 WHERE cst_id=&cst_id;
```

But when these variables are prefixed by double ampersand (&&) then it asks for user input only for first reference and subsequent time it use the same value provided in the first time.

```
SELECT * FROM test1 WHERE cst_id=&&cst_id;
SELECT * FROM test2 WHERE cst_id=&&cst_id;
```

If you do not want user to manually provide the value you can define the value for the substitution variable as below:

```
DEFINE cst_id="10"
```

The result from the following query will be sorted by batch_id:

```
SELECT * FROM batch_log ORDER BY batch_id;
```

The explain plan shows that sorting is used:

OPERATION	OBJECT_NAME	OPTIONS
SELECT STATEMENT		
SORT		ORDER BY
TABLE ACCESS	BATCH_LOG	FULL

How can you avoid sorting? Even though batch_id column is part of the primary key "order by batch_id" uses sorting.

Solution 1

Create index on the batch_id column only. So <u>if you create index</u> on batch_id column only then even if you use order by clause in your query, it will not use sorting. Important to note the "ORDER BY" clause uses the index and hence sorting step is eliminated.

This is the solution using **approach 1** and you employ this approach in certain scenario, but for this case it is not advisable as you have a primary key on "p_grp, **batch_id**, unit_nm"

Solution 2

As explained in **approach 2**, if the "**where**" clause is on indexed columns then you do not need the "**order by**" clause as the data will be returned in index order. There is a huge gain in performance as a result of eliminating the expensive sorting.

```
SELECT *
FROM batch_log
WHERE p_grp='grp1'
AND batch_id BETWEEN 1 AND 10
AND unit_nm='u1';
```

The explain plan shows that sorting is not used but the result-set is inherently sorted:

OPERATION	OBJECT_NAME	OPTIONS
SELECT STATEMENT		
TABLE ACCESS	BATCH_LOG	BY INDEX ROWID
INDEX	PK_BATCH_LOG	RANGE SCAN
Access Predicates		
AND		
P_GRP='grp1'		
BATCH_ID>=1		
UNIT_NM='u1'		
BATCH_ID<=10		
Filter Predicates		
UNIT_NM='u1'		

Solution 3

As explained in **approach 3**, you can use the index hint

```
SELECT /*+ INDEX_ASC(batch_log pk_batch_log) */ * FROM batch_log;
```

The explain plan shows that sorting is not used but the result-set is inherently sorted:

OPERATION	OBJECT_NAME	OPTIONS
⊟ ● SELECT STATEMENT		
⊟ ⊞ TABLE ACCESS	BATCH_LOG	BY INDEX ROWID
└─ ◻ INDEX	PK_BATCH_LOG	FULL SCAN

Equipped with this understanding you can now re-write your query to use "where clause" instead of costly "order by clause" and so improve the performance of your query.

<u>More Advice on eliminating sorting</u>:

> Oracle "**UNION**" clause uses sorting as it returns unique rows,
  "**UNION ALL**" provides all rows (including duplicates) and does not perform sorting.

> Oracle "**DISTINCT**" clause invokes the expensive sorting mechanism. On how to refactor query to avoid "**DISTINCT**" keyword from the query refer Chapter 6 Tips 8: Use Oracle clause IN or EXISTS or DISTINCT And How to Refactor query to avoid "DISTINCT" keyword from the query?

> When using "**DISTINCT**" keyword you do not need "**ORDER BY**" clause if the columns you want to SORT are subset of the columns in the SELECT list and you **use dummy where** clause.

When you use a dummy "WHERE" clause make sure the "**WHERE**" clause column refers to proper data type otherwise if there is any internal data type conversion **you will not get the data sorted**.

Example:

```
CREATE TABLE SORTING_TEST
  (
    SYS_ID        VARCHAR2(30) PRIMARY KEY,
    APARTMENT_NO VARCHAR2(20)
  );


INSERT INTO SORTING_TEST VALUES(1123,'XX/YY');
INSERT INTO SORTING_TEST VALUES(1223,'XX/rY');
INSERT INTO SORTING_TEST VALUES(1823,'XX/pY');
INSERT INTO SORTING_TEST VALUES(1423,'XX/mY');
INSERT INTO SORTING_TEST VALUES(1923,'XX/nY');

COMMIT;
```

Now you can avoid sorting by using "**dummy where clause**" as per **approach 1.**
However, ensure that there is no data type conversion otherwise you will get result-set in incorrect order.

In RDBMS implementation certain data types are automatically converted to other data types based on the data format. This types of conversion is called **IMPLICIT CONVERSION**.

The problem with **implicit data type conversion** is that the corresponding index on the column is ignored in the query.

INCORRECT ORDERING:

Sys_id is **varchar2**, if the WHERE clause is specified as below the data will not be sorted because 0 is number and hence sys_id which is varchar2 will be internally converted into **TO_NUMBER(SYS_ID)** and hence the index will not be used and the ordering will be incorrect

```
SELECT * FROM sorting_test WHERE sys_id >0;
```
The output is as shown below in incorrect order

SYS_ID	APARTMENT_NO
1123	XX/YY
1223	XX/rY
1823	XX/pY
1423	XX/mY
1923	XX/nY

Note: Because of **internal type conversion** the index is not used which may prompt you to use "index hints", however "index hints" is not recommended in this case because, although the index will be used, there will be a full index scan rather **than an index range scan** which slows down performance.

Correct order using proper type of data:
Sys_id is **varchar2** and hence if you use proper data type it will sort the data properly without using the expensive SORT operation.
You can either use input parameter with proper datatype or **convert the input parameter** by means of CAST, TO_CHAR, TO_NUMBER etc. in the **right side** of the operator (>, <,= etc.) as below:

So if the input parameter is coming in the form of variable with data type number (like var_id number: =0) then use
```
SELECT * FROM sorting_test WHERE sys_id>TO_CHAR(var_id);
```
Or use below using CAST operator
```
SELECT * FROM sorting_test WHERE sys_id>CAST(var_id AS VARCHAR2(1));
```

Or simply use as below
```
SELECT * FROM sorting_test WHERE sys_id >'0';
```

This approach has **two benefits**:
- It provides **the data in correct** order
- The query **uses index** and hence gives best response time

The **output** as shown below is in the correct order (<u>even though there is no order by clause</u>)

SYS_ID	APARTMENT_NO
1123	XX/YY
1223	XX/rY
1423	XX/mY
1823	XX/pY
1923	XX/nY

So now you can see that records can be sorted without ORDER BY clause provided you use the proper data type when writing your query.

Note: Based on the above discussion we can suggest the below

- First of all change your data model to create object with proper data type i.e. if a column is supposed to store number you must create the column with number data type instead of varchar2 data type to avoid the implicit conversion.

- If you can not change the data model then you must use either input parameter with proper datatype or **convert the input parameter** by means of CAST, TO_CHAR, TO_NUMBER etc. in the **right side** of the operator (like >, <,=) so that index will be used.
- Regarding the impact of <u>choosing wrong data type</u> **refer to** Chapter 7 Tips 15: Improve performance using Oracle Aliases and impact of choosing wrong datatype

Tips 11: Case study using "Index only scan" and DETERMINISTIC function for performance

Here we will explore how to avoid redundant call and access the whole data from index structure to improve performance of application.

Without touching or accessing the data from a table you can retrieve the data from oracle index tree. This method is called "INDEX FAST FULL SCAN" or "INDEX ONLY SCAN"

Oracle implements this concept in the form of Index organized Table (IOT).
However without IOT you can also use Index only scan and get great performance improvement.

Using "**index only scan**", Oracle does not need to access the table because all the information is present in the index tree. To achieve this you need to build a super index on the columns from "**select list**" and the columns from "**where clause**". <u>However some catches:</u>
- ➤ Index only scan is improved if the table has low clustering factor.
- ➤ High clustering factor means table data is not sequenced. If the table data has high clustering factor, then index only scan performance benefit is almost nominal and not recommended.
- ➤ If you add any extra column in "select clause" or in "where clause" then index only scan does not happen and it takes different execution plan based on many factors at that point of SCN.

Here is one example query <u>which took 5 minute to execute</u> and required to be <u>tuned.</u>

```
SELECT *
  FROM (  SELECT *
            FROM XX_V m
           WHERE m.X = 'LDN' AND m.Y = 'FIN'
         ORDER BY m.q1, m.q2, m.q3)
 WHERE ROWNUM < 2502;
```

Few points about the query:

- ➤ The view in the query is based on some other views
- ➤ The view in the query uses function **f1**:

```
CREATE OR REPLACE
FUNCTION f1(p_in IN NUMBER)
  RETURN VARCHAR2
  AS
  language java name
  'com.xx.utility.rad50ToString(java.math.BigDecimal) return java.lang.String';
```

- ➤ The underlying table has all the suitable indexes and primary key in place properly. There is a unique concatenated index on "q1, q2, q3" columns.

- ➤ This query is used in the GUI for different screens and the response time is very slow. It takes more than 5 min for 1 million data in the underlying tables.

- ➤ The throughput is a benchmark and extraordinary, it process more than 5000 records per seconds.

Now the challenge is to improve the response time without sacrificing the throughput....

Using materialized view instead of view you can we see a **600%** improve in response time, but the throughput is dropped significantly.

The final solution for this is as below
1. Refactor the query using index only scan
2. Use deterministic keyword for the existing function which will internally use the pre-computed result and will be faster

The refactor query looks as below:
```
SELECT *
   FROM XX_V
   WHERE     (q1, q2, q3) IN (SELECT q1, q2, q3
                                FROM (  SELECT q1, q2, q3
                                          FROM XX_V m
                                         WHERE m.X = 'LDN' AND m.Y = 'FIN'
                                       ORDER BY m.q1, m.q2, m.q3)
                              WHERE ROWNUM < 2502)
         AND X = 'LDN'
         AND Y = 'FIN'
ORDER BY q1, q2, q3;
```

Note instead of accessing all the table columns you select only q1, q2 and q3 column and hence invoke the "INDEX ONLY SCAN" and improve performance.

And the function is rewritten as below using DETERMINISTIC keyword:

```
CREATE OR REPLACE
FUNCTION fl(p_in IN NUMBER)
 RETURN VARCHAR2
 DETERMINISTIC
 AS
 language java name
 'com.xx.utility.rad50ToString(java.math.BigDecimal) return java.lang.String';
```

The **DETERMINISTIC** option helps the optimizer avoid redundant function calls. If a stored function was called previously with the same arguments, the optimizer can select to use the previous result.

The number of distinct values of "**P_IN**" argument which are passed to the function is only 20 and it returns **20** distinct java.lang.string but this function is used in a view which returns millions of records and hence the function computes the same 20 return value millions of times. However by means of **DETERMINISTIC** keyword you can use the pre computed 20 return values from the function and improve the performance of the view call significantly.
With both these changes the response time come down from 5 minutes to 3 seconds.

Tips 12: Primary key with UNIQUE index or NON-UNIQUE index

Here we will discuss different ways to create association of unique and non-unique index to a primary key constraint in a table. We will have comparative analysis of both the approaches. At the end we will see how to rebuild index in ONLINE and OFFLINE mode.

A **primary key** is a column in a table which uniquely identifies a row. In a sense Primary key is the same as a unique index but the differences are that
  ➢ **Primary key** cannot be null but unique index can be null.
  ➢ You can have one **primary key** in a table but any number of unique indexes in a table.
When a **primary key** is defined for a table oracle will automatically create an associated **unique index** for it.

However a **primary key** can be associated with a **unique index** or a **non-unique index** by decoupling primary key constraint and index as shown.

Approach 1: (Association with unique index):
Here is an example to show this:

```
CREATE TABLE test_constraint_t
  (
    a NUMBER,
    b VARCHAR2(30),
    c VARCHAR2(30),
    PRIMARY KEY(a)
  );
SELECT * FROM all_constraints WHERE table_name ='TEST_CONSTRAINT_T';
```

Output:

CONSTRAINT_NAME	CONSTRAINT_TYPE	TABLE_NAME
SYS_C00149342784	P	TEST_CONSTRAINT_T

```
SELECT * FROM all_indexes WHERE table_name ='TEST_CONSTRAINT_T';
```

93

Output:

INDEX_NAME	INDEX_TYPE	TABLE_OWNER	TABLE_NAME	TABLE_TYPE	UNIQUENESS
SYS_C00149346130 NORMAL		U1	TEST_CONSTRAINT_T TABLE		UNIQUE

Approach 2: (Association with unique or non-unique index):

Here is an example to show how it is done.

```
CREATE TABLE test_constraint_t
  (
    a NUMBER,
    b VARCHAR2(30),
    c VARCHAR2(30)
  );
CREATE INDEX test_constraint_t_idx ON test_constraint_t(a);
ALTER TABLE test_constraint_t ADD CONSTRAINT TEST_CONSTRAINT_T_PK
PRIMARY KEY (a);
```

Note: Here you create a non-unique index for the primary key, however you can create unique index instead of non-unique index. So you can create just one index for the primary key or using approach 1 internally just one unique index is created. Adding the primary key constraint step as mentioned above won't create any additional unique index.

```
SELECT * FROM all_constraints WHERE table_name ='TEST_CONSTRAINT_T';
```
Output:

CONSTRAINT_NAME	CONSTRAINT_TYPE	TABLE_NAME
TEST_CONSTRAINT_T_PK P		TEST_CONSTRAINT_T

```
SELECT * FROM all_indexes WHERE table_name ='TEST_CONSTRAINT_T';
```
Output:

INDEX_NAME	INDEX_TYPE	TABLE_OWNER	TABLE_NAME	TABLE_TYPE	UNIQUENESS
TEST_CONSTRAINT_T_IDX NORMAL		U1	TEST_CONSTRAINT_T TABLE		NONUNIQUE

Steps to associate primary key with different index(different columns from primary key) **test_constraint_t_idx1**:

```
CREATE INDEX test_constraint_t_idx1 ON test_constraint_t(a,b);
ALTER TABLE test_constraint_t MODIFY PRIMARY KEY USING INDEX test_constraint_t_idx1;
DROP INDEX test_constraint_t_idx;
```

Steps to associate primary key with unique index(same column as primary key) **test_constraint_t_idx2** from a non-unique index:

```
CREATE UNIQUE INDEX test_constraint_t_idx2 ON test_constraint_t(a) invisible;
ALTER TABLE test_constraint_t MODIFY PRIMARY KEY USING INDEX test_constraint_t_idx2;
ALTER INDEX test_constraint_t_idx2 VISIBLE;
DROP INDEX test_constraint_t_idx;
```

No matter whether you use approach 1 or approach 2 to associate the primary key with a unique or non-unique index, the primary key constraint always maintains the uniqueness of the column and returns just one record when you have index lookup.

When you associate the primary key with unique or non-unique index the behaviour is as below:
  ➤ Primary key associated with unique index then oracle use INDEX UNIQUE SCAN
  ➤ Primary key associated with non-unique index then oracle use INDEX RANGE SCAN

94

➤ Both the above cases the index lookup returns just 1 row.

It is preferable to use **approach 2** for the following reasons
➤ You can drop or disable the primary key constraint independent of the index
➤ You can make an index unusable independent of primary key constraint and then make it usable by rebuilding the index, in other words you can **decouple** constraint and index and hence independently disable either the constraint or the index. This flexibility helps to overcome severe performance degradation especially for batch loads which might consists of millions of transactions. By dropping the index (or making the index unusable) during batch load the throughput of batch load is improved considerably. After the batch load is completed the index is recreated and analyzed.
➤ You can associate the primary key with either UNIQUE or NON-UNIQUE index. But with **approach 1** you can associate only with UNIQUE index.
➤ You can give user defined name for primary key and indexes
➤ When large volume of data is present and you need to do certain operation which require disable/deferred/drop primary key you can do that using this **approach 2** and it does not require to **rebuild the index**.
➤ **Rebuilding index** is a process to reorganize an existing index. This operation consumes double the space of a single index because REBUILD index uses existing index as a source for reorganizing the index. Rebuild operation takes exclusive locks by default (offline mode)

➤ **Rebuilding of index** can be done using **online** mode and **offline** mode:

ONLINE MODE: In this mode you can rebuild the index and do DML operation in parallel. In other words DML activities are not locked when index rebuild operation is ongoing.
```
ALTER INDEX index_name REBUILD ONLINE PARALLEL;
```
OFFLINE MODE: In this offline mode when you rebuild the index, DML operations are locked until the rebuild operation is finished.
```
ALTER INDEX index_name REBUILD PARALLEL;
```

When deleting an index entry, space is not freed in the index leaf and is just marked as deleted. By rebuilding index you could free up the spaces and improve performance.

While rebuilding the Index in online/offline mode you can **compress** the index also for better performance. This is showcased in Chapter 1, Concepts 10: Table compression/Index compression in 12c

Tips 13: When to use index and when not to use index

Index is required in the following situations:
➤ Columns that are used in WHERE clause, ORDER BY clause and GROUP BY clause
➤ It is recommended to create index on columns with high number of distinct values

Index is avoided in the following situations:
➤ Columns that are very frequently undergoing changes require high maintenance and hence index on those columns should be avoided.
➤ Column that contains high number of NULL values causes data to be skewed towards NULL and hence index on those columns should be avoided.
➤ If a table is small and can be accessed with fewer I/O it is recommended not to use index on that table.
➤ If a column is used in "**WHERE**" clause but return high percentage of data, in that case it is recommended not to use index

Chapter 3: Analytical query and Inter-row Pattern matching (30 pages)

Analytic functions are also called windowing functions, these allow developer to navigate between rows with ease.
Inter-row pattern matching is an enhanced version of the analytic function.
In this chapter we will explore different patterns like stock price fluctuation enabling us to tell which stock followed a certain pattern. Also you will know different kinds of real life patterns and parallel implementation details using analytic function and "match_recognise" clause in oracle 12c.
Prior to 12c in order to detect a specific pattern it was a very difficult and complex job using analytic function, recursive queries using connect by and "WITH" clause and many self joins,
However in 12c using match_recognise clause (this feature was most probably introduced because of the influence of big data) you can achieve the same with an ease.

Tips 1: Inter-rows W Pattern matching for stock price fluctuation using "MATCH_RECOGNISE" clause, big data influence in 12c?

Tips 2: Pivoting rows into column dynamically in 10g/11g

Tips 3: Breaking a concatenated string to display as set of rows and set of columns?

Tips 4: Find Inter-rows Specific colour Pattern for Animal colour registration **prior to** 12c and in 12c using "MATCH_RECOGNISE" Clause?

Tips 5: Find Inter-rows Specific pattern for consecutive same flag for 3 times prior **to** 12c and in 12c using "MATCH_RECOGNISE" Clause?

Tips 6: What is RANK, DENSE_RANK and ROW_NUMBER?

Tips 7: What is LEAD and LAG function?

Tips 8: Top N query using row limiting clause in 12c?

Tips 9: Result from view is different against result from table/mview created from that view, why?

Tips 10: How to get latest version of data from each set of record in a table?

Tips 11: How to pivot and unpivot prior to 11g and in 11g?

Tips 12: How to Display the grouped data in one row?

Tips 13: Assign dynamic page no through query (instead of application coding for the report)?

Tips 14: Nullify the duplicate record for certain attribute only

Here we will explore which stocks have undergone price fluctuation as per "W" pattern using oracle 12c "MATCH_RECOGNISE" clause

With the advent of "BIG data" the requirement for creation and capture of more and more data is increasing day by day.
Along with extra data, the business requirement of finding different patterns in data is growing rapidly.
A pattern is a repetitive series of events. Pattern can be found everywhere and in the current scenario of big data it is very much a business requirement to analyse a specific dataset and find a particular pattern.

Examples of real life scenarios can be
> Finding stock price ups and down pattern
> Finding malicious activity by some intruder
> Crime pattern
> Predict specific phone call pattern
> Fraud detection

Prior to 12c in order to detect a specific pattern it was a very difficult and complex job using analytic function, recursive queries using connect by and "WITH" clause and many self joins.
However in oracle 12c this pattern matching is simplified using "MATCH_RECOGNIZE" clause. This clause lets you take a dataset then group it into sets of data and order it based on timestamp and then look for a specific patterns in those partitions/groups.
Oracle Regular expression match pattern within the same record/row and 12c MATCH_RECOGNIZE match patterns across rows boundaries. So regular expression works for intra-rows whereas 12c match_recognize works for inter-rows.

Example:
Let us take one example of stock price fluctuation and let us find the stocks which have undergone price fluctuation as per pattern "W". This means stock is at certain value then price dips a couple of time and then price goes up and then price goes down and up again forming W shape pattern of price for a specific stock within certain period of time.

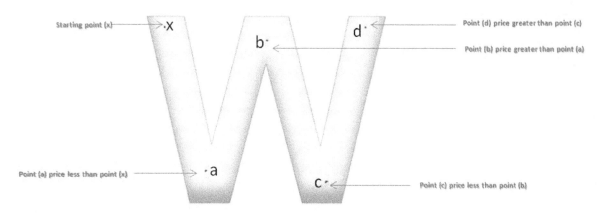

```
create table stock_price(name varchar2(30),price number(10,3),times date);

insert into stock_price values('xyz',80,to_date('15-01-2016 07:10:10','dd-mm-yyyy hh24:mi:ss'));
insert into stock_price values('xyz',90,to_date('15-01-2016 08:10:10','dd-mm-yyyy hh24:mi:ss'));
insert into stock_price values('xyz',25,to_date('15-01-2016 10:10:10','dd-mm-yyyy hh24:mi:ss'));
insert into stock_price values('xyz',24,to_date('15-01-2016 14:10:10','dd-mm-yyyy hh24:mi:ss'));
insert into stock_price values('xyz',27,to_date('16-01-2016 10:10:10','dd-mm-yyyy hh24:mi:ss'));
insert into stock_price values('xyz',26,to_date('16-01-2016 16:10:10','dd-mm-yyyy hh24:mi:ss'));
insert into stock_price values('xyz',28,to_date('16-01-2016 18:10:10','dd-mm-yyyy hh24:mi:ss'));
insert into stock_price values('xyz',20,to_date('17-01-2016 10:10:10','dd-mm-yyyy hh24:mi:ss'));

insert into stock_price values('xyz1',250,to_date('19-01-2016 10:10:10','dd-mm-yyyy hh24:mi:ss'));
insert into stock_price values('xyz1',240,to_date('20-01-2016 14:10:10','dd-mm-yyyy hh24:mi:ss'));
insert into stock_price values('xyz1',270,to_date('21-01-2016 10:10:10','dd-mm-yyyy hh24:mi:ss'));
insert into stock_price values('xyz1',260,to_date('22-01-2016 16:10:10','dd-mm-yyyy hh24:mi:ss'));
insert into stock_price values('xyz1',280,to_date('23-01-2016 18:10:10','dd-mm-yyyy hh24:mi:ss'));
insert into stock_price values('xyz1',200,to_date('24-01-2016 10:10:10','dd-mm-yyyy hh24:mi:ss'));

insert into stock_price values('xyz2',200,to_date('19-01-2016 10:10:10','dd-mm-yyyy hh24:mi:ss'));
insert into stock_price values('xyz2',300,to_date('20-01-2016 14:10:10','dd-mm-yyyy hh24:mi:ss'));
insert into stock_price values('xyz3',400,to_date('21-01-2016 10:10:10','dd-mm-yyyy hh24:mi:ss'));
insert into stock_price values('xyz3',500,to_date('22-01-2016 16:10:10','dd-mm-yyyy hh24:mi:ss'));
insert into stock_price values('xyz3',350,to_date('23-01-2016 18:10:10','dd-mm-yyyy hh24:mi:ss'));
insert into stock_price values('xyz3',500,to_date('24-01-2016 10:10:10','dd-mm-yyyy hh24:mi:ss'));

alter session set nls_date_format='dd-mm-yyyy hh24:mi:ss';
```

Note for **stock xyz** the values 90 to 28 as shown inside an oval shape form the W shape pattern.

Similarly, for **stock xyz1** values 250 to 280 as shown inside an oval shape form the W shape pattern.

But **stock xyz3** does not form the W shape pattern.

In order to find records with W shape pattern here is the solution using MATCH_RECOGNISE clause in 12c,

```
                           select * from stock_price
The MEASURES clause defines the columns to   match_recognize( partition by name order by times
be shown as output produced for each match   measures FIRST(a.times) as first_dips_time,  ←———— Shows the 1st dips time in W shape(point a)
                                                      LAST(d.times) as last_ups_time,    ———— Shows the final ups time in W shape(point d)
              Starting price at point x  ——→ x.price as first_max_price,
              Price in point a in W shape ——→ a.price as first_dips_price,
              Price in point b in W shape ——→ b.price as second_ups_price,
              Price in point c in W shape ——→ c.price as third_dips_price,
              Price in point d in W shape ——→ d.price as fourth_ups_price
                                              ONE ROW PER MATCH  ←————————————    This shows one non duplicate
                                                                                  row for the pattern
                                              PATTERN (x a+ b+ c+ d+) ←————————
                                                                                  This shows the pattern : x is starting point and hence no +
                                              DEFINE --x as (price=max(price)),    A, b, c, d are name of points in W shape and has + means fluctuation here
     Here you define the rule for                   a as (price<PREV(price)),
     each point in the shape, Since x is ————→       b as (price>PREV(price)),
     starting point there is no rule for this        c as (price<PREV(price)),
                                                      d as (price>PREV(price) AND d.times-FIRST(a.times)<=7));
                                                                          ↑
                                                             This shows the pattern only within 7 days span
```

In the pattern clause supported operators and their meaning:

> * for 0 or more iterations
> + for 1 or more iterations
> ? for 0 or 1 iterations
> { n } for exactly n iterations (n > 0)
> { n, } for n or more iterations (n >= 0)
> { n, m } for between n and m (inclusive) iterations (0 <= n <= m, 0 < m)
> { , m } for between 0 and m (inclusive) iterations (m > 0)

The **output** will be as below (the W shape picture is given to explain the output)

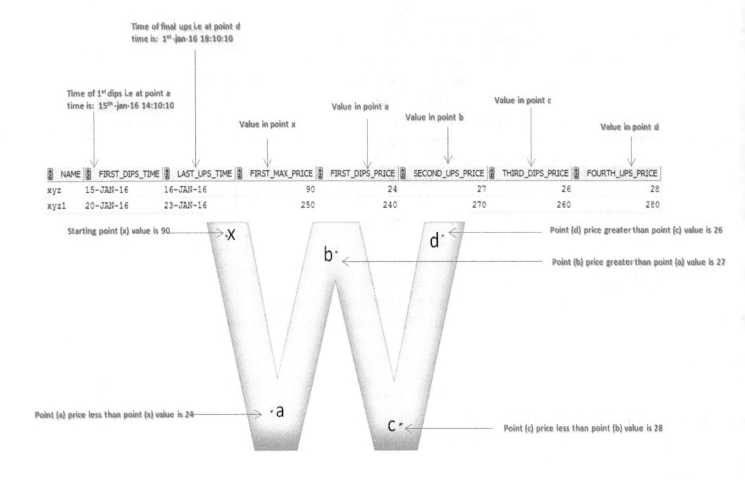

Similarly you can find V shape pattern or any other pattern from the dataset using this new feature in 12c. This seems to be a fairly nice feature as you can refactor the dataset across the rows and display in any format and find any pattern with ease.

Tips 2: Pivoting rows into column dynamically in 10g/11g

Here we will demonstrate how to convert rows into columns with and without PIVOT

Using the 11g PIVOT function you can convert rows into columns. PIVOT does the conversion based on aggregation, however when you have the requirement to purely convert the rows into columns then PIVOT will not work directly, Take the scenario where you have data as below:

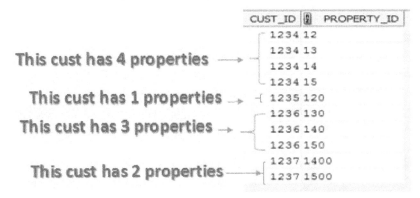

Here in order to turn rows into columns dynamically using PIVOT you need to use inline view using partition by clause. Another solution without PIVOT is: first use WM_CONCAT or XMLAGG or LISTAGG to group all the "property_id" associated with the CUST_ID and then use REGEXP to break the aggregated column (separated by comma) into individual columns.

Note: WM_CONCAT is removed from Oracle 12c onward and hence suggested to use XMLAGG or LISTAGG

Example:

```
CREATE TABLE CUST_PROPERTY
  (
    CUST_ID       NUMBER,
    PROPERTY_ID VARCHAR2(100)
  );

INSERT INTO CUST_PROPERTY VALUES(1234,'12');
INSERT INTO CUST_PROPERTY VALUES(1234,'13');
INSERT INTO CUST_PROPERTY VALUES(1234,'14');
INSERT INTO CUST_PROPERTY VALUES(1234,'15');
INSERT INTO CUST_PROPERTY VALUES(1235,'120');
INSERT INTO CUST_PROPERTY VALUES(1236,'130');
INSERT INTO CUST_PROPERTY VALUES(1236,'140');
INSERT INTO CUST_PROPERTY VALUES(1236,'150');
INSERT INTO CUST_PROPERTY VALUES(1237,'1400');
INSERT INTO CUST_PROPERTY VALUES(1237,'1500');
COMMIT;
```

Solution to convert rows into columns using PIVOT in 11g:

In this solution you need to use inline view to partition the records based on cust_id and then PIVOT the result.

```
SELECT *
FROM
  (SELECT cust_id,
    PROPERTY_ID,
    row_number() over(partition BY cust_id order by PROPERTY_ID DESC) RN
  FROM CUST_PROPERTY
  )
  PIVOT( MAX(PROPERTY_ID)
  FOR RN IN(1 property_1,2 property_2,3 property_3,4 property_4) );
```

Output:

CUST_ID	PROPERTY_1	PROPERTY_2	PROPERTY_3	PROPERTY_4
1234	15	14	13	12
1235	120	(null)	(null)	(null)
1236	150	140	130	(null)
1237	1500	1400	(null)	(null)

Solution to convert rows into columns pre 11g:

Prior to 11g you cannot use PIVOT and hence the solution is as explained:
After aggregating the data using XMLAGG the result-set can be broken down to column level using decode/case, however that approach is very tedious and requires huge effort but with REGEXP_SUBSTR you can achieve the result neatly as below.

```
SELECT cust_id,
  regexp_substr(list_prop,'[^,]+',1,1) AS property_1 ,
  regexp_substr(list_prop,'[^,]+',1,2) AS property_2 ,
  regexp_substr(list_prop,'[^,]+',1,3) AS property_3 ,
  regexp_substr(list_prop,'[^,]+',1,4) AS property_4
FROM
  (SELECT cust_id,
    rtrim(xmlagg(xmlelement(P,property_id
  ||',')).extract('//text()'),',') list_prop
  FROM
    (SELECT DISTINCT cust_id,property_id FROM CUST_PROPERTY ORDER BY cust_id
    )P
  GROUP BY cust_id
  )x;
```

The result will look as below:

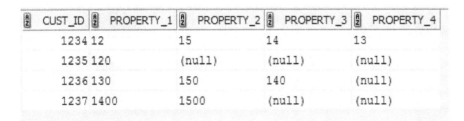

CUST_ID	PROPERTY_1	PROPERTY_2	PROPERTY_3	PROPERTY_4
1234	12	15	14	13
1235	120	(null)	(null)	(null)
1236	130	150	140	(null)
1237	1400	1500	(null)	(null)

So it is possible to dynamically view the rows as any number of columns based on how many property are associated with a cust_id.

Solution to convert row into column in 11g without PIVOT keyword:
Now, if you want to display all the property_1, property_2, property_3 etc. in a certain order you can do it using the LISTAGG (introduced in oracle 11g) analytic function for string aggregation as below:

```
SELECT cust_id,
  regexp_substr(list_prop,'[^,]+',1,1) AS property_1 ,
  regexp_substr(list_prop,'[^,]+',1,2) AS property_2 ,
  regexp_substr(list_prop,'[^,]+',1,3) AS property_3 ,
  regexp_substr(list_prop,'[^,]+',1,4) AS property_4
FROM
  (SELECT DISTINCT cust_id,
  LISTAGG(property_id,',') WITHIN GROUP(
  ORDER BY property_id DESC) OVER(partition BY cust_id)list_prop
  FROM
    (SELECT DISTINCT cust_id,property_id FROM CUST_PROPERTY ORDER BY cust_id
    )P
  )x;
```

This clause pivot the rows

This clause group the data

This clause sort the pivoted column

The same result can be achieved without the "**partition by**" clause as below:

```
SELECT cust_id,
  regexp_substr(list_prop,'[^,]+',1,1) AS property_1 ,
  regexp_substr(list_prop,'[^,]+',1,2) AS property_2 ,
  regexp_substr(list_prop,'[^,]+',1,3) AS property_3 ,
  regexp_substr(list_prop,'[^,]+',1,4) AS property_4
FROM
  (SELECT DISTINCT cust_id,
    LISTAGG(property_id,',') WITHIN GROUP(
  ORDER BY property_id DESC) list_prop --OVER(partition BY cust_id)list_prop
  FROM
    (SELECT DISTINCT cust_id,property_id FROM CUST_PROPERTY ORDER BY cust_id
    )P
  GROUP BY cust_id
  )x;
```

Partition clause is commented and group by is added

The output will look below:

CUST_ID	PROPERTY_1	PROPERTY_2	PROPERTY_3	PROPERTY_4
1234	15	14	13	12
1235	120	(null)	(null)	(null)
1236	150	140	130	(null)
1237	1500	1400	(null)	(null)

Now property_1, property_2 etc come in proper order.

For more on how to convert rows into column refer to Chapter 5 Tips 2: WITH Clause to pivot full rows (all columns rows) into columns

Tips 3: Breaking a concatenated string to display as set of rows or set of Columns?

In this tips we will discuss how to break a string to display the result as set of columns and set of rows.

When you have a concatenated string and you need to break the concatenated string and display as multiple rows or multiple columns here is the steps:

String broken to display as multiple columns:
Use REGEXP_SUBSTR to break the aggregated column (separated by commas) into individual columns.

```
SELECT REGEXP_SUBSTR ('This,12,test,Oracle', '[^,]+', 1, 1) AS val_1 ,
   REGEXP_SUBSTR ('This,12,test,Oracle', '[^,]+', 1, 2)     AS val_2 ,
   REGEXP_SUBSTR ('This,12,test,Oracle', '[^,]+', 1, 3)     AS val_3 ,
   REGEXP_SUBSTR ('This,12,test,Oracle', '[^,]+', 1, 4)     AS val_4
FROM dual;
```

The output will look as below:

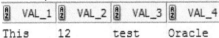

VAL_1	VAL_2	VAL_3	VAL_4
This	12	test	Oracle

String broken to display as multiple rows:
Again use REGEXP_SUBSTR to break the aggregated column (separated by commas) into individual columns then using CONNECT BY you can display the data in rows.

```
WITH concat AS
   (SELECT 'This,12,test,Oracle' AS loc_str FROM dual
   )
SELECT level                               AS rec,
   regexp_substr(loc_str,'[^,]+',1,level) AS val
FROM concat
   CONNECT BY regexp_substr(loc_str,'[^,]+',1,level) IS NOT NULL;
```

The output will look as below:

REC	VAL
1	This
2	12
3	test
4	Oracle

Tips 4: Find Inter-rows Specific colour Pattern for Animal colour registration prior to 12c and in 12c using "MATCH_RECOGNISE" clause?

In this tips we will find all the animals which are registered consecutively as Red, blue, green and yellow prior to oracle 12c and in 12c.

Prior to 12c detecting a specific pattern was a very difficult and complex job using analytic function, recursive queries using connect by, inline views etc.

Example:
Let us take one example of animal registration where each animal has a specific colour.
The requirement is to find the pattern where Red, Blue, Green and Yellow colour appear consecutively based on animal registration id.
Here you can see the specific colour combination appears 2 times.

In order to get the pattern prior to 12 you need to write the following analytic query which will give the animal_ids for which the pattern is found.

Prior to 12c Solution:

```
create table anilmal_colour(animal_id number,colour varchar2(10));
insert into anilmal_colour values(1,'Red');
insert into anilmal_colour values(2,'Yellow');
insert into anilmal_colour values(3,'Green');
insert into anilmal_colour values(4,'Red');
insert into anilmal_colour values(5,'Green');
insert into anilmal_colour values(6,'Yellow');
insert into anilmal_colour values(7,'Red');
insert into anilmal_colour values(8,'Red');
insert into anilmal_colour values(9,'Red');
insert into anilmal_colour values(10,'Red');
insert into anilmal_colour values(11,'Blue');
insert into anilmal_colour values(12,'Green');
insert into anilmal_colour values(13,'Yellow');
commit;
```

The analytic query to get the pattern:

```
SELECT *
FROM anilmal_colour
WHERE (animal_id) IN
  (SELECT regexp_substr(animal_ids_str,'[^,]+',1,level)   ← This will display all the ids in unpivoted rows
  FROM
    (SELECT animal_id
      ||','
      ||next_animal_id
      ||','
      ||second_next_animal_id
      ||','
      ||third_next_animal_id animal_ids_str
    FROM
      (SELECT d.*,
        lead(colour) over(order by animal_id) next_colour,           ← This give next colour, for this case Blue
        lead(animal_id) over(order by animal_id) next_animal_id,
        lead(colour,2) over(order by animal_id) second_next_colour,   ← This give 2nd next colur, for this case Green
        lead(animal_id,2) over(order by animal_id) second_next_animal_id,
        lead(colour,3) over(order by animal_id) third_next_colour,    ← This give 3rd next colour, for this case Yellow
        lead(animal_id,3) over(order by animal_id) third_next_animal_id
      FROM anilmal_colour d
      )
    WHERE colour          ='Red'
    AND next_colour        ='Blue'
    AND second_next_colour='Green'
    AND third_next_colour ='Yellow'
    )
    CONNECT BY regexp_substr(animal_ids_str,'[^,]+',1,level) IS NOT NULL
  );
```

This will display all the ids in unpivoted rows

The output will be:

ANIMAL_ID	COLOUR
10	Red
11	Blue
12	Green
13	Yellow

Oracle 12c solution using match_recognize:

Using Oracle match_recognize it is fairly simple.

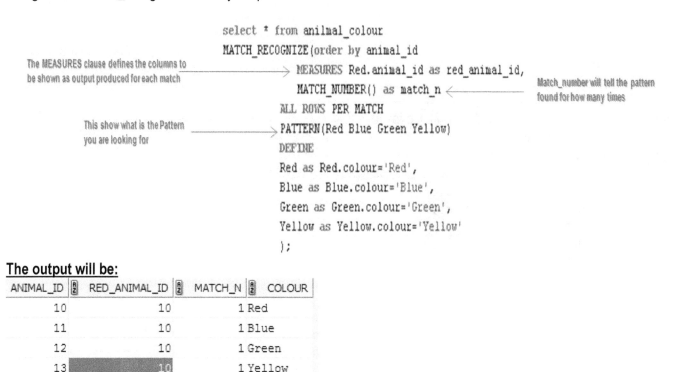

```
select * from anilmal_colour
MATCH_RECOGNIZE(order by animal_id
            MEASURES Red.animal_id as red_animal_id,
            MATCH_NUMBER() as match_n
ALL ROWS PER MATCH
PATTERN(Red Blue Green Yellow)
DEFINE
Red as Red.colour='Red',
Blue as Blue.colour='Blue',
Green as Green.colour='Green',
Yellow as Yellow.colour='Yellow'
);
```

The MEASURES clause defines the columns to be shown as output produced for each match

Match_number will tell the pattern found for how many times

This show what is the Pattern you are looking for

The output will be:

ANIMAL_ID	RED_ANIMAL_ID	MATCH_N	COLOUR
10	10	1	Red
11	10	1	Blue
12	10	1	Green
13	10	1	Yellow

Tips 5: Find Inter-rows Specific pattern for consecutive same flag for 3 times prior to 12c and in 12c using "MATCH_RECOGNISE" clause?

Here we will discuss how to find the rows with same flags for 3 consecutive times in 12c and prior to 12c.

Example:

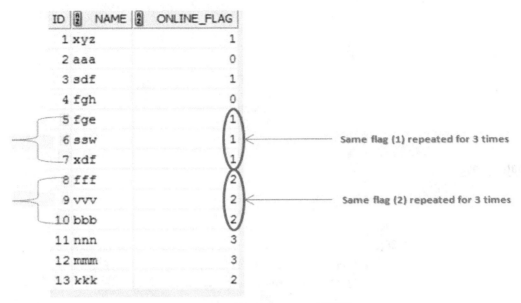

ID	NAME	ONLINE_FLAG
1	xyz	1
2	aaa	0
3	sdf	1
4	fgh	0
5	fge	1
6	ssw	1
7	xdf	1
8	fff	2
9	vvv	2
10	bbb	2
11	nnn	3
12	mmm	3
13	kkk	2

Same flag (1) repeated for 3 times

Same flag (2) repeated for 3 times

So for this case the pattern is seen in ids [5,6,7] and ids [8,9,10]
Prior to 12c you need to use an analytic function to achieve this

Solution prior to 12c:

```
create table dc_customer(id number,name varchar2(30),online_flag number);
insert into dc_customer values(1,'xyz',1);
insert into dc_customer values(2,'aaa',0);
insert into dc_customer values(3,'sdf',1);
insert into dc_customer values(4,'fgh',0);
insert into dc_customer values(5,'fge',1);
insert into dc_customer values(6,'ssw',1);
insert into dc_customer values(7,'xdf',1);
insert into dc_customer values(8,'fff',2);
insert into dc_customer values(9,'vvv',2);
insert into dc_customer values(10,'bbb',2);
insert into dc_customer values(11,'nnn',3);
insert into dc_customer values(12,'mmm',3);
insert into dc_customer values(13,'kkk',2);
```

The analytic query to get the pattern:

```sql
SELECT *
FROM dc_customer
WHERE (id) IN
  (SELECT regexp_substr(cust_ids_str,'[^,]+',1,level)     ← This will display all the ids in unpivoted rows
  FROM
    (SELECT id
      ||','
      ||next_id
      ||','
      ||second_next_id as cust_ids_str
        FROM
      (SELECT d.*,
      lead(online_flag) over(order by id) next_online_flag,     ← This give next consecutive flag
        lead(id) over(order by id) next_id,
      lead(online_flag,2) over(order by id) second_next_online_flag,     ← This give 2nd next consecutive flag
        lead(id,2) over(order by id) second_next_id
      FROM dc_customer d
      )
    where online_flag=next_online_flag     ← 
    and online_flag=second_next_online_flag ←     This make sure 3 consecutive flags are same
    )
    CONNECT BY regexp_substr(cust_ids_str,'[^,]+',1,level) IS NOT NULL
  );
```

The output will be:

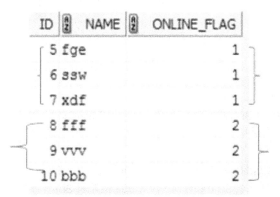

ID	NAME	ONLINE_FLAG
5	fge	1
6	ssw	1
7	xdf	1
8	fff	2
9	vvv	2
10	bbb	2

Oracle 12c solution using match_recognize:

Using Oracle match_recognize it is fairly simple.

```
select * from dc_customer
        MATCH_RECOGNIZE
        (
        order by id
        MEASURES same_flag.online_flag as same_flag_val,
        MATCH_NUMBER() as match_n
        ALL ROWS PER MATCH
        PATTERN(same_flag{3})  <──────── This show pattern is 3 consecutive flag are same
        DEFINE
        same_flag as same_flag.online_flag=first(same_flag.online_flag)
        );
```

The output will be:

ID	SAME_FLAG_VAL	MATCH_N	NAME	ONLINE_FLAG
5	1	1	fge	1
6	1	1	ssw	1
7	1	1	xdf	1
8	2	2	fff	2
9	2	2	vvv	2
10	2	2	bbb	2

Now if you want to find the pattern where 4 consecutive flags are the same then just use this:

```
PATTERN(same_flag{4})  <──────── This show pattern is 4 consecutive flag are same
```

Now for our example four consecutive IDs with the same flag are not present and hence if you run the query based on same_flag {4} the query won't return any output.

Tips 6: what is RANK, DENSE_RANK and ROW_NUMBER?

RANK function provides each row a unique number except for duplicate rows. For duplicate rows it assigns the same rank and the next row rank is not consecutive as there are gaps. Output can be 1,2,2,4

DENSE_RANK function also provides each row a unique number except for duplicate rows. For the duplicate rows it assigns the same ranking value and for the next row it assigns the next rank value, so there are no gaps in the rank value sequence. Output can be 1,2,2,3

ROW_NUMBER function provides each row a unique number over the entire result-set. However if you use optional partition by clause then based on the partition clause the sequencing is done. Output can be 1,2,3,4

E.g.

```
SELECT empno,
  sal,
  DENSE_RANK() OVER (ORDER BY sal DESC) AS dense_ranks,
  RANK() OVER (ORDER BY sal DESC)        AS ranks,
  row_number() OVER (ORDER BY sal DESC) AS row_numbers
FROM emp
WHERE sal IS NOT NULL;
```

Emp_id	sal	dense_ranks	ranks	row_numbers
7839	5000	1	1	1
7902	3000	2	2	2
7788	3000	2	2	3
7566	2975	3	4	4
7698	2850	4	5	5

However if we use optional "partition by" clause against each function the result will be as per the above rule but all the ranking will restart once the value of the partition clause changes.

Here is an example
```
SELECT empno,
  sal,
  deptno,
  DENSE_RANK() OVER (PARTITION BY deptno ORDER BY sal DESC) AS part_dense_ranks,
  RANK() OVER (PARTITION BY deptno ORDER BY sal DESC)        AS part_rank,
  row_number() OVER (PARTITION BY deptno ORDER BY sal DESC) AS part_row_number
FROM emp
WHERE sal IS NOT NULL;
```

Emp_id	sal	deptno	part_dense_ranks	part_ranks	part_row_numbers
7839	5000	10	1	1	1
7782	2450	10	2	2	2
7934	1300	10	3	3	3
7788	3000	20	1	1	1
7902	3000	20	1	1	2
7566	2975	20	2	3	3

Tips 7: What is LEAD and LAG function?

Here we will discuss how to use analytic function to get the next row and previous row against the current row

Analytical function LEAD is used to return data from next row whereas LAG function is used to return data from previous row.
Here is one example:

```
SELECT deptno,
empno,
sal,
LEAD(sal) OVER (PARTITION BY dept ORDER BY sal DESC NULLS LAST) NEXT_LOWER_SAL,
LAG(sal) OVER (PARTITION BY dept ORDER BY sal DESC NULLS LAST) PREV_HIGHER_SAL,
LEAD(sal) OVER (PARTITION BY dept ORDER BY sal ASC NULLS LAST) NEXT_HIGHER_SAL,
LAG(sal) OVER (PARTITION BY dept ORDER BY sal ASC NULLS LAST) PREV_LOWER_SAL
FROM emp
WHERE deptno IN (10, 20)
ORDER BY deptno,sal DESC;
```

The result will look as below and is self-explanatory

DEPTNO	EMPNO	SAL	NEXT_LOWER_SAL	PREV_HIGHER_SAL	NEXT_HIGHER_SAL	PREV_LOWER_SAL
10	7839	5000	2450	0	0	2450
10	7782	2450	1300	5000	5000	1300
10	7934	1300	0	2450	2450	0

Note: When you use LEAD analytic function and ORDER BY DESC inside the OVER clause then it is analogous to LAG analytic function and ORDER BY ASC inside the OVER clause. This is evident from the above output: NEXT_LOWER_SAL (uses LEAD) and PREV_LOWER_SAL (uses LAG)

<u>Generate 10 rows with next 2 records as column:</u>

```
SELECT rownum,
       lead(rownum,1) over ( order by rownum ) AS next_num,
       lead(rownum,2) over ( order by rownum ) AS second_next_num
FROM dual
CONNECT BY level <= 10;
```

The output:

ROWNUM	NEXT_NUM	SECOND_NEXT_NUM
1	2	3
2	3	4
3	4	5
4	5	6
5	6	7
6	7	8
7	8	9
8	9	10
9	10	(null)
10	(null)	(null)

Note: **Lead**(rownum,2) here lead function give the 2nd next record.
Similarly if you use **Lag**(rownum,2) then lag function will give 2nd previous record

Tips 8: Top N query using row limiting clause in 12c?

In this tips we will explore different ways to get top N rows from a table. In other words we will explore how pagination is done in oracle.

Prior to Oracle 12c, to get the top ten salaries of EMP table the following queries were used:
Normal query:

```
SELECT * FROM
  ( SELECT * FROM emp ORDER BY sal DESC
  ) WHERE rownum<11;
```

Analytical query:

```
select * from
(
select a.*,row_number() over (order by sal desc) rn from emp a
)
where rn=1;
```

Basic Syntax for TOP N query **using ROW limiting clause in 12c**:

```
[ OFFSET offset { ROW | ROWS } ]
[ FETCH { FIRST | NEXT } [ { rowcount | percent PERCENT } ]
    { ROW | ROWS } { ONLY | WITH TIES } ]
```

Top 10 records:

```
SELECT * FROM emp ORDER BY SAL DESC
FETCH FIRST 10 ROWS ONLY;
```

If there are duplicate salary values then you can still receive them using "WITH TIES" clause. WITH TIES clause will return more rows if Nth rows value is duplicate.

```
SELECT * FROM emp ORDER BY SAL DESC
FETCH FIRST 10 rows
WITH TIES;
```

In order to get top 10% of salary records from EMP table:

```
SELECT * FROM emp ORDER BY SAL DESC
FETCH FIRST 10 PERCENT ROWS ONLY;
```

In order to get 6th to 10th records from top 10 salaried records:

```
SELECT * FROM emp ORDER BY SAL DESC OFFSET 5 ROWS
FETCH NEXT 5 ROWS ONLY;
```

OFFSET 5 means skip first 5 records.

Note: All the above SQL can be directly used in PL/SQL

E.g.

```
DECLARE
  Type t_sal IS TABLE OF emp.sal%type INDEX BY BINARY INTEGER;
  v_sal t_sal;
BEGIN
  SELECT sal bulk collect INTO v_sal FROM emp ORDER BY sal DESC OFFSET 5 ROWS
  FETCH NEXT 5 ROWS only;
END;
/
```

However in this example if you use bind variable (i.e. in DECLARE section add bind_nr number :=5; and in BEGIN section instead of "5 ROWS" use "bind_nr ROWS") , it will fail with error because of oracle bug in 12c (Bug is related with datatype), when used in "OFFSET/FETCH NEXT" clause. The possible workaround is as below:
Use to_number(bind_nr) ROWS instead of bind_nr ROWS [5 ROWS] in the above PL/SQL block.

Tips 9: Result from view is different from the result from table/mview created from that view, why?

Here in this tips we will demonstrate how view result is different from table/mview created from the view.

A view is just a stored query, the result is never stored. However there is one peculiar scenario I will show you where the result from the view is <u>different</u> from <u>the data held in a table/mview</u> when the table/mview is created from the view.

```
create table app_flag(app_id number,flag varchar2(3));
```
Now insert 1 million records. Each app_id can have 1 and 0 flag.

Now create a view from the table as below:
```
create or replace view app_flag_v as select app_id,List_flag,
DECODE(SUBSTR(List_flag,1,1),1,'Y','N') flag_type
from
(SELECT app_id,
     cast(rtrim (xmlagg (xmlelement (P,flag
     || ',')).extract ('//text()'), ',') as varchar2(3)) List_flag
   FROM
     (SELECT DISTINCT app_id,
        flag
     FROM app_flag
     ORDER BY flag DESC
     ) P
   GROUP BY app_id
);
```

The result of the view may look as below:

114

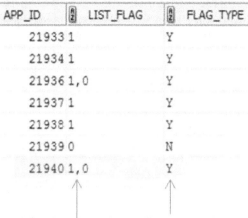

APP_ID	LIST_FLAG	FLAG_TYPE
21933	1	Y
21934	1	Y
21936	1,0	Y
21937	1	Y
21938	1	Y
21939	0	N
21940	1,0	Y

List_flag is displayed as 1,0 and accordingly flag_type become 'Y'

Now when you create a table or materialized view from the view the table/mview data may or may not look exactly the same as the view (**even if there is no change in the underlying table**). This all depends upon how the data is structured/ordered in the inline view as any table is a heap structure and hence it aggregates the data as each block becomes available.

```
create table app_flag_v_t as select * from app_flag_v;
```

```
select * from app_flag_v_t;
```

APP_ID	LIST_FLAG	FLAG_TYPE
21933	1	Y
21934	1	Y
21936	1,0	Y
21937	1	Y
21938	1	Y
21939	0	N
21940	0,1	N

List_flag is displayed as 0,1 and accordingly flag_type become 'N'

This is quite intriguing/erroneous as people using the view will get different result from people using the table directly.

Here is the explanation for this unexpected behavior and the solution to resolve this:

Note in the view the "order by" clause is used to get the flag displayed against app_id. And then all the flags are pivoted as single row against each app_id and at this stage the flag concatenation is not ordered.

So this process does not guarantee the order of flag displayed against app_id. And hence in the view you see

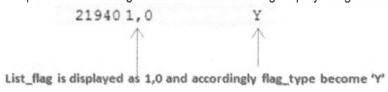

21940 1,0   Y

List_flag is displayed as 1,0 and accordingly flag_type become 'Y'

115

However against table you may see a different result as below because when you create the table from the view the ordering is not guaranteed.

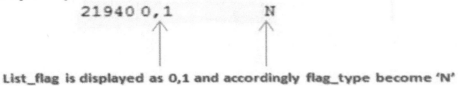

List_flag is displayed as 0,1 and accordingly flag_type become 'N'

Solution
You need to order the flag during pivot process as below:

```
CREATE OR REPLACE VIEW app_flag_v
AS
  SELECT app_id,
    List_flag,
    DECODE(SUBSTR(List_flag,1,1),1,'Y','N') flag_type
  FROM
    (SELECT DISTINCT app_id,
      listagg(flag,',') within GROUP (ORDER BY flag DESC)←————— This will guarantee the flag ordering during pivot
      over (partition BY app_id) List_flag
    FROM
      (SELECT DISTINCT app_id, flag FROM app_flag ORDER BY flag DESC ←—This will guarantee the flag ordering before pivot
      ) P
    );
```

This will guarantee the flag ordering for each row in the view as flags are pivoted in proper order and hence when you create the table or materialized view from the view the **output** will be consistent.

Tips 10: How to get latest version of data from each set of records in a table?

Here we will discuss how to get latest version of data for each set of similar records (CST_IDENTIFIER).

Let's say you have table "test_tab1" with data as below:

```
CREATE TABLE test_tab1
  (cst_identifier NUMBER,status VARCHAR2(1), ver NUMBER
  );
insert into TEST_TAB1 values(111,'U',5);
insert into TEST_TAB1 values(111,'A',3);
insert into TEST_TAB1 values(112,'B',6);
insert into TEST_TAB1 values(112,'U',4);
insert into TEST_TAB1 values(112,'C',2);
insert into TEST_TAB1 values(113,'U',5);
insert into TEST_TAB1 values(113,'P',10);
insert into TEST_TAB1 values(114,'D',2);
insert into TEST_TAB1 values(114,'U',5);
insert into TEST_TAB1 values(114,'F',2);
```

Here for each cst_identifier there are multiple versions present with different statuses.

In order to get the latest version for each cst_identifier, we have to group by cst_identifier and order the result based on version then display the latest version as shown by the arrows.

116

The query will look as below:

```
SELECT cst_identifier,
  status,
  ver
FROM
  (SELECT cst_identifier,
    status,
    ver,
    row_number() OVER(PARTITION BY a.cst_identifier order by a.ver DESC)rn
  FROM test_tab1 a
  )
WHERE rn=1;
```

And the output will be as below:

CST_IDENTIFIER	ST...	VER
111 U		5
112 B		6
113 P		10
114 U		5

Tips 11: How to pivot and unpivot prior to 11g and in 11g?

Here we will explore with simple example how to convert rows into columns and vice versa with and without PIVOT/UNPIVOT

Let's say we have table test_tab3 with data as below:

```
CREATE TABLE test_tab3
  (cust_id NUMBER,region NUMBER,area NUMBER(10,4)
  );
INSERT INTO test_tab3 VALUES(4,1,0);
INSERT INTO test_tab3 VALUES(4,2,100.5);
INSERT INTO test_tab3 VALUES(4,3,34.6);
INSERT INTO test_tab3 VALUES(5,4,29.8);
INSERT INTO test_tab3 VALUES(5,2,44);
INSERT INTO test_tab3 VALUES(6,3,678);
INSERT INTO test_tab3 VALUES(6,4,90);
INSERT INTO test_tab3 VALUES(6,2,89);
INSERT INTO test_tab3 VALUES(6,3,876);
INSERT INTO test_tab3 VALUES(7,2,768);
INSERT INTO test_tab3 VALUES(7,4,56.4);
INSERT INTO test_tab3 VALUES(8,3,567.90);
INSERT INTO test_tab3 VALUES(8,4,90.9);
INSERT INTO test_tab3 VALUES(8,1,89.5);
COMMIT;
```

Here we can see each cust_id belongs to multiple region.

So if we need to know how many regions are associated with each cust_id we write:
```
SELECT cust_id,COUNT(*) FROM test_tab3 GROUP BY cust_id;
```

To know how many region 1, region 2, region 3 and region 4 are associated with each cust_id we write simply as below

```
SELECT cust_id,
   COUNT(*) AS region_1_count
FROM test_tab3
WHERE region=1
GROUP BY cust_id;
```

Output

CUST_ID	REGION_1_COUNT
4	1
8	1

Similarly for region 2:

```
SELECT cust_id,
   COUNT(*) AS region_2_count
FROM test_tab3
WHERE region=2
GROUP BY cust_id;
```

CUST_ID	REGION_2_COUNT
6	1
4	1
5	1
7	1

For region 3 output (just replace region=3):

CUST_ID	REGION_3_COUNT
6	2
4	1
8	1

Foe Region 4 output (just replace region=4)

CUST_ID	REGION_4_COUNT
6	1
5	1
8	1
7	1

However when it is required to display all the output in a single query and in 1 row for each cust_id we have to re write the query as below using **traditional sql join**:

```
SELECT a.cust_id,
  a.total_region_cnt,
  reg_1.region_1_count,
  reg_2.region_2_count,
  reg_3.region_3_count,
  reg_4.region_4_count
FROM
  (SELECT cust_id,COUNT(*) total_region_cnt FROM test_tab3 GROUP BY cust_id
  )a
FULL OUTER JOIN
  (SELECT cust_id,
    COUNT(*) AS region_1_count
  FROM test_tab3
  WHERE region=1
  GROUP BY cust_id
  )reg_1
ON a.cust_id=reg_1.cust_id
FULL OUTER JOIN
  (SELECT cust_id,
    COUNT(*) AS region_2_count
  FROM test_tab3
  WHERE region=2
  GROUP BY cust_id
  )reg_2
ON a.cust_id=reg_2.cust_id
FULL OUTER JOIN
  (SELECT cust_id,
    COUNT(*) AS region_3_count
  FROM test_tab3
  WHERE region=3
  GROUP BY cust_id
  )reg_3
ON a.cust_id=reg_3.cust_id
FULL OUTER JOIN
  (SELECT cust_id,
    COUNT(*) AS region_4_count
  FROM test_tab3
  WHERE region=4
  GROUP BY cust_id
  )reg_4
ON a.cust_id=reg_4.cust_id
```

And the **output** will look as below

CUST_ID	TOTAL_REGION_CNT	REGION_1_COUNT	REGION_2_COUNT	REGION_3_COUNT	REGION_4_COUNT
6	4	(null)	1	2	1
4	3	1	1	1	(null)
5	2	(null)	1	(null)	1
8	3	1	(null)	1	1
7	2	(null)	1	(null)	1

We can write the same query using CASE statement as below:

```
SELECT cust_id,
COUNT(CASE WHEN region in(1,2,3,4) THEN region END) tot_reg_cnt,
COUNT(CASE WHEN region in(1) THEN region END) region_1_count,
COUNT(CASE WHEN region in(2) THEN region END) region_2_count,
COUNT(CASE WHEN region in(3) THEN region END) region_3_count,
COUNT(CASE WHEN region in(4) THEN region END) region_4_count
FROM test_tab3
GROUP BY cust_id;
```

And the **output** will be as below:

CUST_ID	TOT_REG_CNT	REGION_1_COUNT	REGION_2_COUNT	REGION_3_COUNT	REGION_4_COUNT
6	4	0	1	2	1
4	3	1	1	1	0
5	2	0	1	0	1
8	3	1	0	1	1
7	2	0	1	0	1

However from Oracle 11g onward we can simplify this using PIVOT command
As below:

```
SELECT *
FROM
  (SELECT cust_id,region FROM test_tab3
  ) PIVOT (COUNT(*) reg_cnt FOR region IN(1,2,3,4));
```

And the output will look exactly the same, just the header name is dynamically formed.

CUST_ID	1_REG_CNT	2_REG_CNT	3_REG_CNT	4_REG_CNT
6	0	1	2	1
4	1	1	1	0
5	0	1	0	1
8	1	0	1	1
7	0	1	0	1

However if you want to name the header as you wish you need to just alias the column name as below
```
SELECT *
FROM
  (SELECT cust_id,region FROM test_tab3
  ) PIVOT (COUNT(*) reg_cnt FOR region IN(1 as reg_1,2 as reg_2,3 as reg_3,4 as reg_4));
```

And the output will be

CUST_ID	REG_1_REG_CNT	REG_2_REG_CNT	REG_3_REG_CNT	REG_4_REG_CNT
6	0	1	2	1
4	1	1	1	0
5	0	1	0	1
8	1	0	1	1
7	0	1	0	1

So using PIVOT function we can convert row into column.

In reverse way using UNPIVOT we can convert column into row.
Here is an example

```
CREATE TABLE test_unpivot
  (
    cust_id   NUMBER,
    reg_1_cnt NUMBER,
    reg_2_cnt NUMBER,
    reg_3_cnt NUMBER,
    reg_4_cnt NUMBER,
    area      NUMBER(10,4)
  );
INSERT INTO test_unpivot VALUES(4,0,0,2,2,1000);
INSERT INTO test_unpivot VALUES(17,2,0,2,2,2000);
INSERT INTO test_unpivot VALUES(52,2,2,2,2,3000);
COMMIT;

SELECT *
FROM test_unpivot
UNPIVOT (region_count FOR region IN(reg_1_cnt AS 1,reg_2_cnt AS 2,
reg_3_cnt AS 3,reg_4_cnt AS 4)
)
WHERE region_count<>0;
```

Note here in the unpivot "IN" clause we use the name of the column instead of actual value
The output will look as below:

CUST_ID	AREA	REGION	REGION_COUNT
4	1000	3	2
4	1000	4	2
17	2000	1	2
17	2000	3	2
17	2000	4	2
52	3000	1	2
52	3000	2	2
52	3000	3	2
52	3000	4	2

Tips 12: How to Display grouped data in one row?

Here we will discuss how to display individual records of a group in one row.

In this example table TEST_TAB has two columns CUST_ID and HOUSE_NUMBER, with one CUST_ID having more than one NO_OF_HOUSE:

CUST_ID	HOUSE_NUMBER
1234	12
1234	13
1234	14
1235	15
1236	16
1236	17
1236	18

So the below query will return:

```
SELECT cust_id,COUNT(house_number) FROM test_tab GROUP BY cust_id;
```

CUST_ID	COUNT(HOUSE_NUMBER)
1234	3
1236	3
1235	1

To return a single row for each CUST_ID displaying all the associated "HOUSE_NUMBER" run the aggregate query:

```
SELECT cust_id,
  rtrim(xmlagg(xmlelement(P,house_number
  ||',')).extract('//text()'),',') house_number_list
FROM
  (SELECT cust_id,house_number FROM test_tab
  )P
GROUP BY cust_id;
```

Result:

CUST_ID	HOUSE_NUMBER_LIST
1234	12,14,13
1235	15
1236	16,18,17

Alternatively you can use oracle function "wm_concat" to concat the grouped data as below.
However you can use this function from oracle 11g onward.
Note "wm_concat" is unsupported, however oracle 11g onward you can use LISTAGG function as explained in this chapter TIPS-2

```
SELECT cust_id,
  wm_concat(P.house_number) house_number_list
FROM
  (SELECT cust_id,house_number FROM test_tab
  )P
GROUP BY cust_id;
```

This will produce same output.

Tips 13: Assign dynamic page number through query (instead of application coding for the report)?

In this tips we will discuss how to display the page number in a report dynamically based on number of rows.

There are scenarios when a developer requires to create report and display in a certain format. Here is one simple requirement which will take lot of time if it is implemented with Java coding. This is very simple in Oracle.

```
CREATE TABLE Page_breakup
  (
    LP     VARCHAR2(10),
    REG    VARCHAR2(5),
    LPTYP  VARCHAR2(5),
    area   NUMBER(10,3)
  );
insert into Page_breakup values('X1','R1','NNT',12.5);
insert into Page_breakup values('X1','R1','NNT1',10.5);
insert into Page_breakup values('X1','R1','NNT2',9.5);
insert into Page_breakup values('X1','R1','NNT3',12.8);
insert into Page_breakup values('X1','R1','NNT4',15.5);

insert into Page_breakup values('X2','R1','MNT',22.5);
insert into Page_breakup values('X2','R1','MNT1',20.5);
insert into Page_breakup values('X2','R1','MNT2',6.5);


insert into Page_breakup values('X3','R2','PNT3',42.8);
insert into Page_breakup values('X3','R2','PNT4',32.5);
insert into Page_breakup values('X3','R2','PNT4',34.5);
insert into Page_breakup values('X3','R2','PNT4',31.5);
commit;
```

Now the requirement is to display page number against each **record**. The rule is as below:
→ if LP+REG combination repeat for 3 or less than 3 then they should go to Page1
→ if LP+REG combination repeat for more than 3 then 1st 3 will go to Page1 and rest go to Page2

The solution is:

```
SELECT Page_breakup.*,
    DECODE(row_number() over (partition BY LP,REG order by LP),
    1,'Page1',
    2,'Page1',
    3, 'Page1',
    'Page2') Page_number
FROM Page_breakup;
```

This derive the page number

The result will look as below:

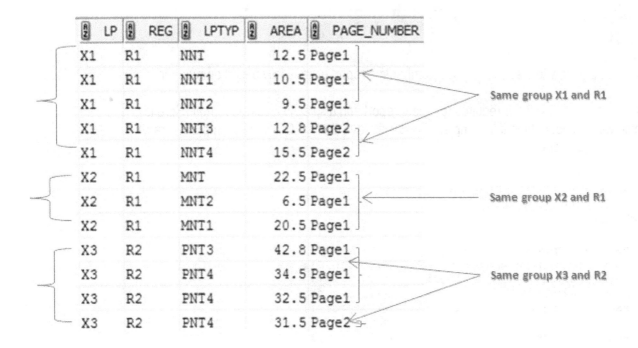

LP	REG	LPTYP	AREA	PAGE_NUMBER	
X1	R1	NNT	12.5	Page1	
X1	R1	NNT1	10.5	Page1	Same group X1 and R1
X1	R1	NNT2	9.5	Page1	
X1	R1	NNT3	12.8	Page2	
X1	R1	NNT4	15.5	Page2	
X2	R1	MNT	22.5	Page1	
X2	R1	MNT2	6.5	Page1	Same group X2 and R1
X2	R1	MNT1	20.5	Page1	
X3	R2	PNT3	42.8	Page1	
X3	R2	PNT4	34.5	Page1	Same group X3 and R2
X3	R2	PNT4	32.5	Page1	
X3	R2	PNT4	31.5	Page2	

Tips 14: Nullify the duplicate record for certain attribute only

Here we will demonstrate how to nullify duplicate attributes in a record.

Consider a situation in which it is required to set the attribute of a column to null if it is duplicated.
For example

```
CREATE TABLE test_tab5
  (
    batch_id  NUMBER,
    record_id NUMBER,
    house_no  VARCHAR2(20),
    area      NUMBER(10,4)
  );

INSERT INTO test_tab5 VALUES(1,12,'AX/11/01',12.5);
INSERT INTO test_tab5 VALUES(2,13,'AX/11/01',12.5);
INSERT INTO test_tab5 VALUES(3,9,'AX/11/01',12.5);
INSERT INTO test_tab5 VALUES(4,12,'BX/Z11/02',19.7);
INSERT INTO test_tab5 VALUES(4,12,'MY/R1/02',29.4);
INSERT INTO test_tab5 VALUES(4,12,'MY/R1/02',29.4);
COMMIT;
```

You are asked to display all the records but for duplicate records based on fld_id you need to display gross area only once and rest of the duplicate records you display null for gross_area.

So for AX/11/01
We need to display gross area 12.5 only for batch_id=1 and for batch_id=2 and 3 we need to display null as gross area

In order to achieve this we need to partition the record based on fld_id and in the partition we will take the corresponding value of gross area for 1st record of the partition and rest of the record you need to set the value to null.

```
SELECT batch_id,
   record_id,
   house_no,
   DECODE(rn,1,area,NULL)area
FROM
   (SELECT batch_id,
     record_id,
     house_no,
     area,
     row_number() over(partition BY house_no order by batch_id DESC) rn
   FROM
     (SELECT batch_id,record_id,house_no,area FROM test_tab5
     )
   );
```

The output look as below now:

BATCH_ID	RECORD_ID	HOUSE_NO	AREA
3	9	AX/11/01	12.5
2	13	AX/11/01	(null)
1	12	AX/11/01	(null)
4	12	BX/Z11/02	19.7
4	12	MY/R1/02	29.4
4	12	MY/R1/02	(null)

This look easy, however if you do not know the technique it will be tricky to nullify certain records through program logic.

Chapter 4: Flashback setup and data Transfer (29 pages)

Flashback transaction was introduced in Oracle 9i. When a query is long running, let us say for 1 hour, then it will display the data when the query was started 1 hour before. Even if some data undergone changes and committed by other transaction it will still display the data for point of time the query was started.

This is because Oracle maintains read consistent image in UNDO segment. So it is possible to get the old version of data till it is present in undo segment and not overwritten. This is how Oracle could show the image of the old version data even if new version of data is present by means of undo segment. So now if there is any mechanism for normal user to retrieve the old version of data from undo segment then we can fire a query and see the data.

However before Oracle 9i there was no such mechanism by which user could see the old version of data even if data was present in undo segment. The quest for helping user to see old version of data led to the introduction of the Flashback transaction in Oracle 9i

In this chapter we will explore all the dimensions of flashback, full examples of setup and data movement to warehouse using flashback mechanism, also we will explore related myth around this.

Tips 1: Why flashback was introduced?
Tips 2: What is the improvement of flashback in Oracle 11g and how to configure flashback?
Tips 3: What is the flashback mechanism?
Tips 4: How to check if flashback is configured in your system and in your tables?
Tips 5: Flashback query using method "timestamp" OR "scn"?
Tips 6: Move all versions of flashback data using STATIC method?
Tips 7: Move all versions of flashback data from dynamically
Tips 8: Restore table which is dropped using flashback?
Tips 9: Move specific date/time flashback data from transactional db to warehouse?
Tips 10: How many time a particular attribute in a row modified using flashback?
Tips 11: Improvement in auditing using flashback in 12c?
Tips 12: Improvement in tracking history for security related table using flashback in 12c?
Tips 13: import and export of flashback version history in 12c?
Tips 14: Free Flashback archive and OPTIMIZE option in 12c?
Tips 15: FLASHBACK magic exposed, Revealed for the first time

Tips 1: Why flashback was introduced?

Here we will discuss how to view old versions of data from undo segment using flashback technology.

Flashback transaction was introduced in Oracle 9i. When a query is long running, let us say for 1 hour, then it will display the data when the query was started 1 hour before. Even if some data undergone changes and committed by other transaction it will still display the data for point of time the query was started.
This is because Oracle maintains read consistent image in UNDO segment. So it is possible to get the old version of data till it is present in undo segment and not overwritten. This is how Oracle could show the image of the old version data even if new version of data is present by means of undo segment. So now if there is any mechanism for normal user to retrieve the old version of data from undo segment then we can fire a query and see the data.
However before Oracle 9i there was no such mechanism by which user could see the old version of data even if data was present in undo segment. The quest for helping user to see old version of data led to the introduction of the Flashback transaction in Oracle 9i
However as you know undo data is not kept forever in undo segment. So based on undo retention period the data is flashed off and overwritten by new data and hence flashback transaction cannot give old version of data if you try to find data beyond undo retention period and the flashback transaction query fail.
So if your undo retention period is 30 min the below will run fine.

2015-11-08 11:51 we run the below flashback transaction query:
```
SELECT versions_startscn, versions_starttime,
       versions_endscn, versions_endtime,
       versions_xid, versions_operation,
       test11.*
  FROM test11
  VERSIONS BETWEEN TIMESTAMP
      TO_TIMESTAMP('2015-11-08 11:25:00', 'YYYY-MM-DD HH24:MI:SS')
  AND TO_TIMESTAMP('2015-11-08 11:50:00','YYYY-MM-DD HH24:MI:SS')
```

This query will give old version of data for the above period. The limitation is it cannot give old version of data before undo retention period (i.e. you cannot get data older than 30 minutes).

Note: This table is not enabled for flashback

Tips 2: What is the improvement of flashback in Oracle 11g and how to configure flashback?

Here we will look into 11g flashback improvement to retrieve old version of data beyond undo retention

Pre 11g you can run flashback query and get old version of data till undo_retention period. However if you try to retrieve data beyond undo retention period then it will fail as below:

2015-11-08 12:06 we run the below flashback query:

```
SELECT versions_startscn, versions_starttime,
       versions_endscn, versions_endtime,
       versions_xid, versions_operation,
       test11.*
  FROM test11
  VERSIONS BETWEEN TIMESTAMP
      TO_TIMESTAMP('2015-11-08 11:25:00', 'YYYY-MM-DD HH24:MI:SS')
  AND TO_TIMESTAMP('2015-11-08 12:05:00', 'YYYY-MM-DD HH24:MI:SS');
```

ORA-30052: invalid lower limit snapshot expression
30052. 00000 - "invalid lower limit snapshot expression"
*Cause: The lower limit snapshot expression was below the UNDO_RETENTION
          limit.
*Action: Specify a valid lower limit snapshot expression.
Error at Line: 7 Column: 11

The above query fails because undo_retention is 30 min and we are trying to retrieve the version data before 30 min.
Note the above query will fail in all the oracle version 9i, 10g, 11g, and 12c as it does not have flashback. However from 11g onward there are some configuration and additional **steps** by which above query can be made to run fine in 11g and subsequent releases.

So it is not possible to get version data beyond the undo_retention using flashback query before oracle 11g. Before Oracle 11g you need to use trigger to store all the old version of data so that you know the workflow of each version of data. This is tedious job and require lot of database activity like trigger related performance impact, context switching, dependency check etc.

To remove the above limitation of flashback, oracle 11g has enhanced flashback mechanism so that you can query the old data beyond undo_retention period.

Here are the steps to do the set up.

Connect to sys as sysdba and run

```
CREATE TABLESPACE DB_FDA_TBS DATAFILE SIZE 1G AUTOEXTEND ON NEXT 1M;
ALTER USER DB QUOTA UNLIMITED ON DB_FDA_TBS;

create flashback archive DB_FDA
tablespace DB_FDA_TBS
quota 1g
retention 1 year
/


GRANT FLASHBACK ARCHIVE ON DB_FDA TO DB;
GRANT FLASHBACK ARCHIVE ADMINISTER TO DB;
GRANT EXECUTE ON DBMS_FLASHBACK_ARCHIVE TO DB; <——————— This can be run only in 12c
```

Now user "DB" is ready to use flashback feature.
To enable FLASHBACK in TABLE "TEST11"

Connect to user "DB" and run
```
alter table test11 flashback archive DB_FDA
/
```

As flashback is configured now, if you run the previous query again (which failed because of the flashback limitation with error ora-30052), it will run fine in 11g and subsequent releases.

```
SELECT versions_startscn, versions_starttime,
       versions_endscn, versions_endtime,
       versions_xid, versions_operation,
       testll.*
  FROM testll
  VERSIONS BETWEEN TIMESTAMP
       TO_TIMESTAMP('2015-11-08 11:25:00', 'YYYY-MM-DD HH24:MI:SS')
  AND TO_TIMESTAMP('2015-11-08 12:05:00', 'YYYY-MM-DD HH24:MI:SS');
```

Tips 3: What is the 11g flashback mechanism?

In this tips we will explain the mechanism to see old versions of data from undo segment.

The 11g flashback mechanism is as below:
When table is changed the old image is stored in flashback archive area (DB_FDA described in previous tips). Oracle internally stores the data in internal history table by flashback mechanism similar to writing trigger to capture pre-image of the data.

The advantages are as below:
a) The internal history table writing by flashback process is not done using trigger but by oracle software code and hence activity like trigger related performance impact, context switching, dependency check etc. are eliminated.
b) You can use the flashback query as before but now this is not restricted to undo retention period.
c) Auditing is asynchronous as flashback archives are written by oracle background process FBDA (Flashback data archiver) and hence transaction performance is not impacted at all.

Tips 4: How to check if flashback is configured in your system and in your tables?

This tips dealt with steps to check flashback setup.

After flashback is configured by DBA as per **Tips 2** in your database you can see the name of flashback drive and flashback tablespace using below command:
```
select * from dba_flashback_archive_ts;
```

This will give output as below:

FLASHBACK_ARCHIVE_NAME	FLASHBACK_ARCHIVE#	TABLESPACE_NAME	QUOTA_IN_MB
DB_FDA	1	DB_FDA_TBS	null

After flashback is configured you can independently enable flashback for a table in your schema as below:
```
alter table tab_nm FLASHBACK ARCHIVE DB_FDA;
```

You can view which are the tables has flashback in your database just run this:
```
select * from dba_flashback_archive_tables;
```
This will return TAB_NM as flashback is set for this table. Also it will provide the corresponding name of **flashback history table**.

After flashback is enabled, if you want to disable the flashback from the specific table just run this
```
alter table tab_nm NO FLASHBACK ARCHIVE;
```

To allow other user (say warehouse user) to run flashback query for the tables present in DB (user 'DB' enabled flashback for all the tables).

```
--Connect to user DB
grant select,flashback on tab_nm to warehouse;
```

Note: In order to DROP a table which has got flashback ebabled you can not DROP the table directly. First you need to disable the flashback for the table and then DROP the table.

However if you need to RENAME the table then you should not DISABLE flashback. If you DISABLE flashback for the table, next RENAME the table and ENABLE flashback for the new table,then you loose all the old flashback data. So be very careful before disabling flashback for a table.

Tips 5: Get version data for a duration using flashback version query

To get version data for a duration we have two approaches

Approach 1: Flashback version query using SCN

We have test11 table which has got flashback enabled. Here is the steps to get the data for a particular period:

Step 1:

Get the SCN number for the particulat timestamp as below:

```
SELECT
timestamp_to_scn(TO_TIMESTAMP('11-12-2016 18:00:00','DD-MM-YYYY HH24:MI:SS')),
timestamp_to_scn(TO_TIMESTAMP('12-12-2016 18:00:00','DD-MM-YYYY HH24:MI:SS'))
FROM dual;
```

TIMESTAMP_TO_SCN(TO_TIMESTAMP('11-12-201618:00:00','DD-MM-YYYYHH24:MI:SS'))	TIMESTAMP_TO_SCN(TO_TIMESTAMP('12-12-201618:00:00','DD-MM-YYYYHH24:MI:SS'))
5834998	5917720

Step 2:

Run the version query:

```
SELECT VERSIONS_STARTTIME,
  versions_operation,
  versions_startscn,
  versions_endscn,
  test11.*
FROM test11 VERSIONS BETWEEN SCN 5834998 AND 5917720
WHERE versions_startscn>= 5834998
AND versions_startscn   <5917720;
```

Approach 2: Flashback version query using Timestamp

```
SELECT VERSIONS_STARTTIME,
  versions_operation,
  versions_startscn,
  versions_endscn,
  test11.*
FROM test11 VERSIONS BETWEEN TIMESTAMP
TO_TIMESTAMP('11-12-2016 18:00:00','DD-MM-YYYY HH24:MI:SS') AND
TO_TIMESTAMP('12-12-2016 18:00:00','DD-MM-YYYY HH24:MI:SS')
WHERE versions_starttime>=
TO_TIMESTAMP('11-12-2016 18:00:00','DD-MM-YYYY HH24:MI:SS') AND
versions_starttime
<TO_TIMESTAMP('12-12-2016 18:00:00','DD-MM-YYYY HH24:MI:SS');
```

Approach 1 i.e. SCN based approach takes less time and henece preferable:

Approach1 is faster because

With the large table data (approx. 100000) and the request for a timestamp based flashback query (using version between TIMESTAMP approach 2) Oracle has to convert the timestamp to an SCN based on the filter used in "where" clause.

130

So in this case the between clause is returning over 100000 records and calling the conversion for each record and this slows down the performance.

However (using approach 1 version between SCN) the SCN approach no conversion is required and the query is returned immediately.

Tips 6: Get latest scn version data for a duration

There are occasion when you have more than one version of data present for a particular timestamp. In order to get the latest SCN data for that particular timestamp we use the below flashback version query:
Here are the steps:
Step 1:Create table:
```
CREATE TABLE test_a
  (pri NUMBER PRIMARY KEY,idx VARCHAR2(30),page_no NUMBER
  );
```

Step 2:Enable Flashback:
```
ALTER TABLE test_a FLASHBACK ARCHIVE DB_FDA;
```

This is optional as we are testing this for 2 minute duration from current time which is within limit of undo_retention

Step 3: Insert data
```
12-12-2016 21:33:05
INSERT INTO test_a VALUES(248,'bulk collect', 108);
COMMIT;
12-12-2016 21:33:05
UPDATE test_a set page_no=107 where pri=248;
COMMIT;

12-12-2016 21:33:23
INSERT INTO test_a VALUES(249,'forall', 108);
COMMIT;
12-12-2016 21:33:29
INSERT INTO test_a VALUES(250,'grant',  108);
COMMIT;
```

Note: at 12-12-2016 21:33:05 we have 2 versions of data, expectation is to get latest versions of data i.e. page_no=107, pri=248

Step 4: Get SCN for the duration
Get the SCN number for the particulat timestamp as below:
```
SELECT
timestamp_to_scn(TO_TIMESTAMP('12-12-2016 21:33:00','DD-MM-YYYY HH24:MI:SS')),
timestamp_to_scn(TO_TIMESTAMP('12-12-2016 21:34:00','DD-MM-YYYY HH24:MI:SS'))
FROM dual;
```

TIMESTAMP_TO_SCN(TO_TIMESTAMP('12-12-201621:33:00','DD-MM-YYYYHH24:MI:SS'))	TIMESTAMP_TO_SCN(TO_TIMESTAMP('12-12-201621:34:00','DD-MM-YYYYHH24:MI:SS'))
5923207	5923234

Step 5: Run the version query:

```
SELECT VERSIONS_STARTTIME,VERSIONS_OPERATION,
  VERSIONS_STARTSCN,
  VERSIONS_ENDSCN,
  test_a.*
FROM test_a VERSIONS BETWEEN SCN 5923207 AND 5923234
WHERE versions_startscn>= 5923207
AND versions_startscn   <5923234
ORDER BY 1;
```

The output:

VERSIONS_STARTTIME	VERSIONS_OPERATION	VERSIONS_STARTSCN	VERSIONS_ENDSCN	PRI	IDX	PAGE_NO
12-DEC-16 21.33.05.000000000	U	5923214	(null)	248	bulk collect	107
12-DEC-16 21.33.05.000000000	I	5923212	5923214	248	bulk collect	108
12-DEC-16 21.33.23.000000000	I	5923221	(null)	249	forall	108
12-DEC-16 21.33.29.000000000	I	5923224	(null)	250	grant	108

As you can see at 12-12-2016 21:33:05 we have 2 versions of data one is "I" and other is "U". However based on SCN you can see latest one is version_operation='U' fpr PRI=248

To get the latest SCN version data solution is:

```
SELECT * FROM
(
SELECT ROW_NUMBER() OVER (PARTITION BY VERSIONS_STARTTIME,pri
                         ORDER BY VERSIONS_STARTSCN DESC) vn,
                         VERSIONS_STARTTIME,
  VERSIONS_STARTSCN,
  VERSIONS_ENDSCN,
  test_a.*
FROM test_a VERSIONS BETWEEN SCN 5923207 AND 5923234
WHERE versions_startscn>= 5923207
AND versions_startscn   <5923234
)
WHERE vn=1;
```

Now you will see the output:

VERSIONS_STARTTIME	VERSIONS_STARTSCN	VERSIONS_ENDSCN	PRI	IDX	PAGE_NO
12-DEC-16 21.33.05.000000000	5923214	(null)	248	bulk collect	107
12-DEC-16 21.33.23.000000000	5923221	(null)	249	forall	108
12-DEC-16 21.33.29.000000000	5923224	(null)	250	grant	108

Tips 7: Get point of time data

In oracle to get data for a particular point of time we have two approaches:
Approach 1: As of timestamp
To get data from a table Tab1, till TO_TIMESTAMP('12-12-2016 18:00:00','DD-MM-YYYY HH24:MI:SS')
```
SELECT *
FROM tab1 AS OF TIMESTAMP
TO_TIMESTAMP('12-12-2016 18:00:00','DD-MM-YYYY HH24:MI:SS');
```

This will give the version of data for this particular point of time. Even if current data is entirely different.

132

Approach 2: As of scn

```
SELECT
timestamp_to_scn(TO_TIMESTAMP('12-12-2016 18:00:00','DD-MM-YYYY HH24:MI:SS'))
FROM dual;
```

This will return: 5917720

```
SELECT *
FROM test_a AS OF SCN 5917720;
```

This will give the version of data for this particular SCN at that point of time. Even if current data is entirely different.

Tips 8: Move all versions of flashback using STATIC method?

Here in this tips we will demonstrate the mechanism to move all versions of old data statically to warehouse db using example.

Here is one typical method used to move data from DB to warehouse using static method.
Rules are as below

> ➤ If a data undergone only INSERT in DB then in warehouse we must insert corresponding record (with **m_start_date** set to **versions_starttime** and **m_end_date** null)
> ➤ If a data undergone only UPDATE in DB then in warehouse we must UPDATE the corresponding record (with end_date set to version start time) in warehouse and insert the new version of the record in warehouse(with meta_start_date set to versions_starttime)
> ➤ If a data undergone only DELETE in DB then in warehouse we must soft DELETE the corresponding record in warehouse by setting **m_delete_date** to versions_starttime and end_date to null.

Step 1: Create necessary table and perform some DML

```
Alter session set nls_date_format='DD_MM_YYYY HH24:MI:SS';

CREATE TABLE dc_cust
  (
ID NUMBER,
NAME VARCHAR2(30 BYTE),
SAL NUMBER(10,3)
  ) ;

CREATE TABLE dc_cust_warehouse
  (
    M_START_DATE   DATE NOT NULL ENABLE,
    M_END_DATE     DATE,
    M_DELETE_DATE  DATE,
    M_LOAD_DATE    DATE NOT NULL ENABLE,
    M_UPDATE_DATE  DATE,
    ID             NUMBER,
    NAME           VARCHAR2(30 BYTE),
    SAL            NUMBER(10,3)
  ) ;

INSERT INTO dc_cust(1,'text',50.5);
COMMIT;
```

```sql
INSERT INTO dc_cust VALUES
  (2,'text1',150.5
  );
COMMIT;
INSERT INTO dc_cust VALUES
  (3,'text2',250.5
  );
COMMIT;
UPDATE dc_cust SET sal=sal*1.1 WHERE id=1;
COMMIT;
UPDATE dc_cust SET sal=sal*1.5 WHERE id=1;
COMMIT;
UPDATE dc_cust SET sal=sal*2.5 WHERE id=1;
COMMIT;
DELETE FROM dc_cust WHERE id=3;
COMMIT;
INSERT INTO dc_cust VALUES
  (3,'text2',290.5
  );
COMMIT;
SELECT * FROM all_objects WHERE object_name ='DC_CUST';
12-02-2016 09:15:09
UPDATE dc_cust SET sal=sal*1.1 WHERE id=2;
COMMIT;
UPDATE dc_cust SET sal=sal*1.5 WHERE id=2;
COMMIT;
DELETE FROM dc_cust WHERE id=2;
COMMIT;


INSERT INTO dc_cust VALUES
  (2,'text1',850.5
  );
COMMIT;
UPDATE dc_cust SET sal=sal*1.3 WHERE id=2;
COMMIT;
UPDATE dc_cust SET sal=sal*2 WHERE id=2;
COMMIT;
```

Step 2: Move data from transaction table to enterprise data warehouse table

Here is the code for this:

```
DECLARE
fr_scn number;
to_scn number;
  CURSOR C1
  IS
    SELECT RN,VERSIONS_STARTTIME,
           versions_operation,
           versions_startscn,
           versions_endscn,
      ID
        FROM
          (SELECT ROW_NUMBER() OVER ( PARTITION BY VERSIONS_STARTTIME,ID ORDER BY VERSIONS_STARTSCN DESC) RN,
           VERSIONS_STARTTIME,
           versions_operation,
           versions_startscn,
           versions_endscn,
           DC_CUST.*
          FROM
           DC_CUST VERSIONS BETWEEN SCN fr_scn AND to_scn
          WHERE versions_startscn>= fr_scn
          AND versions_startscn   <to_scn
        AND versions_operation in('U','D')
          )
        WHERE rn=1
        ORDER BY versions_startscn,
          versions_operation,
          ID;

Type t_dc_cust
IS
  TABLE OF C1%ROWTYPE INDEX BY binary_integer;
  v_dc_cust t_dc_cust;
BEGIN
  SELECT Timestamp_to_scn(p_Start_Timestamp) INTO fr_scn FROM dual;
  SELECT Timestamp_to_scn(p_End_Timestamp) INTO to_scn FROM dual;

  INSERT INTO DC_CUST_WAREHOUSE(M_START_DATE,M_END_DATE,M_DELETE_DATE,M_LOAD_DATE,M_UPDATE_DATE,ID,NAME,SAL)
  SELECT VERSIONS_STARTTIME,NULL,NULL,systimestamp,NULL,ID,NAME,SAL FROM
  (SELECT ROW_NUMBER() OVER ( PARTITION BY VERSIONS_STARTTIME,ID ORDER BY VERSIONS_STARTSCN DESC) RN,
    VERSIONS_STARTTIME,
    versions_operation,
    versions_startscn,
    versions_endscn,
    DC_CUST.*
  FROM
    DC_CUST VERSIONS BETWEEN SCN fr_scn AND to_scn
  WHERE versions_startscn>= fr_scn
  AND versions_startscn   <to_scn
  AND versions_operation in('I','U')
  )
  WHERE rn=1;

  OPEN C1;
  FETCH C1 BULK COLLECT INTO v_dc_cust;
  CLOSE C1;
  FOR i IN 1..v_dc_cust.count
  LOOP
    IF (v_dc_cust(i).versions_operation='U') THEN
      UPDATE DC_CUST_WAREHOUSE
         SET M_END_DATE      =v_dc_cust(i).versions_starttime,
           M_UPDATE_DATE     =systimestamp
         WHERE ID            =v_dc_cust(i).ID
         AND M_END_DATE     IS NULL
         AND M_DELETE_DATE IS NULL
      AND M_START_DATE < v_dc_cust(i).versions_starttime;
```

135

```
    ELSIF v_dc_cust(i).versions_operation ='D' THEN
      UPDATE DC_CUST_WAREHOUSE
      SET M_DELETE_DATE                   =v_dc_cust(i).versions_starttime,
        M_UPDATE_DATE                     =systimestamp
      WHERE ID              =v_dc_cust(i).ID
      AND M_END_DATE                      IS NULL
      AND M_DELETE_DATE                   IS NULL
    AND M_START_DATE < v_dc_cust(i).versions_starttime;

      END IF;
  END LOOP;
END;
/
```

Now when you run the below:

```
SELECT * FROM dc_cust_warehouse order by ID,M_START_DATE;
```

You can see all versions of the data as below **output** format:

M_start_date	M_end_date	M_delete_date	M_load_date	M_update_date	ID	NAME	SAL
1 12_02_2016 09:19:13	12_02_2016 09:20:43	(null)	23_02_2016 09:39:55	23_02_2016 09:39:56	1	text	50.5
2 12_02_2016 09:20:43	12_02_2016 09:20:55	(null)	23_02_2016 09:39:55	23_02_2016 09:39:56	1	text	55.55
3 12_02_2016 09:20:55	12_02_2016 09:21:16	(null)	23_02_2016 09:39:55	23_02_2016 09:39:56	1	text	83.325
4 12_02_2016 09:21:16	(null)	(null)	23_02_2016 09:39:55	(null)	1	text	208.313
5 12_02_2016 09:19:55	12_02_2016 09:49:35	(null)	23_02_2016 09:39:55	23_02_2016 09:39:56	2	text1	150.5
6 12_02_2016 09:49:35	12_02_2016 09:49:47	(null)	23_02_2016 09:39:55	23_02_2016 09:39:56	2	text1	165.55
7 12_02_2016 09:49:47	(null)	12_02_2016 09:50:08	23_02_2016 09:39:55	23_02_2016 09:39:56	2	text1	248.325
8 12_02_2016 09:50:17	12_02_2016 09:50:38	(null)	23_02_2016 09:39:55	23_02_2016 09:39:56	2	text1	850.5
9 12_02_2016 09:50:38	(null)	(null)	23_02_2016 09:39:55	(null)	2	text1	2211.3
10 12_02_2016 09:19:55	(null)	12_02_2016 09:22:46	23_02_2016 09:39:55	23_02_2016 09:39:56	3	text2	250.5
11 12_02_2016 09:22:52	(null)	(null)	23_02_2016 09:39:55	(null)	3	text2	290.5

The above is shown for just one table. However if we want to do it for all the tables in your schema you have to do it individually for each table as above.

Here in this tips we will demonstrate the mechanism to move all versions of old data dynamically to warehouse db using example.

When any database structure changes in source database we have to modify the application code (shown in previous **Tips 6)** to incorporate newly added columns/renamed columns/deleted columns/dropped tables etc. This incurs a huge maintenance cost and hence there will be **frequent outage** (to modify application) and possibility of error and failure is high. If you consider medium scale database where we have some 600 to 800 tables and database is undergoing many changes in each release then the task and effort to maintain will become huge.

However using dynamic query we can automate the work so that no change is required in the application code.
In this approach any data model change will be automatically reflected in the application. Here "mapping_table" is a table in which we store all the table **names** which require to be moved to warehouse.
Rule is as below

> - If a data undergone only INSERT in DB then in warehouse we must insert corresponding record (with meta_start_date set to versions_starttime and meta_end_date null)
> - If a data undergone only UPDATE in DB then in warehouse we must UPDATE the corresponding record (with end_date set to version start time) in warehouse and insert the new version of the record in warehouse (with meta_start_date set to versions_starttime)
> - If a data undergone only DELETE in DB then in warehouse we must soft DELETE the corresponding record in warehouse by setting meta_delete_date to versions_starttime and end_date to null.

Simple scenario:
Transactional DB:
dc_cust (emp_id number primary key, sal number(10,4));

Warehouse db:
dc_cust_warehouse (m_START_DATE date,m_END_DATE date,m_DELETE_DATE date,m_LOAD_DATE date,m_UPDATE_DATE date,emp_id number primary key, sal number(10,4));

Now dc_cust_warehouse need to be populated from transactional DB using flashback between 2 specific dates

Here is partial code snippet (dynamic solution):

```
--connect to warehouse
DECLARE
--declare all variables......
BEGIN

--This will get SCN number for the date from which we would like to process data
SELECT Timestamp_to_scn(sync_from_date) INTO fr_scn FROM dual;

--This will get SCN number for the date to which we would like to process data
SELECT Timestamp_to_scn(sync_to_date) INTO to_scn FROM dual;

--This LOOP contains list of table to be migrated
FOR i IN (SELECT table_name FROM MAPPING_TABLE) LOOP

    --This is the LOOP which get primary key column for a table
    FOR m_data IN (SELECT column_position, ai.column_name
      FROM all_ind_columns ai, all_constraints ac
      WHERE ai.table_name    =ac.table_name
      AND ai.table_name      =i.table_name
      AND ai.table_owner     ='user_nm'
      AND ac.owner           ='user_nm'
      AND ac.constraint_type ='P'
      AND ac.constraint_name =ai.index_name   order by 1) LOOP

        IF m_data.column_position =1 THEN
          sel_stmt    :='select '||m_data.column_name||' as pkey_value1';
          pkey_name1 :=m_data.column_name;
          pkey_count :=1;
        elsif m_data.column_position=2 THEN
          sel_stmt        :=sel_stmt||','|| m_data.column_name||' as pkey_value2';
          pkey_name2    :=m_data.column_name;
          pkey_count    :=2;
        elsif m_data.column_position=3 THEN
           --as above(here the table contain primary key with three columns)
        END IF;
      END LOOP;
      --This is the END LOOP which derived all the primary key column for a table
```

138

```
--This one form the dynamic insert stmt  without the "FROM" clause
 SELECT table_name,
    'insert into '
    ||table_name
    ||'(m_START_DATE,m_END_DATE,m_DELETE_DATE,m_LOAD_DATE,m_UPDATE_DATE,'
    |||LISTAGG(column_name,',') WITHIN GROUP ( ORDER BY COLUMN_ID)||')'||' select versions_starttime,null,null,'
    ||',versions_starttime,null,null,'||',systimestamp,null,'||LISTAGG(column_name,',') WITHIN GROUP (
    ORDER BY COLUMN_ID)
    INTO tab_nm,dyn_ins_stmt
  FROM all_tab_columns  WHERE owner   =pkg_c.f_user  AND TABLE_NAME=i.table_name  GROUP BY table_name;

--This below sel_stmt will form the select statement to extract the version date between 2 scn numbers
--which will be used for update and delete based on primary key column
sel_stmt :=sel_stmt||',versions_starttime,versions_startscn,versions_operation from '||'user_nm'||'.'||i.table_name||' '||'VERSIONS
BETWEEN  SCN '||fr_scn ||' and '|| to_scn ||' WHERE VERSIONS_OPERATION is NOT NULL AND versions_startscn>='||fr_scn ||' AND versions_startscn<'||
to_scn ||' order by versions_startscn,versions_operation';

 --This will do one off insert by appending the "from" clause with dynamic insert
EXECUTE IMMEDIATE dyn_ins_stmt||' from '||'user_nm'||'.'||i.table_name||' '||'VERSIONS  BETWEEN  SCN '||fr_scn ||' and '|| to_scn ||
' WHERE VERSIONS_OPERATION IN('||'''I'''||','||'''U'''||' ) AND versions_startscn>='||fr_scn ||' AND versions_startscn<'|| to_scn
||' order by versions_starttime';

--pkey_count state primary key column consist of how many number of columns
IF pkey_count=1 THEN
--This will bulk collect primary key value, version starttime and version operation for a table.
    EXECUTE immediate sel_stmt bulk collect INTO v_pkey_1_idx_tab,v_ver_starttime_tab,v_ver_startscn_tab,v_ver_operation_tab;
--This will form (only one time for each table)the dynamic update statement with bind variable.
   u_update_stmt :='update '||i.table_name||' set m_END_DATE=:1'||',m_UPDATE_DATE=systimestamp where '||pkey_name1||'=:2'||' and m_END_DATE is NULL
      and m_DELETE_DATE is NULL AND m_START_DATE <:3';
--This will form (only one time for each table)the dynamic update for delete statement with bind variable.
   d_update_stmt :='update '||i.table_name||' set m_DELETE_DATE=:1'||',m_UPDATE_DATE=systimestamp where '||pkey_name1||'=:2'||' and m_END_DATE
      is NULL and m_DELETE_DATE is NULL AND m_START_DATE <:3';

   FOR each_tab_rec IN 1..v_pkey_1_idx_tab.count LOOP --This will update,delete each records in a table between 2 SCNs
      IF v_ver_operation_tab(each_tab_rec) ='U' THEN
--This will update the record in a table based on primary key/startscn(which was derived by select statement)
      EXECUTE immediate u_update_stmt USING v_ver_starttime_tab(each_tab_rec),v_pkey_1_idx_tab(each_tab_rec),v_ver_starttime_tab(each_tab_rec);
      ELSIF (v_ver_operation_tab(each_tab_rec) ='D') THEN
--This will delete the record in a table based on primary key/startscn(which was derived by select statement)
      EXECUTE immediate d_update_stmt USING v_ver_starttime_tab(each_tab_rec),v_pkey_1_idx_tab(each_tab_rec),v_ver_starttime_tab(each_tab_rec);
   END IF;
  END LOOP;--End loop for update and delete of records in a table between 2 SCNs
ELSIF pkey_count=2 THEN----pkey_count=2 state primary key column consist of 2 columns
   --create the dynamic select,update and delete similar to pkey_count=1
END IF;
END LOOP;   --end of main loop which works for each table present in MAPPING_TABLE
END;
/
```

Tips 10: Restore table which is dropped using flashback

This tips dealt with steps to bring back a dropped table.

After dropping a table we can again restore the table by flashback. The syntax for that is:
1. FLASHBACK TABLE <table name> to before drop;
2. FLASHBACK TABLE <table name> TO TIMESTAMP (SYSTIMESTAMP - INTERVAL '1' minute);

Key points to remember:

1. You cannot flash back a table if it has been purged. So as long as the table is present in recyclebin you can restore it. You can find which tables are there in recyclebin by using:
```
select * from dba_recyclebin;
```

However if you have used "**drop table t1 purge;**" then this table won't be present in recycle bin when you fire the above query and hence using flashback you cannot restore the table.

2. You may not get back all of the indexes that were defined on the table you dropped.

3. The database retrieves all triggers and constraints defined on the table except for referential integrity constraints that reference other tables.

Example as shown below:

```
CREATE TABLE test_flash1(a NUMBER);
ALTER TABLE test_flash1 enable row movement;
```

Insert data in the table at certain time and then just DROP the table:
```
Time: 12-12-2016 18:00:00

INSERT INTO test_flash1 VALUES(1);
INSERT INTO test_flash1 VALUES(2);
COMMIT;

DROP TABLE test_flash1;
```

Now to get the dropped table restored run this:
```
FLASHBACK TABLE test_flash1 TO BEFORE DROP;
```

You can see the data:
```
SELECT * FROM test_flash1;
```

A
1
2

Now insert some more data at different timestamp:

140

```
Time: 12-12-2016 19:00:00
INSERT INTO test_flash1 VALUES(3);
INSERT INTO test_flash1 VALUES(4);
COMMIT;
```

And now data look as below:

A
1
2
3
4

Now if you want restore the table to the point before you insert the new data here is the command:
```
FLASHBACK TABLE test_flash1 TO TIMESTAMP
TO_TIMESTAMP('12-12-2016 18:30:00','DD-MM-YYYY HH24:MI:SS');
```

You can see the data is as per the state of the table present at 12-12-2016 18:30:00:
```
SELECT * FROM test_flash1;
```

A
1
2

This is how you can restore your table to old image.

Tips 11: Move specific date/time flashback data from transactional db to warehouse

Here in this steps we will demonstrate ways to move data for specific point of time to warehouse.

In order to move data (in terms of structure and data) from user "DB" to user "DB_2" we can use "as of timestamp" OR "as of SCN" clause to get the specific timestamp data (just one version of data) for that particular point of time.

"As of timestamp" approach:

```
INSERT
INTO DB_2.TAB1
    (
      M_START_DATE,
      M_END_DATE,
      M_DELETE_DATE,
      M_LOAD_DATE,
      M_UPDATE_DATE,
      CODE,
      NAME
    )
SELECT TO_TIMESTAMP('2015-09-24:00:00:00','YYYY-MM-DD HH24:MI:SS'),
   NULL,
   NULL,
   TO_TIMESTAMP('2015-09-24:00:00:00','YYYY-MM-DD HH24:MI:SS'),
   NULL,
   CODE,
   NAME
FROM DB.TEST1 AS OF TIMESTAMP
TO_TIMESTAMP('2015-09-24:00:00:00','YYYY-MM-DD HH24:MI:SS');
```

"As of scn" approach:

```
INSERT
INTO DB_2.TAB1
    (
      M_START_DATE,
      M_END_DATE,
      M_DELETE_DATE,
      M_LOAD_DATE,
      M_UPDATE_DATE,
      CODE,
      NAME
    )
SELECT TO_TIMESTAMP('2015-09-24:00:00:00','YYYY-MM-DD HH24:MI:SS'),
   NULL,
   NULL,
   TO_TIMESTAMP('2015-09-24:00:00:00','YYYY-MM-DD HH24:MI:SS'),
   NULL,
   CODE,
   NAME
FROM DB.TEST1 AS OF SCN
TIMESTAMP_TO_SCN(TO_TIMESTAMP('2015-09-24:00:00:00','YYYY-MM-DD HH24:MI:SS'));
```

Note when you try to retrieve the table details before the table was created or altered we get error:

So if the table was created 2015-10-06 16:40:00 and you try to retrieve flashback details of timestamp 2015-10-06 16:20:00 it will fail

```
select * from test_flash1 as of timestamp TO_TIMESTAMP('2015-10-06 16:20:00',
'YYYY-MM-DD HH24:MI:SS')
```

The above will fail with error:

ORA-01466: unable to read data - table definition has changed
01466. 00000 - "unable to read data - table definition has changed"
*Cause: Query parsed after tbl (or index) change, and executed
        w/old snapshot
*Action: commit (or rollback) transaction, and re-execute
Error at Line: 68 Column: 14

Tips 12: How many times a particular attribute in a row modified using flashback?

As one row may undergo changes based on change in one or more attributes of a row. Here in this tips we will demonstrate how to find number of times a particular attribute in a row is modified.

Now one tricky scenario where we need to find out the number of times a particular column/attributes has been modified. Say we have a table test_payment and data has undergone changes as below

Date: 25-mar 2015 6 AM

ID	version	p_flag	area	phone
1001	1	1	5.2	07412442188
1002	1	1	15.2	07412442198

Date: 25-mar 2015 8 AM

ID	version	p_flag	area	phone
1001	2	1	5.3	07412442188
1002	2	1	15.3	07412442198

Date: 25-mar 2015 9 AM

ID	version	p_flag	area	phone
1001	3	0	5.4	07412442188
1002	3	1	15.4	07412442198

Date: 25-mar 2015 10 AM

ID	version	p_flag	area	phone
1001	4	0	5.4	07412442177
1002	4	1	15.5	07412442198

Date: 25-mar 2015 11 AM

ID	version	p_flag	area	phone
1001	5	0	5.5	07412442177
1002	5	1	15.5	07412442165

Date: 25-mar 2015 11:30 AM

ID	version	p_flag	area	phone
1001	6	1	5.5	07412442177
1002	6	1	15.9	07412442198

In flashback details of each change are stored. Now we have a requirement to find how many records in **test_payment** table have undergone changes for the column p_flag

And, for each record, how many times the change is in p_flag for the period 25-mar-2015 6 AM to 11:30 AM?

So for this case the answer should be as below
The changes in p_flag happens only for **ID=1001 (id=1002 unchanged for this flag)** and changes happen for p_flag at 9 AM from flag value 1 to 0 AND 11:30 AM from flag value 0 to 1.

For ID=1002 there has been other changes but for p_flag there are no changes at all.

We can write the query as below to find out p_flag version history:

```
SELECT DC_1.ID,
   DC_1.VERSIONS_STARTTIME,
   DC_1.VERSIONS_ENDTIME,
   DC_1.p_flag,        <———————————— New value for the flag
   DC_2.p_flag,        <———————————— old value for the flag
   DC_2.VERSIONS_STARTTIME,
   DC_2.VERSIONS_ENDTIME
FROM
   (SELECT VERSIONS_XID,
      VERSIONS_STARTTIME,
      VERSIONS_ENDTIME,
      VERSIONS_OPERATION,
      ID,
      P_FLAG
   FROM test_payment VERSIONS BETWEEN SCN 54723211193 AND 56373687060
   WHERE VERSIONS_STARTSCN >= 54723211193
   AND VERSIONS_STARTSCN    < 56373687060
   AND VERSIONS_OPERATION   = 'U'
   ) DC_1,
   (SELECT VERSIONS_XID,
      VERSIONS_STARTTIME,
      VERSIONS_ENDTIME,
      VERSIONS_OPERATION,
      ID,
      P_FLAG
   FROM test_payment VERSIONS BETWEEN SCN 54723211193 AND 56373687060
   WHERE VERSIONS_ENDSCN >= 54723211193
   AND VERSIONS_ENDSCN    < 56373687060
   ) DC_2
WHERE DC_1.ID                     = DC_2.ID
and dc_1.ID in(1001,1002)
AND DC_1.VERSIONS_STARTTIME       = DC_2.VERSIONS_ENDTIME
AND ( NVL(DC_1.P_FLAG,-1) <> NVL(DC_2.P_FLAG,-1) )
ORDER BY 1,2;
```

Note that in query with (DC_2 alias) we choose the data which has been end dated (endscn) between 6 AM to 11:30 AM And in query with (DC_1 alias) we choose the data which has been started (startscn) between 6 AM to 11:30 AM.

The logic is:
   DC_2.versions_endtime=DC_1.versions_starttime

We get the old/previous value from DC_2 and the new value from DC_1.

The output from the above query will be:

ID	VERSIONS_STARTTIME	VERSIONS_ENDTIME	P_FLAG	P_FLAG_1	VERSIONS_STARTTIME_1	VERSIONS_ENDTIME_1
1001	9 AM	11:30 AM	0	1	6 AM	9 AM
1001	11:30 AM	NULL	1	0	9 AM	11:30 AM

Note p_flag is the new value and p_flag_1 is old value.

Tips 13: Improvement in auditing using flashback in 12c?

Here in this tips we will discuss 12c new feature to see who does the changes in a row.

Pre 12c Oracle flashback FDA can track changes to data however It does not capture who does the changes (**unless this column [updated_by] is present in the respective table**) which is very essential for auditing purpose.
In Oracle 12c FDA tracks complete audit of changes including user environment setting and store them as metadata.
In order to do that in Oracle 12c you need to run the following two commands after flashback is configured as per **Tips 32**

Connect to sys as sysdba
```
GRANT EXECUTE ON DBMS_FLASHBACK_ARCHIVE TO DB;
GRANT CREATE ANY CONTEXT TO DB;
```

Now connect to user "DB" and run the flashback version query

```
SELECT versions_xid,
   DBMS_FLASHBACK_ARCHIVE.get_sys_context(versions_xid, 'USERENV','SESSION_USER')   session_user,
   DBMS_FLASHBACK_ARCHIVE.get_sys_context(versions_xid, 'USERENV','CLIENT_IDENTIFIER') client_identifier,
   versions_starttime,
   versions_endtime,
   versions_operation,
   test2.*
FROM test2 versions BETWEEN TIMESTAMP to_timestamp('2015-01-01 12:30:59','YYYY-MM-DD HH24:MI:SS') AND to_timestamp('2015-06-01 09:39:59','YYYY-MM-DD HH24:MI:SS')
WHERE versions_starttime >= to_timestamp('2015-01-01 12:30:59','YYYY-MM-DD HH24:MI:SS')
AND versions_starttime   < to_timestamp('2015-06-01 09:39:59','YYYY-MM-DD HH24:MI:SS')
and test2.id=1001
ORDER BY versions_starttime;
```

As marked in yellow you can see flashback query could provide the history of data changes and from stored USERENV could provide the corresponding session_user and client_identifier who made the changes.
So from an audit perspective you can find out id=1001 has undergone different changes and changes done from which session user and client_identifier.

Tips 14: Improvement in tracking history for security related table using flashback in 12c?

Here we will demonstrate how to track changes for security sensitive tables.

Oracle 12c has introduced a feature called database hardening which simplifies the management of flashback data archive for a group of security sensitive tables. So in 12c you can have single command to enable FDA for a group of tables and address the need for strong auditing. The management of group of tables is done using below package.
```
DBMS_FLASHBACK_ARCHIVE.
```
Here are the steps to group all the required tables and handle flashback for the set of tables
Start a group:
Here you start a group call APPLICATION associated with flashback drive (DB_FDA).

```
BEGIN
  DBMS_FLASHBACK_ARCHIVE.register_application(
    application_name        => 'APPLICATION',
    flashback_archive_name => 'DB_FDA');
END;
/
```

Assigning table to the group

Here you assign set of tables e.g. T1, T2 and T3 to the group APPLICATION

```
BEGIN
  DBMS_FLASHBACK_ARCHIVE.add_table_to_application (
    application_name => 'APPLICATION',
    table_name       => 'T1',
    schema_name      => 'DB');

  DBMS_FLASHBACK_ARCHIVE.add_table_to_application (
    application_name => 'APPLICATION',
    table_name       => 'T2',
    schema_name      => 'DB');

  DBMS_FLASHBACK_ARCHIVE.add_table_to_application (
    application_name => 'APPLICATION',
    table_name       => 'T3',
    schema_name      => 'DB');

END;
/
```

Enable flashback for the group

```
BEGIN
  DBMS_FLASHBACK_ARCHIVE.enable_application(
    application_name => 'APPLICATION');
END;
/
```

Disable flashback for the group

```
BEGIN
  DBMS_FLASHBACK_ARCHIVE.disable_application(
    application_name => 'APPLICATION');
END;
/
```

Remove certain table from the group

```
BEGIN
  DBMS_FLASHBACK_ARCHIVE.remove_table_from_application(
    application_name => 'APPLICATION',
    table_name       => 'T2',
    schema_name      => 'DB');

END;
/
```

Drop the group from DB

146

```
BEGIN
  DBMS_FLASHBACK_ARCHIVE.drop_application(
    application_name => 'APPLICATION');
END;
/
```

Note: Prior to 12c we could create separate flashback archive drive for security sensitive tables.

Tips 15: import and export of flashback version history in 12c?

Here we will discuss mechanism to import and export flashback version history.

Oracle 12c supports import of user generated history into existing FDA table. So users who have been maintaining history using some other mechanism (like trigger) can now import those history table to oracle 12c FDA as below:

Let us say you want to import "t2_hist" table located in "DB1" schema **into** "DB" schema and flashback table "t2" (T2 has its own flashback data and part of flashback drive DB_FDA).

Step 1
1st import t2_hist table to "DB" schema using normal means like data pump etc.

Step 2
Run the command
```
BEGIN
  DBMS_FLASHBACK_ARCHIVE.import_history (
    owner_name1        => 'DB',
    table_name1        => 'T2',
    temp_history_name  => 'T2_HIST',
    options            => DBMS_FLASHBACK_ARCHIVE.NODELETE);
    -- Allowed values are NODELETE, NODROP, NOCOMMIT,
END;
/
```

Also Oracle 12c supports **export** of existing FDA table's history. Here oracle will automatically create default history table TEMP_HISTORY in the same schema

Let us say you want to export flashback history of "t2" table located in "DB" schema into "DB1" schema
Step 1
Run the command
```
BEGIN
  DBMS_FLASHBACK_ARCHIVE.create_temp_history_table(
    owner_name1 => 'DB',
    table_name1 => 'T2');
END;
/
```

This will create history track table with all version data in default table TEMP_HISTORY

Step 2
Import this temp_history table to DB1 schema using data pump or any other means and you can rename the table.

Tips 16: Free Flashback archive and OPTIMIZE option in 12c?

147

This tips dealt with improvement in flashback archive.

Prior to 12c Flashback data archive was available only with enterprise edition however from 12c onward it is available with all editions.

Also in 12c you have extra parameter to create the flashback archive with compression or no compression option. No Compression option means no optimization and this is the default. However if you use "OPTIMIZE DATA" then it will allow you do compression and this is optimized for performance by means of compression.

Here is the command in 12c to create flashback archive drive:

```
CREATE FLASHBACK ARCHIVE DB_FDA
TABLESPACE DB_FDA_TBS
QUOTA 1G
RETENTION 1 YEAR
NO OPTIMIZE DATA;           This is the extra clause introduced in 12c

CREATE FLASHBACK ARCHIVE DB_FDA
TABLESPACE DB_FDA_TBS
QUOTA 1G
RETENTION 1 YEAR
OPTIMIZE DATA;             This is the extra clause introduced in 12c
```

Tips 17: FLASHBACK magic exposed, Revealed for the first time

This tips dealt with four mysteries regarding flashback and demystifies them.

In Oracle flashback you see some concepts that are still a puzzle for most people, I am going to show you the magic and then gradually explain the mechanism to solve the puzzle.

Puzzle 1: When you use AS OF TIMESTAMP clause it does not give data for the timestamp as expected. So even if your data is committed at that timestamp you may not see that latest version of data.

Puzzle 2: When you use corresponding SCN for a timestamp and use "AS OF SCN" clause it does not give data for corresponding timestamp as expected. So even if your data is committed at that timestamp you may not see that latest version of data.

Puzzle 3: When you use "AS OF TIMESTAMP" clause you will get the column even if the column does not exist at that point of time However when you use "AS OF SCN" clause it will fail if you try to select the non-existent column.

Puzzle 4: You have a table in which you are running flashback version query at 2015-11-08 13:00:00 and it runs fine for a certain duration. The exact same query (same duration) when run at 2015-11-08 15:00:00 fails. Why? This is a simple one and covered earlier (in Tip under flashback), just to reinforce the concept it is repeated here

Here is one example to demonstrate the puzzles:

```
create table test_timestamp_scn(a number,b number,c number);
```

Connect to sys and enable flashback:
```
alter table test_timestamp_scn FLASHBACK ARCHIVE FLASHBACK_FDA_NAME
```

```
timestamp: 17-JAN-16 10.00.37.000000000 run the below:


SELECT Timestamp_to_scn(TO_TIMESTAMP('2016-01-17 10:00:37',
'YYYY-MM-DD HH24:MI:SS')) SCN FROM dual;
63225290057 <───────────── Corresponding SCN for the timestamp


And after few minute do the below operations:

insert into test_timestamp_scn values(1,1,2);
commit;
insert into test_timestamp_scn values(1,1,3);
commit;
insert into test_timestamp_scn values(1,2,3);
commit;
insert into test_timestamp_scn values(1,3,3);
commit;
alter table test_timestamp_scn drop column c;
insert into test_timestamp_scn values(1,9);
alter table test_timestamp_scn add (cl number);
insert into test_timestamp_scn values(2,9,2);
commit;
select to_char(sysdate,'dd-mm-yyyy hh24:mi:ss') from dual;
17-01-2016 10:11:37 <───────────── End of the operation


Corresponding SCN is:
SELECT Timestamp_to_scn(TO_TIMESTAMP('2016-01-17 10:11:37',
'YYYY-MM-DD HH24:MI:SS')) SCN FROM dual;
63225316840 <───────────── Corresponding scn
```

Now just run the version query to get all the version of data for the table for the following SCN range:

```
SELECT scn_to_Timestamp(63225290057) timestamp_val FROM dual;
17-JAN-16 10.00.37.000000000
SELECT scn_to_Timestamp(63225316844) timestamp_val FROM dual;
17-JAN-16 10.11.37.000000000
```

Output of version query

```
SELECT versions_startscn,
   TO_CHAR(VERSIONS_STARTTIME, 'DD-MON-YY HH24:MI:SS') VERSIONS_STARTTIME,
   versions_operation,
   versions_startscn,
   versions_endscn,
   test_timestamp_scn.*
FROM test_timestamp_scn VERSIONS BETWEEN SCN 63225290057 AND 63225316844
WHERE versions_startscn>= 63225290057
AND versions_startscn   <63225316844
ORDER BY 1;
```

The result will look as follows:

VERSIONS_STARTSCN	VERSIONS_STARTTIME	VERSIONS_OPERATION	VERSIONS_STARTSCN_1	VERSIONS_ENDSCN	A	B	C1	D_63225316618_C
63225316627	17-JAN-16 10:11:25	I	63225316627	63225316713	1	1	(null)	2
63225316629	17-JAN-16 10:11:25	I	63225316629	63225316713	1	1	(null)	3
63225316631	17-JAN-16 10:11:25	I	63225316631	63225316713	1	2	(null)	3
63225316633	17-JAN-16 10:11:25	I	63225316633	63225316713	1	3	(null)	3
63225316713	17-JAN-16 10:11:25	U	63225316713	(null)	1	1	(null)	(null)
63225316713	17-JAN-16 10:11:25	U	63225316713	(null)	1	3	(null)	(null)
63225316713	17-JAN-16 10:11:25	U	63225316713	(null)	1	1	(null)	(null)
63225316713	17-JAN-16 10:11:25	U	63225316713	(null)	1	2	(null)	(null)
63225316773	17-JAN-16 10:11:31	I	63225316773	(null)	1	9	(null)	(null)
63225316843	17-JAN-16 10:11:37	I	63225316843	(null)	2	9	2	(null)

Puzzle 1 example:

You can see the data in timestamp `17-JAN-16 10:11:25` as shown above in **Output of version query**
But when you run the below no data will return:

```
select * from test_timestamp_scn as of timestamp
TO_TIMESTAMP('2016-01-17 10:11:25','YYYY-MM-DD HH24:MI:SS');
```

→No data will return

Even if you run to use 10:11:25.999999999 to show that the latest value of timestamp has been requested

```
SELECT * from test_timestamp_scn as of timestamp
TO_TIMESTAMP('2016-01-16 10.11.25.999999', 'YYYY-MM-DD hh24.mi.ss.FF');
```

→No data will return.

Puzzle 2 example:

This function convert timestamp into SCN

```
SELECT Timestamp_to_scn(TO_TIMESTAMP('2016-01-17 10:11:25',
'YYYY-MM-DD HH24:MI:SS')) SCN FROM dual;
63225316618 ←——————— This is the corresponding SCN
```

You can see the data in in timestamp `17-JAN-16 10:11:25` as shown above in **Output of version query,**
but when you run following query using **AS OF SCN** clause for that timestamp (SCN for that timestamp is
`63225316618`).

```
select * from test_timestamp_scn as of scn 63225316618;
```

Return no data

Puzzle 3 example:

When you use "AS OF TIMESTAMP" clause you will get the data with latest column added (C1 at 17-JAN-2016 10:11:37)
even if the column does not exist at that point of time.
However when you use "AS OF SCN" clause for the same timestamp it will fail with invalid column error when you try to
select the non-existent column.

```
desc test_timestamp_scn
Name Null Type
---- ---- ------
A         NUMBER
B         NUMBER
C1        NUMBER
select a,b,cl from test_timestamp_scn as of timestamp
TO_TIMESTAMP('2016-01-17 10:11:25', 'YYYY-MM-DD HH24:MI:SS');
```

This will return no data will without any error.

A	B	C1

However when you run the same against same timestamp using "AS OF SCN" clause it will fail with below error:

```
select a,b,cl from test_timestamp_scn as of scn 63225316618;
```

This is the SCN for corresponding timestamp '2016-01-17 10:11:25'

```
ORA-00904: "C1": invalid identifier
00904. 00000 - "%s: invalid identifier"
*Cause:
*Action:
Error at Line: 80 Column: 11
```

Puzzle 4 example:

The following query is run at 2015-11-08 13:00:00 and it runs fine

```
SELECT versions_startscn, versions_starttime,
       versions_endscn, versions_endtime,
       versions_xid, versions_operation,
       testll.*
  FROM testll
  VERSIONS BETWEEN TIMESTAMP
      TO_TIMESTAMP('2015-11-08 11:25:00', 'YYYY-MM-DD HH24:MI:SS')
  AND TO_TIMESTAMP('2015-11-08 12:05:00', 'YYYY-MM-DD HH24:MI:SS');
```

However when you run the same query again at 2015-11-08 15:00:00 it fails, why?

Do you know the reason behind the 4 mischievous behaviors?

I am going to **reveal the reason** for all the puzzles mentioned.

→For a single timestamp there are many SCN number present in the system. This is obvious because in the same second you can have many committed transaction. So for this case Timestamp 17-JAN-16 10.11.25.000000000 has set of SCN, you can check using below query:

```
SELECT scn_to_Timestamp(63225316618) timestamp_val FROM dual;
17-JAN-16 10.11.25.000000000
SELECT scn_to_Timestamp(63225316713) timestamp_val FROM dual;
17-JAN-16 10.11.25.000000000
```

We have scn ranges from 63225316618
to 63225316713 for timestamp 17-JAN-16 10.11.25

→ However when you try to find the corresponding SCN for a timestamp it will give the **lowest SCN** from the range.

This function convert timestamp into SCN

```
SELECT Timestamp_to_scn(TO_TIMESTAMP('2016-01-17 10:11:25',
'YYYY-MM-DD HH24:MI:SS')) SCN FROM dual;
63225316618
```
← This is the corresponding SCN

So for this case again if you run with precision of second as below you will get same SCN

```
SELECT Timestamp_to_scn(TO_TIMESTAMP('2016-01-17 10.11.25.999999',
'YYYY-MM-DD hh24.mi.ss.FF')) SCN FROM dual;
63225316618
```
← This is the corresponding SCN

Puzzle 1 – the magic exposed:

Now when you run AS OF TIMESTAMP as in Puzzle 1 example then Oracle will internally use the smallest SCN from the list and for the smallest SCN 63225316618 for this case from **Output of version query**, you can see there is no corresponding versions_startscn and hence no output is returned.

So you must be careful when you use AS OF TIMESTAMP because you may miss some actual updates and hence miss the actual version of data for that timestamp.

Puzzle 2 – the magic exposed:

Similarly when you run AS OF SCN as in Puzzle 2 example then Oracle will explicitly use the smallest SCN from the list [because Timestamp_to_scn will return the smallest SCN from the list for that timestamp] and for the smallest SCN 63225316618 for this case from **Output of version query**, you can see there is no corresponding versions_startscn and hence no output is returned.

One more important thing to notice regarding **Puzzle 2** is that when you run the query using clause "AS OF SCN" with ranges of SCN for the same timestamp you will get different results.

```
We have scn ranges from 63225316618
to 63225316713 for timestamp 17-JAN-16 10.11.25
```

So If you run the following queries the output will be different even though they all point to the same timestamp.
```
select * from test_timestamp_scn as of scn 63225316618;
select * from test_timestamp_scn as of scn 63225316627;
select * from test_timestamp_scn as of scn 63225316713;
```

Puzzle 3 – the Magic exposed:

As in Puzzle 3 example when you use AS OF TIMESTAMP clause you will get the data with latest column even if the column does not exist at that point of time, why? This is the oracle behavior, it **always returns current state of table**.

However when you use "AS OF SCN" why does the query fail? The reason is when you use "**AS OF SCN**" clause it gives exact representation of data at that particular SCN.

So for this case "AS OF SCN" 63225316618 the column "C1" did not exist as you can see from **Output of version query** and hence it failed. The column was introduced shortly after this. So when you run the query AS OF SCN 63225316843 the query will run fine.

Puzzle 4 – the Magic exposed:

The reason for this different behavior in **Puzzle 4** example is because there is no flashback in the table **test11** and hence table is using data from **undo_retention**. So as long as the undo data was present you could run the flashback query and once the query is run after the **undo_retention** period it fails with this error:

```
ORA-30052: invalid lower limit snapshot expression
30052. 00000 - "invalid lower limit snapshot expression"
*Cause:   The lower limit snapshot expression was below the UNDO_RETENTION
          limit.
*Action:  Specify a valid lower limit snapshot expression.
Error at Line: 7 Column: 11
```

If you enable flashback in the table "TEST11" the query will run fine every time you run.

Chapter 5: Sub query factoring using WITH clause (13 pages)

The WITH clause referred to as the sub query factoring clause. This clause lets oracle reuse a query when it occurs more than once within the same statement. So instead of storing the query results in a temporary table and performing queries against this temporary table, you can use the WITH clause. By doing this you can avoid a re-read and re-execution of the query which in turn improves overall query execution time and resources utilization. You most frequently use this type of query when querying against large volumes of data e.g. data warehouse

We will explore the enhancement of WITH clause in oracle 12c and alternate approach to resolve the same prior to 12c.

Tips 1: WITH Clause in Oracle query give great performance?
Tips 2: Different ways to pivot full rows (for all columns rows) into columns
Tips 3: WITH Clause improvement in 12c?
Tips 4: Reference a package constant from sql select in 12c?
Tips 5: PRAGMA UDF to improve function call from SQL in 12c?

Tips 1: WITH Clause in Oracle query gives great performance

Here we will discuss how to reuse a query to avoid re-execution multiple times, instead execute one time and use the result multiple times.

Till Oracle 10gR2 we have seen using WITH clause gives huge performance benefit.
Here is a query which used to take 4 hrs. Now it takes hardly 1 minute to execute.

Please note you should not take this as a rule of thumb and change all queries to use WITH clause (temporary table). Performance is an iterative process and hence you should apply all the refactoring techniques and check the explain plan before deciding which technique is best for your database.
So it is better we acquaint ourselves with all the refactoring techniques and choose the one which is most fitted for each situation.
The WITH clause is referred to as the sub query factoring clause. This clause lets oracle reuse a query when it occurs more than once within the same statement. So instead of storing the query results in a temporary table and performing queries against this temporary table, you can use the WITH clause. By doing this you can avoid a reread and re-execution of the query which in-turn improves overall query execution time and resource utilization. You most frequently use this type of query when querying against large volumes of data e.g. data warehouse.

Here is a code snippet with and without "WITH" clause (Temporary table sub query)

```
SELECT PO_ID,
  TO_CHAR(sysdate, 'DD/Mon/YYYY HH24:MI:SS') AS "Current_Time",
  ERR_CODE,
  FILE_NAME,
  TIME_RECEIVED,
  DATE_RECEIVED,
  NET_SETT_AMT,
  SETTLER,
  SENDER,
  ERR_TYPE,
  ERR_RECORD_TYPE,
  COUNT (err_code) AS err_count
FROM r_validation_errs_v r
WHERE r.po_id                = NVL (NULL, r.po_id)
AND TRUNC (r.po_date_created) >= NVL (NULL, TRUNC (r.po_date_created))
AND TRUNC (r.po_date_created) <= NVL (NULL, TRUNC (r.po_date_created))
AND r.err_type               = 'non-critical'
AND r.file_name NOT          IN
  (SELECT c.file_name FROM r_validation_errs_v c WHERE c.err_type = 'critical'
  )
GROUP BY PO_ID,
  ERR_CODE,
  FILE_NAME,
  TIME_RECEIVED,
  DATE_RECEIVED,
  NET_SETT_AMT,
  SETTLER,
  SENDER,
  ERR_TYPE,
  ERR_RECORD_TYPE
ORDER BY FILE_NAME,
  ERR_CODE;
```

This query took some 4 hrs. In Oracle 10g, Please note the view r_validation_errs_v is based on six tables and there are complex joins involved.

Now when the query is re-written using the "WITH" clause as below, it took less than 1 minute to execute.

```sql
WITH groupings AS
  (SELECT
    /*+ USE_HASH_AGGREGATION */
    PO_ID,
    TO_CHAR(sysdate, 'DD/Mon/YYYY HH24:MI:SS') AS "Current_Time",
    ERR_CODE,
    FILE_NAME,
    TIME_RECEIVED,
    DATE_RECEIVED,
    NET_SETT_AMT,
    SETTLER,
    SENDER,
    ERR_TYPE,
    ERR_RECORD_TYPE,
    COUNT (err_code) AS err_count
  FROM r_validation_errs_v r
  WHERE r.po_id                    = NVL (NULL, r.po_id)
  AND TRUNC (r.po_date_created) >= NVL (NULL, TRUNC (r.po_date_created))
  AND TRUNC (r.po_date_created) <= NVL (NULL, TRUNC (r.po_date_created))
  AND r.err_type                   = 'non-critical'
  AND r.file_name NOT              IN
    (SELECT c.file_name FROM r_validation_errs_v c WHERE c.err_type = 'critical'
    )
  GROUP BY PO_ID,
    ERR_CODE,
    FILE_NAME,
    TIME_RECEIVED,
    DATE_RECEIVED,
    NET_SETT_AMT,
    SETTLER,
    SENDER,
    ERR_TYPE,
    ERR_RECORD_TYPE
  )
SELECT * FROM groupings ORDER BY FILE_NAME, ERR_CODE;
```

The performance improvement is realized because of 2 reasons:
1. Use of use_hash_aggregation hint which enforce HASH GROUP BY instead of the costly SORT GROUP BY in the execution plan
2. Sub query refactoring using "WITH" clause which eleminate reread and re-execution of the query and enhance performance.

Tips 2: Different ways to pivot full rows (for all columns rows) into columns

Here we will discuss different ways to pivot all columns in a table.

As discussed in Chapter 3 Tips 2: Pivoting rows into column dynamically in 10g/11g

We can convert rows (for a single column) into columns using **Pivot** and without **pivot** (by using LISTAGG and then break the string using REGEXP_SUBSTR).

Here we will explore how to pivot rows (for all columns) into columns.

Take one example:

```
CREATE TABLE cust_house_det
  (
    cust_id          NUMBER,
    house_no         NUMBER,
    area             NUMBER(14,4),
    registered_flag NUMBER
  );
INSERT INTO cust_house_det(cust_id,house_no,area,registered_flag) values(1234,12,1371.5,1);
INSERT INTO cust_house_det(cust_id,house_no,area,registered_flag) values(1234,13,1471.5,0);
INSERT INTO cust_house_det(cust_id,house_no,area,registered_flag) values(1234,14,1571.5,0);
```

The data look as below:

CUST_ID	HOUSE_NO	AREA	REGISTERED_FLAG
1234	12	1371.5	1
1234	13	1471.5	0
1234	14	1571.5	0

Objective:
Pivot the whole 3 rows into 1 row.

Approach 1: Using PIVOT:

Using Pivot

```
WITH t1 AS
  (SELECT cust_id,
    house_no,
    area,
    registered_flag,
    row_number() over(partition BY cust_id order by rownum) AS rn
  FROM cust_house_det
  WHERE cust_id=1234
  )
SELECT *
FROM t1
PIVOT( MAX(house_no) AS house_no,MAX(area) AS area, MAX(registered_flag)
AS registered_flag FOR rn IN(1,2,3)
);
```

The output:

CUST_ID	1_HOUSE_NO	1_AREA	1_REGISTERED_FLAG	2_HOUSE_NO	2_AREA	2_REGISTERED_FLAG	3_HOUSE_NO	3_AREA	3_REGISTERED_FLAG
1234	12	1371.5	1	13	1471.5	0	14	1571.5	0

Approach 2: Using normal subquery:

```
SELECT x.cust_id,
  x.house_no house_no_1,
  x.area area_1,
  x.registered_flag registered_flag_1,
  y.house_no house_no_2,
  y.area area_2,
  y.registered_flag registered_flag_2,
  z.house_no house_no_3,
  z.area area_3,
  z.registered_flag registered_flag_3
FROM
  (SELECT *
  FROM
    (SELECT cust_id,
      house_no,
      area,
      registered_flag,
      row_number() over(partition BY cust_id order by house_no DESC) AS rn
    FROM cust_house_det
    WHERE cust_id=1234
    )
  WHERE rn=1
  )x,
  (SELECT *
  FROM
    (SELECT cust_id,
      house_no,
      area,
      registered_flag,
      row_number() over(partition BY cust_id order by house_no DESC) AS rn
    FROM cust_house_det
    WHERE cust_id=1234
    )
  WHERE rn=2
  )y,
  (SELECT *
  FROM
    (SELECT cust_id,
      house_no,
      area,
      registered_flag,
      row_number() over(partition BY cust_id order by house_no DESC) AS rn
    FROM cust_house_det
    WHERE cust_id=1234
    )
  WHERE rn=3
  )z
WHERE x.cust_id=y.cust_id
AND x.cust_id =z.cust_id;
```

The output:

CUST_ID	HOUSE_NO_1	AREA_1	REGISTERED_FLAG_1	HOUSE_NO_2	AREA_2	REGISTERED_FLAG_2	HOUSE_NO_3	AREA_3	REGISTERED_FLAG_3
1234	14	1571.5	0	13	1471.5	0	12	1371.5	1

157

Approach 3: <u>Using multiple WITH clause</u>

Using "WITH" clause . This gives the great performance (as compared to approach 2) as oracle materializes the temporary tables that are created inside the "WITH" clause.

```
WITH t1 AS
  (SELECT *
  FROM
    (SELECT cust_id,house_no,area,registered_flag,
      row_number() over(partition BY cust_id order by house_no DESC) AS rn
    FROM cust_house_det WHERE cust_id=1234
    )
  WHERE rn=1
  ),
t2 AS
  (SELECT *
  FROM
    (SELECT cust_id,house_no,area,registered_flag,
      row_number() over(partition BY cust_id order by house_no DESC) AS rn
    FROM cust_house_det WHERE cust_id=1234
    )
  WHERE rn=2
  ) ,
t3 AS
  (SELECT *
  FROM
    (SELECT cust_id,house_no,area,registered_flag,
      row_number() over(partition BY cust_id order by house_no DESC) AS rn
    FROM cust_house_det WHERE cust_id=1234
    )
  WHERE rn=3
  )
SELECT
t1.cust_id,t1.house_no house_no_1,t1.area area_1,
t1.registered_flag registered_flag_1,t2.house_no house_no_2,
t2.area area_2,t2.registered_flag registered_flag_2,
t3.house_no house_no_3,t3.area area_3,t3.registered_flag registered_flag_3
FROM t1,t2,t3
WHERE t1.cust_id=t2.cust_id
AND   t1.cust_id=t3.cust_id;
```

The output:

CUST_ID	HOUSE_NO_1	AREA_1	REGISTERED_FLAG_1	HOUSE_NO_2	AREA_2	REGISTERED_FLAG_2	HOUSE_NO_3	AREA_3	REGISTERED_FLAG_3
1234	14	1571.5	0	13	1471.5	0	12	1371.5	1

All the three temp tables have same cust_id value but different area,house_no,registered_flag etc.
Using "WITH" clause you can see the result of temporary tables t1, t2 and t3 have been placed in single row. This is very handy in many scenarios where you must get multiple rows output in a single row.

I have shown the example for one "CUST_ID" if you remove the "WHERE CUST_ID=1234" clause the above query will work for all the records in your table.

Out of the 3 approaches, **approach 1** is most favorable in terms of coding/maintainance and performance.

158

Tips 3: WITH Clause improvement in 12c

Here we will discuss how inlining of PL/SQL function/procedure is done in 12c without using Pragma inline.

Inlining is the process by which oracle internally replaces the stored program code in the calling program, this in-turn removes context switching and so results in better performance.

Prior to 12c inlining was possible <u>only for a view</u>, to inline a function/procedure you needed to use PRAGMA (Example of how to use PRAGMA **INLINE** is described in **(Chapter-8: Tips: PL/SQL code optimization by "inlining" in 11g?)**.

However **in 12c** you can INLINE function/procedure using **"WITH"** clause. You can have faster running procedure or function if they are defined and declared inside "WITH" clause of SQL statement.
In order to use "WITH" clause in **PL/SQL** you need to use dynamic sql.

Let us take one example to demonstrate how it works:
(**Note:** PL/SQL function using "WITH clause" <u>does not work</u> in some version of **SQLDEVELOPER**, so you must use sql*plus in case it does not work in your SQLDEVELOPER version for trying out all the examples given here.
)

```
SQL> create table test1(id number);

Table created.

SQL> insert into test1 values(1);

1 row created.

SQL> insert into test1 values(2);

1 row created.

SQL> insert into test1 values(3);

1 row created.

SQL> commit;

Commit complete.

SQL> WITH FUNCTION with_fun(v_id IN NUMBER) RETURN NUMBER IS BEGIN RETURN v_id;
  2    END;
  3    SELECT with_fun(id) FROM test1 WHERE rownum=1
  4    /

WITH_FUN(ID)
------------
           1
```

In order to call the WITH clause from subquery you must use WITH_PLSQL hint as below:

```
SQL> select /*+ WITH_PLSQL */ * from
  2  (
  3  WITH FUNCTION with_fun(v_id IN NUMBER) RETURN NUMBER IS BEGIN RETURN v_id;
  4  END;
  5  SELECT with_fun(id) FROM test1 WHERE rownum=1
  6  )
  7  /

WITH_FUN(ID)
_____
           1
```

If you do not use "WITH_PLSQL" hint then SQL SELECT statement will fail with error:

```
SQL> select * from
  2  (
  3  WITH FUNCTION with_fun(v_id IN NUMBER) RETURN NUMBER IS BEGIN RETURN v_id;
  4  END;
  5  SELECT with_fun(id) FROM test1 WHERE rownum=1
  6  )
  7  /
```

```
ORA-32034: unsupported use of WITH clause
```

To use procedure and function together use the below (I have formatted the output in SQLDEVELOPER for rest of the examples):

Set serveroutput on
```
WITH PROCEDURE with_proc(v_id IN NUMBER) IS
BEGIN DBMS_OUTPUT.put_line('v_id is:'
  || v_id);
END;
FUNCTION with_fun(
    v_id IN NUMBER)
  RETURN NUMBER
IS
BEGIN
  with_proc(v_id);
  RETURN v_id;
END;
SELECT with_fun(id) FROM test1 WHERE rownum = 1
/
```

This will return
```
WITH_FUN(ID)
-----------------

1
v_id is:1
```

In PL/SQL if you want to use a procedure or function using a "WITH" clause, you must use dynamic sql.
Normal functions/procedures are stored in the server, the procedure/function using "WITH" clause is inline which means the SQL engine does not need to do context switching and hence performs faster, greatly improving performance.

Here is a PL/SQL example:

160

Set serveroutput on

```
DECLARE
  v_sql VARCHAR2(2000);
  v_cur SYS_REFCURSOR;
  v_val NUMBER;
BEGIN
  v_sql := 'WITH
FUNCTION with_fun(v_id IN NUMBER) RETURN NUMBER IS
BEGIN
RETURN v_id;
END;
SELECT with_fun(id)
FROM   testl
WHERE  rownum = 1';
  OPEN v_cur FOR v_sql;
  FETCH v_cur INTO v_val;
  DBMS_OUTPUT.put_line('v_val is:' || v_val);
  CLOSE v_cur;
END;
/
```

You can compare the performance yourself by calling stored function and inline function using "WITH" clause in a **PL/SQL** block and loop it for larger set of records.

You can use the WITH FUNCTION/PROCEDURE in update statement using "WITH_PLSQL" operator. This operator is used like an oracle hints by embedding in UPDATE statement. If you do not use the operator then the statement will fail:

```
UPDATE testl a
SET a.id =
(
WITH FUNCTION with_fun(p_id IN NUMBER) RETURN NUMBER IS
BEGIN RETURN p_id;
END;
SELECT with_fun(a.id) FROM dual
);
```
Output:
```
ORA-32034: unsupported use of WITH clause
```

Here is the solution to update using "WITH_PLSQL" operator:

161

```
UPDATE /*+ WITH_PLSQL */ test1 a
SET a.id =
(
WITH FUNCTION with_fun(p_id IN NUMBER) RETURN NUMBER IS
BEGIN RETURN p_id;
END;
SELECT with_fun(a.id) FROM dual
);
```

This will update table "test1" successfully. Actually this "WITH_PLSQL" operator will let you define the function/procedure as temporary object using "WITH" clause.

Note: PL/SQL function using WITH clause does not work in some version of SQLDEVELOPER, so you must use sql*plus in case it does not work in your SQLDEVELOPER version.
You can further improve the performance of inline PL/SQL function using WITH clause by including **PRAGMA UDF** in the declaration section of inline functions.

```
WITH FUNCTION with_fun(v_id IN NUMBER) RETURN NUMBER IS
PRAGMA UDF;
BEGIN RETURN v_id;
END;
SELECT with_fun(id) FROM test1 WHERE rownum=1;
```

Use of **PRAGMA UDF** you will see in this **Chapter**, **Tips 5**.

So in oracle 12c you need not store "**one time use only**" kind of functions in data dictionary but use them as local object directly by means of "WITH" clause.
Another **note:** "WITH" clause cannot be used directly in PL/SQL but can be used in PL/SQL using Native dynamic sql as shown.

Tips 4: Reference a package constant from sql select in 12c?

Here we will discuss how to call a package constant from SQL select, it is not possible to directly call this prior to 12c.

Prior to 12c you could not refer a package constant from SQL SELECT.
However in 12c you can call a package constant from select statement.
e.g.

```
CREATE OR REPLACE PACKAGE test_pkg
    IS
        v_app_scheme_type CONSTANT number  :=1;
        v_rej_scheme_type CONSTANT number := 2;
    END;
    /
```

If you try to call the package constant from SQL select it fails:

```
SELECT test_pkg.v_app_scheme_type FROM customer_tab WHERE id=111;
```

It fails **prior to 12c with error PLS-221** v_scheme_type is not a function

To resolve this **prior to oracle 12c** there are two options:
Approach1:
→Alter the package to add a function

162

→Create the package body in which the new function returns v_app_scheme_type.
→Then you can call the package constant from sql select via a function call.

Approach 2
Call the select from PL/SQL block.

However **in 12c** it is very simple, just call the package constant as below.

```
WITH FUNCTION v_app_scheme_type RETURN NUMBER IS BEGIN
RETURN test_pkg.v_app_scheme_type;
END;
SELECT v_app_scheme_type FROM customer_tab WHERE id=111;
```

The "WITH CLAUSE" feature is very useful SQL enhancement in oracle 12c.

Tips 5: PRAGMA UDF to improve function call from SQL in 12c?

Here we will discuss compiler directive UDF to remove context switch between SQL and PL/SQL for function. This Pragma UDF is used to rearrange/inline a code for better performance.

SQL and PL/SQL has different memory representation and hence when a PL/SQL function is called from a select statement there are context switches between SQL and PL/SQL engines.
To resolve this Oracle 12c has introduced inlining using "WITH FUNCTION" clause which will invoke the function instantly in the SELECT statement with no context switching.
Also to resolve the context switching Oracle 12c has introduced "PRAGMA UDF". This is a compiler directive which states that the function is a "user defined function" and this function is used primarily in SQL select statement.

So the "WITH FUNCTION" and "PRAGMA UDF" similarity is that both are inlining the function and reduce the context switches between SQL and PL/SQL engines.
Difference between the two is:
"WITH FUNCTION" defines the PL/SQL subprogram **inside** the SQL statement.
"PRAGMA UDF"   defines the PL/SQL subprogram **outside** the SQL statement.

Converting a normal function to PRAGMA UDF function is the better approach because:

1. Using Pragma UDF you can make the code procedural and hence maintenance is easy and
   Less chance of making mistake
2. Get the advantage of inlining function which reduces context switches.
3. Moving from existing normal function to UDF function is fairly straightforward as against
   "**WITH FUNCTION**" clause which requires massive code changes where there is a function call in your application.

However if you are not worried about point **1 and 3** mentioned here then it is advisable to use "WITH FUNCTION" rather than "PRAGMA UDF" as I have seen "WITH FUNCTION" outperform "PRAGMA UDF" many times. In any case you must try all the approaches before finalizing your choice.

Both "**WITH FUNCTION**" and "**PRAGMA UDF**" method perform better than conventional function as long as these functions are called from SQL select statement. However if the "PRAGMA UDF" function is called from PL/SQL using direct call e.g. v1:=fun_pragma_udf (para1) then "PRAGMA UDF" method will drastically reduce the performance compared to a normal function. This is because Oracle "PRAGMA UDF" definition itself states the usage of this clause is beneficial only if the function is called from SQL SELECT.

Here is one example how to use "PRAGMA UDF"

```
CREATE OR REPLACE
  FUNCTION func_upper_udf(
      v_empid NUMBER)
    RETURN VARCHAR2
  IS
    PRAGMA UDF;          ———————— This is the only change in the function
    v_ename VARCHAR2(30);
  BEGIN
    SELECT upper(ename) INTO v_ename FROM emp WHERE empid=v_empid;
    RETURN v_ename;
  END func_upper_udf;
  /
```

In order to call the UDF function it is advisable to call it from SQL SELECT **as below** to get best performance:

```
DECLARE
  v_sql VARCHAR2(32767);
  v_cur SYS_REFCURSOR;
TYPE t_tab_name
IS
  TABLE OF VARCHAR2(30) INDEX BY BINARY_INTEGER;
  v_tab_name t_tab_name;
BEGIN
  v_sql :='SELECT func_upper_udf(empid) from emp';
  OPEN v_cur FOR v_sql;
  FETCH v_cur BULK COLLECT INTO v_tab_name;
  CLOSE v_cur;
END;
/
```

However if you call it as below the UDF function **performs slowly in fact it runs slightly slower than normal function without UDF PRAGMA**

```
DECLARE
  v_ename VARCHAR2(30);
BEGIN
  FOR i IN
  (SELECT empid FROM emp
  )
  LOOP
    v_ename :=func_upper_udf(i.empno);
  END LOOP;
END;
/
```

To get best benefit of "WITH clause function" and "function with PRAGMA UDF", you must call those functions from SQL SELECT statement.

So here are the suggestions in the order of best performance
→1st Try with SQL select if you can achieve the same functionality as the function.
→2nd Try a **function** using **Result cache or user**
→3rd Try with SQL select and "WITH FUNCTION" clause if you are not worried about maintenance

Cost.

→4th Use "PRAGMA UDF" in your function

→5th Use conventional function

Note: This is just a suggestion, however before choosing any approach you must try all the options mentioned and accordingly take a call for your situations.

Restriction of PRAGMA UDF

When IN or OUT parameter of a function is of data type "DATE" then UDF performs slowly

When the IN parameter data type (varchar2) has got any default value then UDF performs slowly.

Chapter 6: Integration of similar concepts (28 pages)

In database there are different ways of doing the same task but one should know the related concepts associated with a specific challenge in order to gain the best throughput and response time. Knowing a concept is easy but the ability to determine the specific approach to implement in order to achieve the best results for your application is difficult.

In this chapter you will correlate similar concepts and get an insight as to how you can derive the best approach for a particular challenge.

Tips 1: Oracle Object CACHE Using "Cache" **or** "Keep buffer pool" **or** Oracle 12c "IN-MEMORY column store"?

Tips 2: Result cache function **or** deterministic function **or** PL/SQL collection?

Tips 3: Function result cache **or** Oracle user Cache?

Tips 4: Correlated update **or** merge **or** different approach to update?

Tips 5: Oracle NOT IN clause **or** MINUS or JOIN or NOT EXISTS clause?

Tips 6: nested loop Join **or** hash join **or** parallelism **or** multi-threading?

(Covered in chapter 1): Function Based Index **or** Indexed Virtual column in 11g?

Tips 7: Use "Where" clause **or** "Having" clause?

Tips 8: Use Oracle clause IN **or** EXISTS **or** DISTINCT And How to Refactor query to avoid "DISTINCT" keyword from the query?

Tips 9: Oracle IN clause **or** INTERSECT or JOIN clause?

(Covered in chapter 1): INDEX order in composite index **or** INDEX only access?

Tips 10: Materialized view **or** SQL Result Cache in 11g?

(Covered in chapter 3): Flashback query using method "timestamp" **or** "scn"?

Tips 11: How to Convert a PL/SQL For loop update into SQL update **or** Merge for performance improvement?

Tips 12: Query refactoring for Hierarchical query "OR" clause **or** "UNION" clause?

Tips 13: Mutating trigger resolution using collection **or** Global temporary table?

(Covered in chapter 1): Primary key with UNIQUE index **or** NON-UNIQUE index?

Tips 1: Oracle Object CACHE Using "Cache", "Keep buffer pool" or Oracle 12c "IN-MEMORY column store"?

Here we will discuss different ways of pinning an object (or part of the object) in memory for better performance.

When you run a query multiple times in the same session the response time reduces because blocks are cached and, as per LRU algorithm, are subsequently aged out of the cache block. Caching means pinning the data.
So when you talk about "Caching object" it means you PIN the object in memory. So here we will discuss 3 different ways of Caching using a simple example

Approach 1
```
alter table tl cache;
```
In this approach you will pin a frequently used small table in memory. But in real sense this is not fully in memory. The table is kept in general buffer cache but it stays at the most recently used end of LRU list, that means it is not susceptible to being aged out of cache very frequently. It stays in the cache longer but based on system demand it is aged out for sure sooner or later. Here the full table is pinned even if you need some section of the table to be pinned

Approach 2
```
alter table tl storage (buffer_pool Keep);
```
In this approach also you will pin a frequently used small table in memory. Here the table is placed in the special section of the cache called the KEEP buffer pool and hence the table is never aged out from the cache. Here the full table is pinned even if you need some section of the table to be pinned.

Approach 3
In-memory Column-store (IM-COLUMN) is a mechanism (introduced in Oracle 12c) by which performance critical subset of a table is placed in the "in-memory column store" which is the new section of the SGA in Oracle 12c. This "in-memory area" can be configured using "INMEMORY_SIZE" initialization parameter. You can store whole table, set of columns, specific group of columns, materialized view, table partition etc. in the IM-COLUMN store.
In-memory storage not only helps accessing data in memory (approach 1 and approach 2 which are based fundamentally on accessing data from memory cache only) it helps reporting, business intelligence and high performance analytical queries run faster by its internal algorithm to keep the data in columnar format instead of traditional row format.

Example how to configure:
```
ALTER SYSTEM SET SGA_TARGET=4G SCOPE=SPFILE;
ALTER SYSTEM SET INMEMORY_SIZE=2G SCOPE=SPFILE;      <——— Enabling the IN-MEMORY
SHUTDOWN IMMEDIATE;
STARTUP;

                                                     Disabling the IN-MEMORY SYSTEM level
ALTER SYSTEM SET INMEMORY_SIZE=0;  <——————
ALTER SESSION SET INMEMORY_SIZE=0;<
                                                     Disabling the IN-MEMORY SESSION level
SHUTDOWN IMMEDIATE;
STARTUP;
```

Example how to use IM-COLUMN store (IMDB in short):

```
CREATE TABLE tl
  (
    id NUMBER,
    a  NUMBER,
    b  NUMBER,
    c  NUMBER,
    d  NUMBER,
    e  NUMBER,
    f  NUMBER
  )
  INMEMORY;
```
INMEMORY; ← This clause keep the table in IMDB

In-memory (IM) <u>setting for this table can be changed</u> as below:

```
ALTER TABLE tl NO INMEMORY;
```
← Table out of IMDB

```
ALTER TABLE tl INMEMORY;
```
← Full Table in IMDB

```
ALTER TABLE tl  NO INMEMORY(b,c,d);
```
← Only b, c, d columns are out of IMDB

```
ALTER TABLE tl  INMEMORY(b,c);
```
← b, c, columns are again in IMDB

For materialized view the command is:
```
CREATE MATERIALIZED VIEW tl_mview INMEMORY
AS SELECT * FROM tl;
```
As per Oracle documentation:

IM column store is good in the following scenarios:

- Large scans using "=", "<", ">" and "IN" filters, IN-MEMORY join use bloom filter.
- When it selects few columns from a table with large number of columns.
- Join small tables to large tables.
- In-memory aggregation.

IM column store is not good in the following scenarios:

- Complex predicates in the join
- Join returning large set of columns and large number of rows.
- Join large table to large table.

Approach 3 gives tremendous performance as compared to **approach 1** and **approach 2**

However you must weigh all the options before finalizing the solution for different scenarios.

In oracle there are different ways to store a value in memory and implement complex logic. Here we will discuss different approaches to do that.

Approach 1: Function result-cached:

This is a function whose argument values and corresponding result-set are stored in the cache in SGA area. Function result cache is mostly used when the function contain lots of complex sql query inside it. In oracle 11g PL/SQL function result cache is <u>cross session result cache</u>.

```
CREATE OR REPLACE FUNCTION f2_result_cache(
                p_first_name IN VARCHAR2
                ) RETURN VARCHAR2
                  RESULT_CACHE
                  RELIES_ON (cust)
                IS
                v_id_name varchar2(60);
    BEGIN
       select upper(id||'-'||last_name) INTO v_id_name from cust
       where first_name=p_first_name and rownum<2;
       RETURN v_id_name;
    END f2_result_cache;
/
```

Now if you execute
```
select first_name,last_name,f2_result_cache(first_name) from cust;
```
It will take approx. 10 sec in my testing even if you run it from different sessions (As result cache is applicable for cross session).

Approach 2: Function NO-cached:
In this approach we use conventional function to return the result.
```
CREATE OR REPLACE FUNCTION f2_no_cache(
                p_first_name IN VARCHAR2
                ) RETURN VARCHAR2
                IS
                v_id_name varchar2(60);
    BEGIN
       select upper(id||'-'||last_name) INTO v_id_name from cust
       where first_name=p_first_name and rownum<2;
       RETURN v_id_name;
    END f2_no_cache;
/
```
You can execute as below:
```
select first_name,last_name,f2_no_cache(first_name) from cust;
```

This takes little longer than 19 sec:

Approach 3: Deterministic Function:

A deterministic function uses the pre-computed result for a specific session.

169

```
CREATE OR REPLACE FUNCTION f2_deterministic(
            p_first_name IN VARCHAR2
            ) RETURN VARCHAR2 DETERMINISTIC
            IS
            v_id_name varchar2(60);
    BEGIN
        select upper(id||'-'||last_name) INTO v_id_name from cust
        where first_name=p_first_name and rownum<2;
        RETURN v_id_name;
    END f2_deterministic;
/
```

When you execute:
```
select first_name,last_name,f2_deterministic(first_name) from cust;
```

If this is executed 2nd time in same session it takes approx. 10 second as it takes for result cache function (approach 1). However if it is executed in different session it takes around 19 sec.

Approach 4: PL/SQL collection:

PL/SQL collection is similar to array in C. The data of PL/SQL collection is stored in PGA memory and PL/SQL runtime engine can directly access it. Note, this data storage happens in each and every session independently which means cross session interoperability is not there for PL/SQL collection.
As you know PL/SQL function results are stored in SGA (not in PGA) and PL/SQL collection stores the data in PGA. Since getting data from PGA (RAM) is much faster than getting data from SGA we have seen PL/SQL collection is faster than function result cache. *However you have to store the collection result of each session in PGA and hence you may run out of total PGA memory in a multi-user environment. This should be taken into consideration when deciding which approach to use.*

The following example uses PL/SQL collection instead of a function result cache

```
DECLARE
  v_id_name DBMS_SQL.VARCHAR2_TABLE;
  v_first_names DBMS_SQL.VARCHAR2_TABLE;
  v_last_names DBMS_SQL.VARCHAR2_TABLE;
BEGIN
  SELECT first_name,
    last_name,
    upper(id
    ||'-'
    ||last_name) BULK COLLECT
  INTO v_first_names,
    v_last_names,
    v_id_name
  FROM cust;
  FOR i IN 1 .. v_first_names.COUNT
  LOOP
    dbms_output.put_line('v_id_name is:'||v_id_name);
  END LOOP;
END;
/
```
This block will take less than 6 sec to execute.

170

So in a nutshell:

- o Use function result cache when the function has complex sql logic embedded. The function result cache is referred as a cross session function result cache because it caches the result-set across the sessions.
- o Use function result cache over deterministic when you work in multi user environment where you want to get the benefit of running the same function in different sessions.
- o When it comes to use result cache function or associative array (PL/SQL table) you have seen PL/SQL table(PL/SQL collection) is better than function result cache because PL/SQL table gets the data from PGA and function result cache gets the data from SGA. However there is a trade-off between performance and memory usage.
- o When your underlying table in the function undergoes frequent DML changes then function result cache is not ideal for the function as DML change will force the database to invalidate the result set.
- o Most importantly consider using function result cache if the time spent in specific function business logic is more than time spent in result cache mechanism. If time spent in evaluating the business logic is less than the time spent in evaluating the result cache mechanism it is advisable not to use the result cache. Classic example for this scenario is when you need to concatenate two inputs by comma or do some simple arithmetic on the data. In these kinds of scenario you should not use result cache function.

One more example to demonstrate the performance of no cache, function result cache and deterministic function:

We will create simple function using these 3 methods and show the result after processing all the rows.

```
CREATE OR REPLACE FUNCTION fl_result_cache(
                p_first_name IN VARCHAR2,
                p_last_name  IN VARCHAR2
                ) RETURN VARCHAR2
                  RESULT_CACHE
                  RELIES_ON (cust)
                IS
     BEGIN
        RETURN p_first_name || ' ' || p_last_name;
     END fl_result_cache;
/
CREATE OR REPLACE FUNCTION fl_no_cache(
                p_first_name IN VARCHAR2,
                p_last_name  IN VARCHAR2
                ) RETURN VARCHAR2
                    IS
     BEGIN
        RETURN p_first_name || ' ' || p_last_name;
     END fl_no_cache;
/
CREATE OR REPLACE FUNCTION fl_deterministic(
                p_first_name IN VARCHAR2,
                p_last_name  IN VARCHAR2
                ) RETURN VARCHAR2
                  DETERMINISTIC
                  IS
     BEGIN
        RETURN p_first_name || ' ' || p_last_name;
     END fl_deterministic;
/
```

Once these functions are created, we are ready to execute each functions and note down time as show in Below example:

```
set serverout on 20000000
DECLARE
  v_cust_name VARCHAR2(60);
  v_first_names DBMS_SQL.VARCHAR2_TABLE;
  v_last_names DBMS_SQL.VARCHAR2_TABLE;
  v_cnt NUMBER :=1500;
  t1     NUMBER;
  t2     NUMBER;
  t3     NUMBER;
  t4     NUMBER;
BEGIN
  SELECT first_name,
    last_name BULK COLLECT
  INTO v_first_names,
    v_last_names
  FROM cust WHERE rownum<1501;
  t1          :=dbms_utility.get_time;
  FOR i       IN 1 .. v_first_names.COUNT
  LOOP
    FOR j IN 1 .. v_cnt LOOP
      v_cust_name := fl_result_cache( v_first_names(i), v_last_names(i) );
    END LOOP;
  END LOOP;
  t2:=dbms_utility.get_time;
  dbms_output.put_line('time taken to execute with result cache is:'||(t2-t1));
  FOR i                          IN 1 .. v_first_names.COUNT
  LOOP
    FOR j IN 1 .. v_cnt LOOP
      v_cust_name := fl_no_cache( v_first_names(i), v_last_names(i) );
    END LOOP;
  END LOOP;
  t3:=dbms_utility.get_time;
  dbms_output.put_line('time taken to execute with no cache is:'||(t3-t2));
  FOR i                          IN 1 .. v_first_names.COUNT
  LOOP
    FOR j IN 1 .. v_cnt LOOP
      v_cust_name := fl_deterministic( v_first_names(i), v_last_names(i) );
    END LOOP;
  END LOOP;
  t4:=dbms_utility.get_time;
  dbms_output.put_line('TIME taken TO EXECUTE WITH deterministic IS:'||(t4-t3));
END;
/
```

The output is

```
time taken to execute with result cache is:126
time taken to execute with no cache is:90
TIME taken TO EXECUTE
WITH deterministic IS:89
```

So this shows the time spent in evaluating result cache result is more than time spent in evaluating the business logic and hence there is no performance improvement rather we get performance penalty. In fact in this kind of scenario deterministic performs the best.

However consider a scenario as below which has only a few distinct return values (let us say 20-30 values) however this function is used in a view which returns millions of records then you must use result cache function to use the pre-computed value.

So in this case p_type has only 20 distinct values and it returns 20 distinct java.lang.string
However **complex_view** has more than 1 million records based on join on multiple base tables including tab1.

```
create or replace
function f1(p_type in number)
return VARCHAR2
RESULT_CACHE
RELIES ON(tab1)
as language java name 'com.xx.utility.rad50ToString(java.math.BigDecimal)
return java.lang.String';
/
```

So when we fire the following query
```
SELECT id,name,p_type,f1(p_type) FROM complex_view;
```
                          ↑   ↑
         This function return 20 distinct name   This View return millions of rows

It does not compute the function f1 more than a million times. Instead it compute only 20 times (by eliminating redundant function calls) and the remaining times it uses the pre-computed result not only in 1 session but across other sessions and gives huge performance benefit.

Here are the restriction on using function result cache:
- It cannot be used in invoker's rights code or in an anonymous block.
- It cannot be used in a pipelined table function.
- It cannot be used in a function which has OUT or IN OUT parameters.
- It cannot be used in a function whose IN parameter has one of the following types,
- BLOB, CLOB, NCLOB, REF CURSOR, Collection Object, Record.
- It cannot be used in a function which has return type BLOB, CLOB, NCLOB, REF CURSOR, Object, Record or PL/SQL collection that contains one of the preceding unsupported return types.

Here we will discuss and compare different mechanisms to eliminate the expensive read from kernel/physical disk.

Approach 1: Function result-cache:

This is a function whose argument values and corresponding result-set are stored in the cache in SGA area. Function result cache is mostly used when the function contain lots of complex sql query inside it. In oracle 11g PL/SQL function result cache is <u>cross session result cache</u>.

Approach 2: Function NO-cached:

In this approach we use conventional function to return the result.

Approach 3: Oracle user cache:

Oracle user cache is the mechanism by which a value in an oracle package is stored as a variable and we can retrieve that value from buffer cache which eliminates the expensive read from kernel/physical disk.
Here you will see the Cache mechanism is best when compared with no cache.

However *oracle user cache* is slightly better than *function result cache (This was discussed in earlier Tips).*

```
CREATE OR REPLACE PACKAGE user_cache AS
FUNCTION f2_user_cache(
                p_first_name IN VARCHAR2
                ) RETURN VARCHAR2;
FUNCTION f2_result_cache(
                p_first_name IN VARCHAR2
                ) RETURN VARCHAR2
                  RESULT_CACHE;
                  --RELIES_ON (cust);
FUNCTION f2_no_cache(
                p_first_name IN VARCHAR2
                ) RETURN VARCHAR2;
END user_cache;
/
```

```
CREATE OR REPLACE PACKAGE body user_cache AS
      TYPE user_cache_t IS TABLE OF varchar2(100) INDEX BY varchar2(100);
      g_user_cache user_cache_t;

   FUNCTION f2_user_cache(
               p_first_name IN VARCHAR2
               ) RETURN VARCHAR2
               IS
    BEGIN
    IF NOT g_user_cache.EXISTS(p_first_name) THEN
       select upper(id||'-'||last_name) INTO g_user_cache(p_first_name)
       from cust
       where first_name=p_first_name and rownum<2;
     END IF;
       RETURN g_user_cache(p_first_name);
    END f2_user_cache;

   FUNCTION f2_result_cache(
               p_first_name IN VARCHAR2
               ) RETURN VARCHAR2
                 RESULT_CACHE
                 RELIES_ON (cust)
               IS
               v_id_name varchar2(60);
     BEGIN
       select upper(id||'-'||last_name) INTO v_id_name from cust
       where first_name=p_first_name and rownum<2;
       RETURN v_id_name;
     END f2_result_cache;

   FUNCTION f2_no_cache(
               p_first_name IN VARCHAR2
               ) RETURN VARCHAR2
               IS
               v_id_name varchar2(60);
     BEGIN
       select upper(id||'-'||last_name) INTO v_id_name from cust
       where first_name=p_first_name and rownum<2;
       RETURN v_id_name;
     END f2_no_cache;
END user_cache;
/
```

Now when we execute all the 3 functions from PL/SQL we can see the performance difference as shown:

```
declare
  t1    NUMBER;
  t2    NUMBER;
  t3    NUMBER;
  t4    NUMBER;
  v_id_name varchar2(60);
begin
  t1:=dbms_utility.get_time;
for i in (select first_name from cust) loop
  v_id_name :=user_cache.f2_no_cache(i.first_name);
end loop;
  t2:=dbms_utility.get_time;
dbms_output.put_line('Time taken with no cache:'||(t2-t1));
for i in (select first_name from cust) loop
  v_id_name :=user_cache.f2_result_cache(i.first_name);
end loop;
  t3:=dbms_utility.get_time;
dbms_output.put_line('Time taken with result cache:'||(t3-t2));
for i in (select first_name from cust) loop
  v_id_name :=user_cache.f2_user_cache(i.first_name);
end loop;
  t4:=dbms_utility.get_time;
dbms_output.put_line('Time taken with user cache:'||(t4-t3));
end;
/
```

The output look as below:

```
Time taken with no cache:13513
Time taken with result cache:7375
Time taken with user cache:6654
```

So this suggests Caching is good for performance, for this example Oracle cache is the best. However you should not jump to conclusions, you should consider all the options for your business scenario and finally decide which option is best for you.

Tips 4: Correlated update or merge or different approach to update?

Here we will discuss different approaches for "update" to get better performance. Also we will look how a correlated query can be re-written using different approaches and specifically highlight the advantage of using **Oracle 12c** new construct "**LATERAL**" to achieve that.

A correlated update is an update in which an inner table is joined with the outer table for each row.
Let us take one example and see different ways of doing the update and obvious issues.

The data looks as below:

```
CREATE TABLE test_s
  (cust_id VARCHAR2(8),house_no NUMBER,buying_date DATE
  );
INSERT INTO test_s VALUES('Asim 01',1,TO_DATE('06-01-2015','DD-MM-YYYY'));
INSERT INTO test_s VALUES('Arun 01',2,TO_DATE('06-01-2015','DD-MM-YYYY'));
INSERT INTO test_s VALUES('Ani 01',3,TO_DATE('06-01-2015','DD-MM-YYYY'));
INSERT INTO test_s VALUES('Aditi 01',44,TO_DATE('06-01-2015','DD-MM-YYYY'));
COMMIT;


CREATE TABLE test_tgt
  (cust_id VARCHAR2(8),house_no NUMBER,buying_date DATE
  );
INSERT INTO test_tgt VALUES('Asim 01',1,TO_DATE('07-01-2015','DD-MM-YYYY'));
INSERT INTO test_tgt VALUES('Arun 01',2,TO_DATE('07-01-2015','DD-MM-YYYY'));
INSERT INTO test_tgt VALUES('Ani 01',3,TO_DATE('07-01-2015','DD-MM-YYYY'));
INSERT INTO test_tgt VALUES('Aditi 01',44,TO_DATE('07-01-2015','DD-MM-YYYY'));
INSERT INTO test_tgt VALUES('PPPP 01',10,TO_DATE('07-01-2015','DD-MM-YYYY'));
COMMIT;
```

Note cust_id PPPP 01 is not present in table "test_s" however it is present in table "test_tgt".

Now you need to update test_tgt with the value from test_s
Here is the update statement:

```
UPDATE test_tgt a
SET (house_no,buying_date)=(SELECT house_no,buying_date FROM test_s b
WHERE b.cust_id=a.cust_id);
```

Do you find any issue in the update?

This will update the cust_id PPPP 01 in test_tgt with house_no and buying_date as null because this cust_id is not present in test_s source table.

The data in test_tgt look as below after the update.

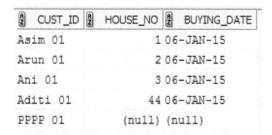

CUST_ID	HOUSE_NO	BUYING_DATE
Asim 01	1	06-JAN-15
Arun 01	2	06-JAN-15
Ani 01	3	06-JAN-15
Aditi 01	44	06-JAN-15
PPPP 01	(null)	(null)

To resolve this here is the correct update statement:

Approach 1:

Using correlated update:

```
UPDATE test_tgt a
SET (house_no,buying_date)=(SELECT house_no,buying_date FROM test_s b
WHERE b.cust_id=a.cust_id)
WHERE EXISTS (SELECT 1 FROM test_s c
              WHERE c.cust_id=a.cust_id);
```

However this approach is inefficient because "test_s" table is queried twice.
To resolve the performance issue here are 2 approaches to update the test_tgt table

Approach 2:
Here we update the joined version of both tables by issuing update on the inline view as below:

However there are some restriction in this approach. You must make sure both the table test_s and test_tgt are joined on primary key column. If the tables are not joined using primary key column it will fail with error

```
UPDATE
  (SELECT a.house_no src_hou,
    a.buying_date src_dt,
    b.house_no tgt_hou,
    b.buying_date tgt_dt
  FROM test_s a,
    test_tgt b
  WHERE a.house_no=b.house_no
  )
SET tgt_hou=src_hou,
  tgt_dt   =src_dt;
```

```
SQL Error: ORA-01779: cannot modify a column which maps to a non key-preserved table
01779. 00000 -  "cannot modify a column which maps to a non key-preserved table"
*Cause:     An attempt was made to insert or update columns of a join view which
            map to a non-key-preserved table.
*Action:    Modify the underlying base tables directly.
```

So this approach is used when you have same kind of table or has some backup table of the original table.

Approach 3:
We can use Oracle Merge to do this as below:
```
MERGE INTO test_tgt tgt
USING
test_s src
ON (tgt.cust_id=src.cust_id)
WHEN MATCHED THEN
UPDATE SET
tgt.house_no=src.house_no,
tgt.buying_date=src.buying_date;
```

178

I personally opt for approach 3 because of ease of use, no restriction as seen in approach 2, less amount code and better response time, however it is suggested to try all approaches before deciding on final approach.

Note: In this context let me explain **Correlated subquery**. When a subquery reference a column from outer table it is called correlated subquery. Simple example to find the deptno, employee name and maximum salary of that department you can use **correlated subquery**.

Solution using correlated subquery:

```
SELECT ename,dept_id,sal
FROM emp a
WHERE sal=
  (SELECT MAX(sal) FROM emp b WHERE a.dept_id=b.dept_id
  );
```

Here in the subquery, inner table "**EMP b**" joins with outer table "**EMP a**".

Solution using LATERAL keyword in 12c:

Oracle 12c has introduced LATERAL syntax to correlate inline views. In other words using LATERAL keyword let you reference an item similar to normal join.
The above correlated subquery can be re-written using LATERAL keyword:

```
SELECT a.*,x.ename
FROM  (SELECT MAX(sal) salary,dept_id FROM emp GROUP BY dept_id)a,
 LATERAL
 (SELECT sal,dept_id,ename FROM emp b WHERE a.dept_id=b.dept_id AND b.sal=a.salary
 )x;
```

Note you are able to refer to "**table alias a**" within an "**inline view x**" by virtue of LATERAL keyword.

Solution using inline view:

If you do not use the "LATERAL" keyword then you can not refer other table inside an inline view "alias x" you have to join the inline view with other table seperately as below:

```
SELECT a.*,x.ename
FROM  (SELECT MAX(sal) salary,dept_id FROM emp GROUP BY dept_id)a,
 (SELECT sal,dept_id,ename FROM emp b)x
where
a.dept_id=x.dept_id AND a.salary=x.sal
```

Solution using normal subquery:
```
SELECT ename,dept_id,sal
FROM emp
WHERE (dept_id,sal) IN
  (SELECT dept_id,MAX(sal) FROM emp GROUP BY dept_id
  );
```

Regrding the use of "LATERAL" keyword let us take one more example:

```
CREATE TABLE task_t(task_name VARCHAR2(10),no_of_activity NUMBER
  );
INSERT INTO task_t VALUES('Task 1',5);
INSERT INTO task_t VALUES('Task 2',3);
INSERT INTO task_t VALUES('Task 3',4);
INSERT INTO task_t VALUES('Task 4',6);
INSERT INTO task_t VALUES('Task 5',2);
```

Now the requirement is to construct and display activity name based on number of activity against each task name. So if "no_of_activity" is 5 for a task then you need to construct 5 activities.

Here is the **solution** using LATERAL clause in 12c:
```
SELECT t.task_name,t.no_of_activity,act_break.activity_name
FROM task_t t,
LATERAL
(SELECT 'activity '||rownum AS activity_name FROM dual CONNECT BY rownum<t.no_of_activity+1) act_break
ORDER BY t.task_name,
   act_break.activity_name;
```
The output look as below:

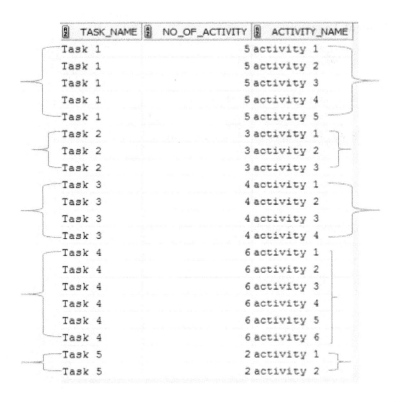

The above query will fail without the LATERAL keyword with error:
ORA-00904: "T"."NO_OF_ACTIVITY": invalid identifier

So without LATERAL clause it will be little tricky to derive the solution as shown in following example:

```
SELECT t.task_name,t.no_of_activity,act_break.activity_name
FROM task_t t,
   (SELECT rownum AS rn,'activity '||rownum AS activity_name FROM dual CONNECT BY rownum<10)act_break
WHERE rn<t.no_of_activity+1
ORDER BY t.task_name,
   act_break.activity_name;
```

This is simple example however when you have some complex query where you need to derive rowset based on other table in the "FROM" clause then it will be tricky to write code without "LATERAL" keyword.

So as you can see "LATERAL" keyword is very powerful in terms of ease of use as you just need to place "LATERAL" keyword between two tables/inline views. In the inline view you are able to refer to other tables as you do in corelated subquery.

Tips 5: Oracle NOT IN or MINUS or JOIN or NOT EXISTS clause?

Here we will discuss different ways to refactor a query for better performance.

When you have requirement to derive a set of values from a set of source tables, there are different ways to derive the same result based on the complexity of the requirement.

To demonstrate the relative performance of each method here is a simple example. Please note in order to see considerable difference in performance you need to use a complex query with multiple joins and a minimum 3-4 tables. For a simple query on a small data set, performance will be similar whichever method is chosen. All the methods return the same result but there will be difference in response time. Explain plan will show the reason for the differences.

"NOT IN" method
```
SELECT a.app_id
FROM app a
WHERE a.app_id  =2
AND app_id NOT IN
   (SELECT app_id FROM app_parcel WHERE a.app_id=2
   );
```

This takes approx. 4 seconds (as it does not use the index). In Oracle NOT IN clause trigger the full table scan even if there is index in app_id column.

Note: Oracle **does not use index** with **NOT predicates** e.g. NOT IN, NOT LIKE, NOT BETWEEN, <>, NOT >=. Also NULL predicate will not use index. (However for **NOT EXISTS** clause it uses index)

"NOT EXISTS" method
```
SELECT a.app_id
FROM app a
WHERE a.app_id  =2
AND not exists
   (SELECT 1 FROM app_parcel b WHERE b.app_id=a.app_id);
```

This takes approx. 2 seconds as it uses the index.

"JOIN" method

```
SELECT DISTINCT a.app_id
FROM app a,
  app_parcel b
WHERE a.app_id =b.app_id(+)
AND b.app_id  IS NULL;
```

Note here you need to use distinct clause to eliminate the duplicate records,
This takes approx. 6 seconds

"MINUS" method

```
SELECT a.app_id
FROM app a
MINUS
SELECT b.app_id
FROM app_parcel b;
```

This takes approx. 2 seconds

So in a nutshell
1. if your requirement is to display the result irrespective of whether there are any duplicates then it is better to use JOIN or MINUS or NOT EXISTS rather than "NOT IN" clause. MINUS is more preferable.
2. If your requirement is to display the result without duplicates it is better to use NOT IN or NOT EXISTS or MINUS instead of JOIN clause. NOT EXISTS is better than NOT IN. MINUS is most preferable. However you must try all approaches before deciding any specific approach as performance tuning is an iterative process. There is no "one size fits all" solution in Oracle. These are just recommendations.

Tips 6: nested loop Join OR hash join OR parallelism OR multi-threading?

Here we will discuss different types of internal join methods and option to run your code in multi-threaded mode.

Let us take one example to see the performance of each process

We have 2 tables
Small table is "apps" which has around 60,000 records and
Big table "shop" which has around 1,100,000 records

And after joining the final result-set returns around 162,000 records, please note for this case both tables are almost equally big and hence it is preferable to use HASH join over nested loop join
However we will discuss all the alternate ways to get the resultset.

Approach 1: "Nested loop join" method

Nested loop join is good for small result-set where one table is small and by using index range scan we can derive the final result-set quickly.

```
SELECT /*+ use_nl(S L)*/
S.product_id,L.shop_id
from apps S,shop L
where S.apps_id=L.apps_id
and L.shop_region='ASIA';
```

This takes roughly 20 sec

Approach 2: "Hash join" method

Hash join is good when larger result-set is expected and both the tables are big as using nested loop join for this scenario will require numerous index range scans.

```
SELECT /*+ use_hash(L S)*/
S.product_id,L.shop_id
from apps S,shop L
where S.apps_id=L.apps_id
and L.shop_region='ASIA';
```

This will take roughly 12 sec as expected because for this scenario Hash join is better alternative than nested loop join.

Approach 3: "Parallelism" method

Parallelism can be done on both hash join and nested loop join. It is a mechanism by which multiple process execute the same job. Multiple process creation is determined by degree of parallelism which is discussed in this book.

```
SELECT /*+ PARALLEL(L,6) use_hash(L S)*/
S.product_id,L.shop_id
from apps S,shop L
where S.apps_id=L.apps_id
and L.shop_region='ASIA';
```

This will take roughly 3 sec

Note that here in big table "shop" (alias L) we have imposed the parallelism of degree 6.

Approach 4: "Multithreading" method

Multi-threading is done on nested loop join. It is a mechanism by which multiple process execute the same job. Multiple process creation is determined by degree of parallelism which is discussed in this book.
The difference between parallelism and multi-threading is that parallelism usually involves full table/index scan and multi-threading involves sequential read of single block obviously via index scan.
Let us take one example to see the performance of each process

```
SELECT /*+ PARALLEL(S 30) use_nl(S L)*/
S.product_id,L.shop_id
from apps S,shop L
where S.apps_id=L.apps_id
and L.shop_region='ASIA';
```

This will take roughly 0.2 sec.

Note that here in small table "apps" (alias S) we have imposed the parallelism of degree 30. This is the opposite of what we do in the parallelism (approach 3) where in the big table only we impose parallelism.

This approach 4 (nested loop multi-threading using parallelism) does not work when the query contains "WHERE IN" clause or "WHERE EXISTS" clause because oracle apparently cannot divide the work and coordinate the nested loop slaves.

Also note approach 3 implements parallelism whereas approach 4 implements multi-threading. The difference between parallelism and multi-threading is that parallelism usually involves full table/index scan and multi-threading involves sequential read of single block obviously via index scan. Both approach 3 and 4 uses parallelism but in <u>opposite</u> ways.

Note: One more thing I would like to add on top of the methods mentioned: I have seen that sometimes hash join is better than nested loop join even if it completely fits the nested loop join criteria. E.g. when you use in the where clause "(cola, colb) IN (select x, y from tab...) "oracle uses a nested loop join and takes hours however if you convert this "(cola||colb) IN (select x||y from tab...) "it uses a hash join and finish in few minutes only. Have this trick in your hand and check if it helps in some of your solutions.

Tips 7: Use "WHERE" clause or "HAVING" clause?

As a rule "WHERE" clause is used to filter the normal data and "HAVING" clause is used to filter the <u>grouped data</u> and <u>also to filter normal data</u>. So both are useful in their own way.
However when there is a question to use "WHERE or HAVING" clause to filter data you must make sure you use "WHERE" clause to filter normal data and should not use "HAVING" clause to filter normal data.

Approach 1: Using "HAVING" clause
The "HAVING" clause filters group of rows after they have been grouped. So this grouping operation will take some time to execute and consume some resource. Now if you do not need some grouped data as a matter of understanding one should not group that data in the first place.
For e.g.
```
SELECT deptno,
   COUNT(*)
FROM emp
GROUP BY Deptno
HAVING deptno NOT   IN(2,3)
AND COUNT(       *)>500;
```

In this example you are unnecessarily grouping deptno for deptno in (2, 3) and then in "HAVING" clause you discard the data.

Approach 2: Using "WHERE" clause

184

To make the query in approach 1, efficient and reduce the overhead of grouping unnecessary deptno you need to first filter the deptno in "WHERE" clause instead of "HAVING" clause.

The restructured query look as below:

```
SELECT deptno,
   COUNT(*)
FROM emp
WHERE deptno NOT IN(2,3)
GROUP BY Deptno
HAVING COUNT(*)>500;
```

The execution path of a query is as follows:
WHERE → GROUP BY → HAVING → ORDER BY
So ensure that filtering activities are executed as early as possible rather than leaving them all to the final "HAVING" step.

This is a very simple tip which is often ignored resulting in a huge performance penalty, especially in an environment where these kinds of query are executed millions of times and hence are resource intensive.

Tips 8: Use Oracle clause IN or EXISTS or DISTINCT And How to Refactor query to avoid "DISTINCT" keyword from the query?

Here we will discuss ways to refactor query to eliminate costly sorting which is incurred when you use "DISTINCT".

From experience we have seen that "EXISTS" is better than "IN". Also many times we can avoid the very expensive "DISTINCT" keyword and use "EXISTS" clause to get the distinct value from Oracle.

You use "IN" clause to check if the value is present in a table or in a data-set whereas you use "EXISTS" clause to check only the existence of row (not any actual data).

You can display the unique value in a table by using "DISTINCT" keyword. The "DISTINCT" keyword internally sorts the retrieved rows (all data) and then removes the duplicates and displays the unique values. This is a very expensive operation. However using "EXISTS" you can display only the distinct values without using "DISTINCT" keyword.

We will check all the 3 examples here
In app table you have all the unique app_id (i.e. product id), let's say you have 10000 app_id
In purchase table you have all the app_id which has been purchased by any customer. So app_id may be present in purchase table more than 1 time or it may not present at all if no one purchased that product. Let us say in purchase you have 100000 records.

Now our objective is to display all the unique product id (app_id) which has been at least purchased by 1 person.

We can achieve this by 3 methods:

Method "IN"

```
SELECT app_id FROM app a WHERE app_id IN
   (SELECT app_id FROM purchase b
   );
```

This will take 5 seconds...

Method "DISTINCT"

185

```
SELECT DISTINCT a.app_id
FROM app a, purchase b
WHERE a.app_id=b.app_id;
```

This will take 130 seconds...

Method "EXISTS"
```
SELECT app_id
FROM app a
WHERE EXISTS
   (SELECT 1 FROM purchase b WHERE b.app_id=a.app_id
   );
```
This will take 1 second...

So it is evident from the example that "EXISTS" is better than "IN" and "DISTINCT" and you know how you can refactor your query to use "EXISTS" instead of the very expensive "DISTINCT" clause in many scenarios.

Tips 9: Oracle IN clause or EXISTS clause or INTERSECT or JOIN clause?

Here we will discuss again more ways to refactor a query for better performance.

When you have requirement to derive a set of values from two or more source tables there are different ways to derive the result based on the complexity of the requirement.
To demonstrate the relative performance of each method here is a simple example. Please note in order to see considerable difference in performance you need to use complex query with multiple joins and a minimum of 3-4 tables. For a simple query it does not make any difference whether you use any of the 4 methods.

Approach 1: Using "IN" method
You use "IN" clause to check if the value is present in a table

```
SELECT a.app_id
FROM app a
WHERE a.app_id=2345
AND app_id   IN
   (SELECT b.app_id FROM app_repository b WHERE b.app_id =2345
   );
```

This takes approx. 3 seconds

Approach 2: Using "EXISTS" method

You use "EXISTS" clause to check only the existence of row (not any actual data).

```
SELECT a.app_id
FROM app a
WHERE a.app_id=2345
AND EXISTS
   (SELECT 1 FROM app_repository b WHERE b.app_id=a.app_id AND b.app_id =2345
   );
```

This takes approx. 1 seconds

Approach 3: Using "JOIN" method

```
SELECT DISTINCT a.app_id
FROM app a,
   app_repository b
WHERE a.app_id=b.app_id
AND a.app_id  =2345;
```

Note here you need to use distinct clause to eliminate duplicate records.
This takes approx. 4 seconds

Approach 4: Using "INTERSECT" method

```
SELECT a.app_id FROM app a WHERE a.app_id=2345
INTERSECT
SELECT b.app_id FROM app_repository b WHERE b.app_id=2345;
```

This takes approx. 1 second

From analysis we found instead of using "IN" clause to derive the final set of rows from different sources it is advisable to use JOIN or INTERSECT. However many a time if you use JOIN you need to use DISTINCT keyword to remove the duplicate, but INTERSECT will internally remove the duplicates.

So it is suggested to use a set operator like INTERSECT to combine different criteria and get the result quickly.
So in a nutshell
1. If your requirement is to display the result irrespective of whether there are any duplicates then it is better to use JOIN or INTERSECT rather than "IN" clause. INTERSECT is preferable.
2. If your requirement is to display the result without duplicates it is better to use IN or EXISTS or INTERSECT instead of JOIN clause. INTERSECT is most preferable. However you must try all approaches before deciding which to use as performance tuning is an iterative process. There is no one size fits all solution in Oracle. These are just recommendations.

Tips 10: Materialized view Or SQL Result Cache in 11g?

Here we will discuss how to get the result of a query stored in permanent form but always provide the latest data.

Materialized view is a database object which physically stores the pre-joined complex views and pre-computed result of a complex query. So when user tries to select from the mview, Oracle does not re-execute the underlying query but directly displays the pre-computed results from the stored mview. The mview is refreshed only then the underlying query is re-executed. So data in the mview is as accurate as the point of time of refresh but not accurate at the current point of time. So when taking a decision to use mview you must consider whether the mview being out of sync for certain period will impact the business. [Please note by using Automatic fast refresh of materialized views we can resolve the out of sync data issue, however it impacts throughput of application as it has to write into mview log on each commit and hence is very expensive]

In Oracle 11g we can overcome the issue of out of sync data in materialized view by means of
"**Result_cache**" hint.
Also by using "**Result_cache**" hints you avoid the overhead of setting up and maintaining a materialized view.

```
SELECT /*+ result_cache */
  a.*.b.* FROM tab1, tab2 WHERE a.id=b.id;
```

So here when the query is executed for the 1st time it stores the result in a result cache similar to storing pre-computed/pre-joined query result and hence subsequent execution will use the result cache instead of re-executing the query.
However there is another advantage of using result cache: it will automatically refresh the result cache when the underlying base table's data are modified. So this result into getting accurate data as of current point of time with high response time without impacting throughput.

Tips 11: How to Convert a PL/SQL For loop update into SQL update or Merge for performance improvement

Here we will discuss how to convert PL/SQL code to SQL merge to get huge performance boost.

People generally use Oracle "for loop" when we have two big tables with millions of rows and would like to update one of the tables based on the other table for some complex scenario with multiple complex joins with other tables.

However we have seen better performance using Sql update or Merge.
Here is simple example showing how to convert a "for loop" update into Sql update and merge.

```
BEGIN
   FOR j IN
   (SELECT SYS_ID, OBJECTID, CODE FROM Tab1
   )
   LOOP
     UPDATE tab2
     SET CODE      =j.CODE
     WHERE SYS_ID =j.SYS_ID
     AND objectid =j.objectid
     AND N_CD      <>12;
   END LOOP;
END;
/
```

Note: Inside the FOR LOOP the "UPDATE" statement is executed 1 million times if the "SELECT" statement returns 1 million rows. Here the "UPDATE" statement evaluates the condition **N_CD<>12** 1 million times and this causes performance bottleneck. So to improve performance you can pull the filter condition **N_CD<>12** from "UPDATE" and place it in FOR LOOP as below:

```
SELECT sys_id,objectid,code FROM tab1 WHERE N_CD<>12
```

So now **N_CD<>12** will be evaluated only for 1 time instead of million times and give huge performance benefit. **N_CD** column is present both in Tab1 and Tab2. Refactoring a code give huge performance boost. So try to refactor your code when possible.

In order to convert this PL/SQL block to a "MERGE" statement you need to define target table based on all the columns referred in above update. Source table will be as per "FOR LOOP" SELECT.
The Join clause should be Main join clause used in the update as below:

```
MERGE INTO
( SELECT CODE, SYS_ID, objectid, N_CD FROM tab2 WHERE N_CD <>12
) D USING
( SELECT SYS_ID, OBJECTID, CODE FROM Tab1
) S ON ( D.SYS_ID =S.SYS_ID AND D.objectid =S.objectid )
WHEN MATCHED THEN
  UPDATE SET D.CODE = S.CODE;
```

This gives more than 1000% improvement on performance.
With complex update we have seen the time taken in the update "for loop" was 1 hour, and using Merge command it comes down to 1 minute.

You can use direct update also for this purpose to improve the performance

```
UPDATE
  (SELECT src.SYS_ID ,
    src.OBJECTID ,
    src.CODE tgt.SYS_ID ,
    tgt.OBJECTID ,
    tgt.CODE ,
    tgt.N_CD
  FROM Tab1 src ,
    Tab2 tgt
  WHERE src.SYS_ID =tgt.SYS_ID
  AND src.objectid =tgt.objectid
  AND tgt.N_CD      <>12
  )
SET tgt.CODE= src.CODE;
```

This co-related update is almost as good as the Merge. However I have seen Merge perform better than the co-related update in many situations.

Tips 12: Query refactoring for Hierarchical query "OR" clause or "UNION" clause?

Here we will discuss how to refactor a query to use "UNION" clause instead of "OR" clause to get better performance.

When you want to derive the result from a hierarchical query do not use OR clause as it makes the optimizer use FULL table scan and query performance is affected badly.
In fact Oracle suggest not to use OR clause and their advice is to use UNION instead.

Example: OR clause with hierarchical query

```
SELECT *
FROM tab1
WHERE id=6
OR
ID IN
  (SELECT id
  FROM tab1
    START WITH parent_id IN
    (SELECT id FROM tab1 WHERE id=7
    )
    CONNECT BY prior id=parent_id
  );
```

This uses full table scan and it takes **10 min** to return the data,

189

However if you use normal sub query or direct values in the "IN" clause it will work fast.

So what is the solution to get the result on the same query with some refactoring?

Solution for OR clause with hierarchical query

Just use "UNION" instead of "OR" clause as below:

```
SELECT * FROM tab1 WHERE id=6
UNION
SELECT *
FROM tab1
WHERE id IN
  (SELECT id
  FROM tab1
    START WITH parent_id IN
    (SELECT id FROM tab1 WHERE id=7
    )
    CONNECT BY prior id=parent_id
  );
```

This uses index scan and finishes in 5 sec.

The reason behind the performance improvement is because "UNION" just combine two simple operations and hence quick However "OR" clause confuses the optimizer and force it to use sub-optimal explain plan.
Note: Hierarchical query has been discussed in detail in Chapter 1 Concepts 17: **Hierarchical Query**

Tips 13: Mutating trigger resolution using collection OR Global temporary table?

A trigger select from a table which is undergoing change results in an error. Here we will discuss different approaches to resolve this.

Mutation means changing. When a table is undergoing changes and a row level trigger tries to select from or modify that table, then oracle throws mutating table error (ORA-4091).
So when the table is getting modified and subsequently the trigger is fired and the trigger body uses SELECT or any DML on the triggering table, then the trigger will not get the correct value. So mutating error is issued to maintain the data integrity.

Example
One Organization has equipment storage system. In that organization so far only new equipment comes to the repository. However a new need arises: As per the agreement some of the existing equipment may be replaced with some better equipment based on terms and condition.

Requirement is: System should check if the equipment code (OPTCODE+NOMBLOC) is present in the table or not. If it is not present then insert the full details of equipment , If the equipment code is present then remove the existing details of the equipment and insert only the new details with same equipment code (OPTCODE+NOMBLOC)

To resolve this you need to use a trigger, but if we use normal trigger to check if the code being inserted into table is already present in the table then you will get mutating trigger ORA-04091 error.

You can remove the mutating trigger error by using autonomous transaction. However if you make the trigger autonomous then the trigger cannot see the changes done by the insert statement and hence business validation fails and we will get erroneous data (**but no error!**).

There are 2 ways to resolve this:

Solution 1 (Use PL/SQL collection)

This solution is to use one package inside which you will store the details fetched by the row level trigger. Then in a statement level trigger you will loop through each record of the table and match against the details inserted by the insert statement and stored in package collection variable. Here is the full code (modified to show the lighter version)

```
CREATE TABLE COMP_INVENTORY_T
  ( OPTCODE NUMBER(10), NOMBLOC VARCHAR2(100)
  );


CREATE OR REPLACE
PACKAGE pack_1
AS
Type rec IS TABLE OF COMP_INVENTORY_T%ROWTYPE INDEX BY binary_integer;
  L_inv_rec rec;
END;
/


CREATE OR REPLACE TRIGGER mutate_row_level_trig Before
  INSERT ON COMP_INVENTORY_T FOR EACH row
  DECLARE
  I NUMBER :=pack_1.L_inv_rec.count+1;
  BEGIN
    pack_1.L_inv_rec(i).OPTCODE :=:new.OPTCODE;
    pack_1.L_inv_rec(i).NOMBLOC :=:new.NOMBLOC;
  END;
  /
```

```
CREATE OR REPLACE TRIGGER mutate_statement_level_trig AFTER
  INSERT ON COMP_INVENTORY_T DECLARE X NUMBER;
 v_count NUMBER;
 -- PRAGMA AUTONOMOUS_TRANSACTION;
 BEGIN
   FOR I IN 1..pack_1.L_inv_rec.count
   LOOP
     IF(pack_1.L_inv_rec(i).NOMBLOC = 'OPTION REMISE')
       THEN
       SELECT COUNT(*)
       INTO v_count
       FROM COMP_INVENTORY_T
       WHERE OPTCODE= pack_1.L_inv_rec(i).OPTCODE
       AND NOMBLOC IN ('OPTION INCLUSE','OPTION SOUSCRITE') ;
       dbms_output.put_line('v_count value is:'||v_count);
       IF ( v_count = 0 ) THEN
         NULL;
       END IF ;
       IF ( v_count > 0 ) THEN
         DELETE
         FROM COMP_INVENTORY_T
         WHERE OPTCODE= pack_1.L_inv_rec(i).OPTCODE
         AND NOMBLOC  =pack_1.L_inv_rec(i).NOMBLOC;
       END IF ;
     END IF;
   END LOOP;
 END;
 /
```

Solution 2 (Use temporary table)
Alternatively you can use Global temporary table to resolve the nuisance of mutating table

```
CREATE GLOBAL TEMPORARY TABLE inventory_temp_t(
   OPTCODE       NUMBER(10),
   NOMBLOC   VARCHAR2(10)
) ON COMMIT DELETE ROWS;

CREATE OR REPLACE TRIGGER mutate_row_level_trig Before
  INSERT ON COMP_INVENTORY_T FOR EACH row BEGIN
  INSERT
  INTO inventory_temp_t
    (
      OPTCODE,
      NOMBLOC
    )
    VALUES
    (
      :new.OPTCODE,
      :new.NOMBLOC
    );
  END;
error.  /
```

```
CREATE OR REPLACE TRIGGER mutate_statement_level_trig AFTER
  INSERT ON COMP_INVENTORY_T DECLARE X NUMBER;
  v_count NUMBER;
  -- PRAGMA AUTONOMOUS_TRANSACTION;
  BEGIN
    FOR I IN
    (SELECT * FROM inventory_temp_t)
    LOOP
      IF(I.NOMBLOC = 'OPTION REMISE') THEN
        SELECT COUNT(*)
        INTO v_count
        FROM COMP_INVENTORY_T
        WHERE OPTCODE= I.OPTCODE
        AND NOMBLOC IN ('OPTION INCLUSE','OPTION SOUSCRITE') ;
        dbms_output.put_line('v_count value is:'||v_count);
        IF ( v_count = 0 ) THEN
          NULL;
        END IF ;
        IF ( v_count > 0 ) THEN
          DELETE FROM COMP_INVENTORY_T
          WHERE OPTCODE= I.OPTCODE AND NOMBLOC =I.NOMBLOC;
        END IF ;
      END IF;
    END LOOP;
  END;
  /
```
Using one of these approaches you can resolve mutating table error. However the Global temporary table approach (solution 2) seems to be better solution than PL/SQL collection (solution 1) as when you rollback any DML then the PL/SQL table contents will not be cleaned up.

Chapter 7: Generic know how on Oracle SQL for developer (26 Pages)

In database development knowing how a feature can be implemented in different versions of the database is a matter of necessity.

When I started using oracle versions 10g, 11g and 12c in parallel in multiple projects I found it extremely difficult to navigate between different versions of Oracle releases.

There are a lot of additional features in Oracle 12c which require an alternative approach to derive similar functionality in database versions prior to 12c.

In this chapter we will cover **SQL** tips not covered in previous chapters so that you will know the different approaches employed in different releases of database to achieve the same functionality.

Tips 1: Invisible column in 12c

Tips 2: Session level sequence in 12c?

Tips 3: Extended data type in Oracle 12c?

Tips 4: Truncate table cascade in 12c and prior to 12c solution?

Tips 5: Create default value for NULL column in 12c?

Tips 6: Auto-populate column using Sequence as Column default value in 12c?

Tips 7: Default primary key column value using IDENTITY type in 12c?

Tips 8: Occurrence of substring in a string using new regular expression in 11g and prior to 11g solution?

Tips 9: Recursively expand sqltext of a view and find how parser rewrite the SQL in 12c?

Tips 10: Get distinct count of values across columns

Tips 11: Fully qualified column reference in Oracle SQL

Tips 12: Advantage and disadvantage of Truncate and steps to check and reclaim unused space

Tips 13: Ignore the LEFT OUTER JOIN result (unwanted records) from 3 or more table JOIN

Tips 14: Control trigger firing using "FOLLOWS" and "PRECEDES" clause in 11g

Tips 15: Improve performance using Oracle Aliases and impact of choosing wrong datatype

Tips 16: Minimize number of table look up and improve response time

Tips 17: Un-interrupted database testing using SET TRANSACTION

Tips 18: Connection to sqlplus from command line and example of multiversioning and read consistency.

Tips 19: Danger of using "NOT IN" clause

Tips 1: Invisible column in 12c?

Here we will discuss how to make a column invisible to all and visible to those who are aware of the existence of the column.

Invisible index and virtual column were introduced in oracle 11gR1 and **Invisible column** was introduced in Oracle 12c. **Invisible column** concept came from the requirement of data hiding which used to be done using Oracle view or some kind of security filter using FGAC.

In Oracle 12c R1 you can have an invisible column in a table. So once you define a column as invisible that column will not appear in generic query (i.e. SELECT * FROM ...).
You **can see the column**
- By explicitly referring to the column name in "**select**" or "**insert**" statement
- By describing the table (provided you use SET command in sql*plus in 12c
  SET COLINVISIBLE ON|OFF)

Any normal column, **virtual column** and partition column can be defined as **invisible**
However external table, temporary table and cluster table will not support invisible column.

Here is the syntax to create invisible column
```
CREATE TABLE emp
 (empno NUMBER,
 ename VARCHAR2(40),
 sal NUMBER(9,4) INVISIBLE
 );
```

In order to convert a column from invisible to visible use:
```
ALTER TABLE emp MODIFY (sal VISIBLE );
```

In order to convert a column from visible to invisible again use:
```
ALTER TABLE emp MODIFY (sal INVISIBLE );
```

Finding hidden column:
You can find the list of invisible columns using:
```
SELECT owner,table_name,column_name,hidden_column
FROM all_tab_cols
WHERE owner     = 'U1'
AND table_name = 'EMP';
```

Notes:
- In 12c, **even in a view** you can make a column invisible:
  ```
  CREATE OR REPLACE VIEW emp_vw (empno, ename, sal INVISIBLE)
  AS
     SELECT empno, ename, sal FROM emp;
  ```

- In 12c you can make a **virtual column** also visible and invisible similar to a normal column.

- Invisible columns are not considered when you use TABLE_NAME%ROWTYPE

195

Tips 2: Session level sequence in 12c?

Here we will discuss how to reset a sequence value for any new session automatically.

In oracle 12c you can create session level sequence by using keyword "session". The default one is global. Session level sequence produces unique values for a session and once the session ends the sequence is reset, unlike global level session.
Session sequence performs better than global sequence because session sequence does not keep anything in data dictionary. However session sequence can be used only in a few specific scenarios

- During loading to staging table where the sequence is used by single session.
- As a surrogate key in <u>global temporary</u> table

The syntax for creating and converting to session and global level is given below:

```
CREATE SEQUENCE session_seq START WITH 1 INCREMENT BY 1 SESSION;

ALTER SEQUENCE session_seq GLOBAL|SESSION;
```

Tips 3: Extended data type in Oracle 12c?

Here we will discuss how in 12c database table the size of VARCHAR2 can be of size 32767 byte as against 4000 byte in 11gR2.

Prior to Oracle 12c maximum size of RAW, VARCHAR2, NVARCHAR2 data type table columns were 2000, 4000 and 4000 respectively.
In oracle 12c the size of these data types has been extended up to 32767 bytes in database table column.
In order to use the extended character size in 12c you need to set the initialization parameter **MAX_STRING_SIZE** to EXTENDED. The default value is STANDARD. If default value STANDARD is used then the size of these column will be same as it was prior to 12c.

Steps to set the parameter:

```
SHUTDOWN;
STARTUP UPGRADE;
ALTER system SET max_string_size = EXTENDED scope=spfile;
Run $ORACLE_HOME/rdbms/admin/utl32k.sql
SHUTDOWN IMMEDIATE;
STARTUP;
```

Once you upgrade your database to use setting EXTENDED you cannot revert it to STANDARD.

Advantage of using extended data types is that it will reduce the requirement to use LOB data types most of the time.

Note: From 11g onward PGA memory allocation is dynamic if you declare a VARCHAR2 variable of size greater than 4000. If you declare a variable less than or equal to 4000 byte then PGA memory is fully allocated (i.e. not dynamic). And hence it is suggested to declare a variable to a size greater than 4000 in case you are not sure of approx. length of the variable. By declaring the VARCHAR2 bigger you save large amount of PGA memory.
How to calculate the amount of PGA memory allocation refer to Chapter 1 Concepts 18: SGA, UGA and PGA

Tips 4: Truncate table cascade in 12c and prior to 12c solution

Here we will discuss how to truncate a parent table which has a relation with child table.

Prior to oracle 12c if any table is referred to by a child table using foreign key relationship then you cannot truncate the parent table.
Even if there is no data present in child table, still the truncate option will not work for parent table, it will give an error:
```
TRUNCATE table P1

SQL Error: ORA-02266: unique/primary keys in table referenced by enabled foreign
02266. 00000 -  "unique/primary keys in table referenced by enabled foreign keys
*Cause:     An attempt was made to truncate a table with unique or
            primary keys referenced by foreign keys enabled in another table.
            Other operations not allowed are dropping/truncating a partition of a
            partitioned table or an ALTER TABLE EXCHANGE PARTITION.
*Action:    Before performing the above operations the table, disable the
            foreign key constraints in other tables. You can see what
            constraints are referencing a table by issuing the following
            command:
            SELECT * FROM USER_CONSTRAINTS WHERE TABLE_NAME = "tabnam";
```

So prior to oracle 12c you have <u>two **options**</u> **(As you cannot use truncate when you have child table)**
  ➢ Delete all the dependencies and then delete the parent table:
    E.g.

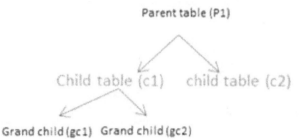

Parent table (P1)

Child table (c1)   child table (c2)

Grand child (gc1) Grand child (gc2)

In the above scenario in order to delete "P1" table you need to traverse the tree and find out all the dependencies and then you need to delete in the following sequence only
gc1->gc2->c1->c2>P1
I have shown only 2 levels however the dependency tree can go to any level and there may be interdependency between child tables. So it can be very tricky to find all the recursive dependencies and execute the delete.

  ➢ Foreign key is implemented using below command by default:
```
ALTER TABLE C1 ADD CONSTRAINT EMP_FK1 FOREIGN KEY (dept_id)
REFERENCES P1(dept_id);
```
And hence if you fire
```
DELETE FROM P1;
```

It will fail with error
```
02292. 00000 - "integrity constraint (%s.%s) violated - child record found"
```

So the solution is:

Recreate the foreign key constraint with "ON DELETE CASCADE"

```
ALTER TABLE C1 ADD CONSTRAINT EMP_FK1 FOREIGN KEY (dept_id)
REFERENCES P1(dept_id) ON DELETE CASCADE;
```

And then fire:

```
DELETE FROM P1;
```

This will delete records from child tables too.

However in Oracle 12c you can use Truncate as below:

```
TRUNCATE table P1 CASCADE
```

This will automatically initiate recursive truncate of all the child tables and then the parent table.
However note for this option to work you must have foreign key present in all the child tables with reference as ON DELETE CASCADE using the command as below (here "emp" is child table and "DEPT" is parent table)

```
ALTER TABLE C1 ADD CONSTRAINT EMP_FK1 FOREIGN KEY (dept_id)
REFERENCES P1(dept_id) ON DELETE CASCADE;
```

Note: since "ON DELETE CASCADE" silently, without any warning, deletes rows from child tables it is sometime a business requirement not to delete the child rows and instead update the child rows setting parent column **value to null**. In order to do that use below step:

```
ALTER TABLE C1 DROP CONSTRAINT EMP_FK1;

ALTER TABLE C1 ADD CONSTRAINT EMP_FK1 FOREIGN KEY (dept_id)
REFERENCES P1(dept_id) ON DELETE SET NULL;
```

So this will not remove rows from child tables, rather it will just update the reference parent column to null in the child tables.

Tips 5: Create default value for NULL column in 12c

Here we will explore how to use a default value even if you mistakenly insert null for a table column.

Prior to Oracle 12c when you want to keep a default value for the nullable column you use DEFAULT keyword in table creation. However when you insert null the default value is lost.

```
CREATE TABLE t
  (a NUMBER PRIMARY KEY,
  b NUMBER DEFAULT 12
  );

INSERT INTO t(a) VALUES(1);
INSERT INTO t(a,b) VALUES(2,NULL);
INSERT INTO t(a,b) VALUES(3,23);
COMMIT;
```

Now when you run a select you will see

```
SELECT * FROM t;
```

	A		B
1	1		12
2	2		(null)
3	3		23

Note in 1st insert statement we have omitted the default column and hence it takes the default column value 12 for A=1
In 3rd Insert statement I have explicitly mentioned column value 23 for column "b" and hence it has taken that value 23 for A=3

Now the problem is in 2nd insert. When we insert null in column "b" the default value 12 is ignored.

In order to resolve this before Oracle 12c you have to have logic in your application to check if the value is null then set it to default.

However in Oracle 12c you need not do this, it will automatically use the default value if you insert NULL in that column. This is possible because of the construct "DEFAULT ON NULL"

```
CREATE TABLE t
  (a NUMBER PRIMARY KEY,
  b NUMBER DEFAULT ON NULL 12
  );

INSERT INTO t(a) VALUES(1);
INSERT INTO t(a,b) VALUES(2,NULL);
INSERT INTO t(a,b) VALUES(3,23);
COMMIT;
```

Now when you run a select you will see
```
SELECT * FROM t;
```

	A		B
1	1		12
2	2		12
3	3		23

Note: If the table "t" is created with "b number default 12" (instead of "b number default ON NULL 12" introduced in 12c) then if you insert "NULL" then it will store "NULL". If you do not insert anything in the column "b" then it will use the default value "12".

Tips 6: Auto-populate column using Sequence as Column default value in 12c?

Here we will discuss mechanism to auto populate primary key column using sequence without the use of trigger.

Prior to Oracle 12c you cannot use sequence_name.nextval to create a default column value. In order to do that you need to make use of a trigger as below:

```
CREATE SEQUENCE t_seq START WITH 1;
DROP TABLE t;
CREATE TABLE t
  (a NUMBER PRIMARY KEY,
   b NUMBER DEFAULT 12
   );
CREATE OR REPLACE TRIGGER t_trig BEFORE INSERT ON t FOR EACH ROW
BEGIN
  IF :new.a IS NULL THEN :new.a :=t_seq.nextval;
END IF;
END t_trig;
/
```

Now if you run
```
INSERT INTO t(b) VALUES(24);
```
Table "t" will have a record as below where column A has been populated by the trigger:

A	B
1	24

In Oracle 12c you need not use a trigger as you can directly use **nextval** attribute of sequence to create default column value as shown below:

```
CREATE SEQUENCE t_seq START WITH 1;
DROP TABLE t;
CREATE TABLE t
  (a NUMBER DEFAULT t_seq.nextval PRIMARY KEY,
   b NUMBER DEFAULT ON NULL 12
   );
```

Now if you insert a record it will populate the primary key "a" from the sequence t_seq

```
SET serveroutput ON
DECLARE
  var_a NUMBER;
BEGIN
  INSERT INTO t(b) VALUES(17) RETURNING a INTO var_a;
  dbms_output.put_line('value is:'||var_a);
END;
/
```
Output:
```
PL/SQL procedure successfully completed.

value is:1
```

Note: Throughput of application improve dramatically when you use sequence.nextval instead of trigger based approach to populate a default column in 12c.

Tips 7: Default primary key column value using IDENTITY type in 12c

Here we will discuss mechanism to auto populate primary key column using IDENTITY type in 12c without the use of trigger.

Prior to Oracle 12c if you want to default the primary key column value you need to take the help of trigger as shown in the above Tips,
In Oracle 12c you can default the primary key column value using .NEXTVAL attribute of sequence as shown in the above Tips.
Alternatively in 12c you can use IDENTITY type for the same purpose. So without using a sequence you can populate the primary key with default value as shown below:

```
CREATE TABLE t
  (
    a NUMBER GENERATED AS IDENTITY PRIMARY KEY,
    b NUMBER DEFAULT ON NULL 12
  );
```

You can set the default column value and choose the next number

```
CREATE TABLE t
  (
    a NUMBER GENERATED BY DEFAULT AS IDENTITY (
    START WITH 10 INCREMENT BY 2) PRIMARY KEY,
    b NUMBER DEFAULT ON NULL 12
  );
```

Basically Identity type will internally create a sequence similar to a database sequence and assign that value to the default primary key column.

Tips 8: Occurrence of substring in a string using new regular expression in 11g and prior to 11g solution?

Here we will discuss number of occurrences of a substring inside a string with and without regular expression.

Prior to 11g to get the number of occurrences of a substring in main string you need to develop a user defined function as below

```
  CREATE OR REPLACE
  FUNCTION f_Count_occurrences(
      p_string    IN CLOB,
      p_substring IN VARCHAR2)
    RETURN NUMBER
  IS
    l_occurrences NUMBER;
  BEGIN
    IF ( p_string   IS NOT NULL AND p_substring IS NOT NULL ) THEN
      l_occurrences := ( LENGTH(p_string) - ( NVL(LENGTH(REPLACE(p_string,
      p_substring)), 0) ) ) / LENGTH(p_substring) ;
    END IF;
    RETURN ( l_occurrences );
  END f_count_occurrences;
  /
```

Now when you run

```
SELECT f_Count_occurrences('This is the test for the code', 'the') from dual;
```

You will get output as **2**

Oracle 11g solution

However in 11g oracle has introduced new regular expression function REGEXP_COUNT. This function will return the number of occurrences of a substring in a string.

When you run:

```
SELECT REGEXP_COUNT('This is the test for the code', 'the') from dual;
```

You will get output as **2**

Tips 9: Recursively expand sqltext of a view and find how parser rewrite the SQL in 12c?

Ever struggled to get the definition of recursive views? Here we will discuss how to view full text for all the recursive views and also find the re-written SQL by oracle parser.

A view is used to hide the complexity of code from the developer and also to reduce redundant code in an application as 1 view can be referred to by multiple other views. Prior to oracle 12c to debug any issue you need to expand the sql of all the dependent views of the main view and analyse. This is very tedious exercise especially when recursive depth is large. Good news, Oracle 12c R1 provides the facility to expand the sql text to see the full SQL reference of the view with full reference of dependent recursive views.

Here is very simple dummy example to demonstrate how it works:

```
CREATE TABLE t1
   (owner VARCHAR2(10),object_name VARCHAR2(30),created DATE
   );
CREATE OR REPLACE VIEW v1
AS
   SELECT owner,object_name,created FROM t1;

CREATE OR REPLACE VIEW v2
AS
   SELECT * FROM v1 WHERE created BETWEEN sysdate-5 AND sysdate;

CREATE OR REPLACE VIEW v3
AS
   SELECT * FROM v2 WHERE object_name LIKE 'TEST%';
```

Now to expand v3 we use dbms_utility.expand_sql_text as below:

Make sure you give grant execute on dbms_utility to your user.

```
SET SERVEROUTPUT ON
DECLARE
  v_output CLOB;
BEGIN
  DBMS_UTILITY.expand_sql_text ( input_sql_text => 'SELECT * FROM v3',
                                 output_sql_text => v_output );
  DBMS_OUTPUT.put_line(v_output);
END;
/
```

The output will look like:

```
SELECT "A1"."OWNER" "OWNER","A1"."OBJECT_NAME" "OBJECT_NAME","A1"."CREATED" "CREATED" FROM
(SELECT "A2"."OWNER" "OWNER","A2"."OBJECT_NAME" "OBJECT_NAME","A2"."CREATED" "CREATED" FROM
(SELECT "A3"."OWNER" "OWNER","A3"."OBJECT_NAME" "OBJECT_NAME","A3"."CREATED" "CREATED" FROM
(SELECT "A4"."OWNER" "OWNER","A4"."OBJECT_NAME" "OBJECT_NAME","A4"."CREATED" "CREATED" FROM SYS."T1" "A4") "A3"
WHERE "A3"."CREATED">=SYSDATE-5 AND "A3"."CREATED"<=SYSDATE) "A2" WHERE "A2"."OBJECT_NAME" LIKE 'TEST%') "A1"
```

Note **DBMS_UTILITY.expand_sql_text** not only replaces recursively all the views referred in the input SQL query but it also provides how oracle parser rewrite the code while doing the expansion of SQL.
E.g.
As provided in Chapter 3: Tips 8: Top N query using row limiting clause in 12c
Let us take the same example to show how oracle rewrite the code internally:
```
SELECT * FROM emp ORDER BY SAL DESC
FETCH NEXT 5 ROWS ONLY;
```

You pass this SQL statement to the **expand_sql_text** as below:
```
SET serveroutput ON
DECLARE
  v_output CLOB;
BEGIN
  DBMS_UTILITY.expand_sql_text( input_sql_text => 'select * from emp order by sal desc fetch next 5 rows only', output_sql_text=>v_output);
  DBMS_OUTPUT.put_line(v_output);
END;
/
```

The output will expand the SQL and shown below how your SQL has been rewritten by oracle parser:

```
SELECT "A1"."EMPLOYEE_ID" "EMPLOYEE_ID",
  "A1"."EMPLOYEE_NAME" "EMPLOYEE_NAME",
  "A1"."JOB" "JOB",
  "A1"."MANAGER_ID" "MANAGER_ID",
  "A1"."HIREDATE" "HIREDATE",
  "A1"."SAL" "SAL",
  "A1"."COMMISSION" "COMMISSION",
  "A1"."DEPARTMENT_ID" "DEPARTMENT_ID"
FROM
  (SELECT "A2"."EMPLOYEE_ID" "EMPLOYEE_ID",
    "A2"."EMPLOYEE_NAME" "EMPLOYEE_NAME",
    "A2"."JOB" "JOB",
    "A2"."MANAGER_ID" "MANAGER_ID",
    "A2"."HIREDATE" "HIREDATE",
    "A2"."SAL" "SAL",
    "A2"."COMMISSION" "COMMISSION",
    "A2"."DEPARTMENT_ID" "DEPARTMENT_ID",
    "A2"."SAL" "rowlimit_$_0",
    ROW_NUMBER() OVER ( ORDER BY "A2"."SAL" DESC ) "rowlimit_$$_rownumber"
  FROM "EMP" "A2"
  ) "A1"
WHERE "A1"."rowlimit_$$_rownumber"<=5
ORDER BY "A1"."rowlimit_$_0" DESC;
```

Tips 10: Get distinct count of values across columns

Here we will discuss how can you count values horizontally i.e. on column level.

Generally you get the count of values for rows. However when you need to get the count of values across columns you need to convert column to row using **UNPIVOT** option and display the result.
Here is one simple scenario

```
create table working_country(empid number,country1 varchar2(30),
country2 varchar2(30),country3 varchar2(30));

insert into working_country values(100,'India','Netherland','India');
insert into working_country values(200,'India','Canada','Edinburgh');
insert into working_country values(300,'Canada','Canada','Canada');
insert into working_country values(400,'India','Edinburgh','Edinburgh');
commit;
```

```
select * from working_country;
```

EMPID	COUNTRY1	COUNTRY2	COUNTRY3
100	India	Netherland	India
200	India	Canada	Edinburgh
300	Canada	Canada	Canada
400	India	Edinburgh	Edinburgh

Now requirement is to get the distinct count for each column against each empid so for 1st row the distinct count should be 2 as empid 100 works only in India and Netherland.

100 India   Netherland India   2

Here is the query to achieve this:

```
SELECT a.*,
  b.distinct_cntry_cnt
FROM working_country a,
  (SELECT empid,
    COUNT(*) distinct_cntry_cnt
  FROM
    ( SELECT DISTINCT empid,
      country_name
    FROM working_country UNPIVOT (country_name FOR col IN(country1,country2,country3))
    )
  GROUP BY empid
  )b
WHERE a.empid=b.empid;
```

The result will look as below:

EMPID	COUNTRY1	COUNTRY2	COUNTRY3	DISTINCT_CNTRY_CNT
100 India	Netherland	India		2
400 India	Edinburgh	Edinburgh		2
300 Canada	Canada	Canada		1
200 India	Canada	Edinburgh		3

Note: Few basics regarding usage of COUNT function

Count (*):
This will give total number of records in a table by retrieving all the fields in a table.

Count (1):
This will give total number of records in a table by retrieving the numeric value 1 for each row.

Count (column_name):
This will give total number of records in a table where **column_name is not null**. So if any value of column_name is null then the count (column_name) will evaluate to different value than count (1).To get the total count (including NULL values for the column) you can use **COUNT(NVL(column_name, 1))**

Count (distinct column_name):
This will give total number of **distinct, NOT NULL values of column_name** in a table.

Approx_count_distinct (column_name):
This will give **approximate** total number of **distinct, NOT NULL values** of column_name in a table. This function is introduced in oracle 12c. Performance improvement using this function is significant as compared to **Count** (distinct column name) and hence when you do not have requirement to display the exact distinct count then you can make use of this function for any of your reporting requirements.

Remember that **COUNT (name)** returns the count of an expression but when the expression evaluates to NULL then that particular record is **not included** in the total.

Tips 11: Fully qualified column reference in Oracle SQL?

Here we will discuss how to make Oracle do less work by associating the column with a table alias.

When you are joining multiple tables and selecting certain columns you must make sure you specify the column by prefixing the table or table alias. If we do not specify the table alias against the column Oracle will search each table in the "from" clause to find out the actual table from which the column is present.

Generally we need not prefix the table alias against a column if it is present in only single table. However if it is present in more than 1 table it is must to prefix the table alias against the column otherwise it will fail with oracle error (duplicate column found).

But by referencing table alias against each column (no matter if the column is unique or not) you are instructing oracle not to search for each column in each table mentioned in the FROM clause.

e.g.
```
SELECT col1,col2,col3 FROM tab1 a,tab2 b,tab3 c WHERE a.id=b.id AND b.id=c.id;
```

This example does not fully qualify the column references and hence Oracle needs to search for the existence of col1, col2, col3 in all 3 tables.

In order to fully qualify the column reference here is the code
```
SELECT a.col1,
   b.col2,
   c.col3
FROM tab1 a,
   tab2 b,
   tab3 c
WHERE a.id=b.id
AND b.id =c.id;
```

Tips 12: Advantage and disadvantage of Truncate and steps to check and reclaim unused space

Want to remove data from table? Use Truncate but be aware of pros and cons. Also will discuss how to reset high watermark and claim the unused space.

Advantage:
1. It does the auto commit as it is DDL command
2. It reset the high water mark for the table. **High water mark** is the space used by object. By resetting high water mark to zero we de-allocate all the space and let other object/transactions use the space. This is not possible using delete.
3. It is very fast as compared to delete.

Disadvantage:
1. You cannot rollback the transaction.
2. If the parent table has got the primary key which is referred to by child table then you cannot truncate the table even if the child table does not have any records.
3. You cannot truncate part of the data. You have to either delete all data or none. However if the table is partitioned then you can truncate a single partition instead of whole table.

Note: The table with high water mark not only occupy huge space which cannot be used by oracle but this issue affect the performance of application because now oracle has to do full table scan of the table with more number of blocks (**more than the actual number of blocks because of unused blocks**) to get the required data.

Here is one example to display how "DELETE" operation create unused space and "TRUNCATE" de-allocate the unused space. The solution to reclaim space if you use "DELETE"

```
CREATE TABLE t2 AS
SELECT * FROM all_objects;
```

This has 1 million records.

Note: [Without collecting statistics if you would like to know the high water mark (size in blocks occupied by a table) use:
```
SELECT COUNT(DISTINCT dbms_rowid.rowid_block_number(rowid)) no_of_blocks
FROM t2;
```
This is explained in Chapter 9 Tips 25: understanding ORA_ROWSCN and block number for table rows]

Collect statistics:
```
ANALYZE TABLE T2 compute statistics;
```

Now see the **actual size of table** and **high_water_mark_in_bytes** (**projected size of the table**).
Note the column "**BLOCKS**" signify the high water mark i.e. the projected size of table.
8192 is the size of each BLOCKS (in bytes) in your database.

```
SELECT table_name,
    AVG_ROW_LEN*NUM_ROWS actual_size_in_bytes,
    blocks       *8192 high_water_mark_in_bytes
FROM dba_tables
WHERE owner   ='SCHEMA_NAME'
AND table_name='T2';
```

Now if you use "TRUNCATE" the projected size is showing correctly as high water mark (**blocks**) is reset.

```
TRUNCATE TABLE T2;
ANALYZE TABLE T2 compute statistics;
```

Now see the **actual size of table** and **high_water_mark_in_bytes** (**projected size of the table**) after the truncate operation.

```
SELECT table_name,
    AVG_ROW_LEN*NUM_ROWS actual_size_in_bytes,
    blocks       *8192 high_water_mark_in_bytes
FROM dba_tables
WHERE owner   ='SCHEMA_NAME'
AND table_name='T2';
```

You can see the high water mark is reset and hence projected size and actual size are almost same.

However if you use "**DELETE**" the projected size (high water mark) shows more than actual size.

```
DELETE FROM T2;
ANALYZE TABLE T2 compute statistics;
```

Now see the **actual size of table** and **high_water_mark_in_bytes** (**projected size of the table**) after the DELETE operation.

```
SELECT table_name,
  AVG_ROW_LEN*NUM_ROWS actual_size_in_bytes,
  blocks     *8192 high_water_mark_in_bytes
FROM dba_tables
WHERE owner   ='SCHEMA_NAME'
AND table_name='T2';
```

You can see the high water mark is **not reset** this time and hence projected size is showing huge space occupied but actual size is zero as all the records has been deleted.

Solution to reclaim space:
In order to reclaim the unused space here are the steps:

```
ALTER TABLE t2 enable row movement;
ALTER TABLE t2 shrink space;
ANALYZE TABLE t2 compute statistics;
```

Note: If the table has flashback enabled then you must first disable flashback and then shrink the space.

You can shrink the space associated with any index segments also using the CASCADE clause:

```
ALTER TABLE t2 shrink space CASCADE;
```

See the **actual size of table** and **high_water_mark_in_bytes** (**projected size of the table**) after shrinking the space to reclaim the unused space. Here is the query:

```
SELECT table_name,
  AVG_ROW_LEN*NUM_ROWS actual_size_in_bytes,
  blocks     *8192 high_water_mark_in_bytes
FROM dba_tables
WHERE owner   ='SCHEMA_NAME'
AND table_name='T2';
```

Now you will find the high water mark is **reset** and unused space is reclaimed even if records has been deleted using "DELETE" command. By resetting high water mark there is **significant improvement in application** as oracle has to scan less number of block (**high_water_mark_in_bytes**) to fetch the data.

Note: Using row movement and shrink space command you can reclaim the unused space which changes the clustering factor and change the rowids as rows are moved to different data blocks which in turn may cause slight performance issue (However performance gain is significantly high as compared to performance penalty because of rowids movement) and hence DBA may use **dbms_redefinition** package to organize the table online. This package mainly creates a snapshot of the table and then apply all the table changes to a new table and as part of final step remove the new table.

Tips 13: Ignore the LEFT OUTER JOIN result (unwanted records) from 3 or more table JOIN

Here we will discuss how to eliminate unwanted record from a result-set generated from left outer joins.

Using LEFT OUTER JOIN you will get all the data from main table which does not exist on all the tables which are joined using LEFT OUTER JOIN method.

Let us take one simple scenario
You have main table A with 1000 records,
And you want to join this table with Table B (800 records) and Table C (700 records). The intention is to get the data from Table A, B and C which is present either in Table B or in Table C or both in Table B & C, However if the data of Table A is not present in both Table B & C then do not return the corresponding data.

Approach 1
If you use only normal JOIN for all the 3 tables you will miss some data from B and C.

```
SELECT a.cust_id,
  b.house_no,
  c.area_code
FROM A
JOIN B
ON A.cust_id=B.cust_id
JOIN C
ON A.cust_id=C.cust_id;
```

So not correct approach.

Approach 2
If A is joined with B and C using LEFT OUTER JOIN you will get all the data from A, B and C tables.
However the result-set using this approach contain some data from table A which is not present both in B and C table.

```
SELECT a.cust_id,
  b.house_no,
  c.area_code
FROM A
LEFT OUTER JOIN B
ON A.cust_id=B.cust_id
LEFT OUTER JOIN C
ON A.cust_id=C.cust_id;
```

So this approach also fails to return the required data. It returns extra data when **B.cust_id and C.area_code** are both null.

Approach 3
A is joined with B and C using LEFT OUTER JOIN and then eliminate the selected record if they are not present in both B and C.
So this way you will get the result-set as below
Table A data is present in B but not present in C
Table A data is present in C but not present in B
Table A data is present in both B & C

Basically you want to get all the data **except** when both **B.cust_id and C.area_code** values are null.
Here is the basic code for this scenario

```
SELECT a.cust_id,
  b.house_no,
  c.area_code
FROM A
LEFT OUTER JOIN B
ON A.cust_id=B.cust_id
LEFT OUTER JOIN C
ON A.cust_id=C.cust_id
WHERE (B.cust_id IS NULL OR C.cust_id IS NOT NULL)
  OR
  (B.cust_id IS NOT NULL OR C.cust_id IS  NULL)
  OR
  (B.cust_id IS NOT NULL OR C.cust_id IS NOT NULL);
```

This is too much code and is not good for performance.

Approach 4:
Instead of the above WHERE clause use this:
```
B.cust_id IS NOT NULL OR C.cust_id IS NOT NULL
```

Approach 5
```
SELECT a.cust_id,
  b.house_no,
  c.area_code
FROM A
LEFT OUTER JOIN B
ON A.cust_id=B.cust_id
LEFT OUTER JOIN C
ON A.cust_id=C.cust_id
WHERE NVL(B.cust_id,-9)||NVL(C.cust_id,-8)<> '-9-8';
```

You can use any value when handling NVL, here I used -9 and -8 for this.

Tips 14: Control trigger firing using "FOLLOWS" and "PRECEDES" clause in 11g?

Here we will discuss how to control which order similar kind of trigger executed.

Prior to 11g there was no way you could control the order of firing the same kind of triggers, hence the result after execution of similar kinds of trigger was unpredictable.
However in 11g you can control the order of firing using FOLLOWS clause as below:

```
CREATE TABLE t1(
   id    NUMBER,
   name VARCHAR2(30)
);

CREATE OR REPLACE TRIGGER t1_trig_2
BEFORE INSERT ON t1
FOR EACH ROW
BEGIN
   DBMS_OUTPUT.put_line('ti_trig_2 is Executed');
END;
/

CREATE OR REPLACE TRIGGER t1_trig_1
BEFORE INSERT ON t1
FOR EACH ROW
FOLLOWS t1_trig_2    ⟵————————————————————  This control the firing, trig_2 is fired before trig_1
BEGIN
   DBMS_OUTPUT.put_line('ti_trig_1 is Executed');
END;
/
```

Now when you execute the insert
```
set serveroutput on
insert into t1 values(1,'test');
```

The fire ordering is as per the below **output**
```
1 rows inserted.
ti_trig_2 is Executed
ti_trig_1 is Executed
```

You can use "FOLLOWS" clause can be used in every kind of triggers.
However, you can use PRECEDES clause ONLY in Reverse cross edition triggers.
 ("Reverse cross-edition" triggers are created on non-schema object type).

You can find the sequence of trigger firing from dictionary table all_trigger_ordering
```
SELECT trigger_owner,
   trigger_name,
   referenced_trigger_owner,
   referenced_trigger_name,
   ordering_type
FROM all_trigger_ordering;
```

The **output** will be:

TRIGGER_OWNER	TRIGGER_NAME	REFERENCED_TRIGGER_OWNER	REFERENCED_TRIGGER_NAME	ORDERING_TYPE
U1	T1_TRIG_1	U1	T1_TRIG_2	FOLLOWS

That mean T1_TRIG_2 is fired first and then T2_TRIG_1 is fired.

Tips 15: Improve performance using Oracle Aliases and impact of choosing wrong datatype

Here we will discuss advantage of using Oracle Alias and how improper datatype in your data model impacts performance.

An ALIAS is a way to give a shorthand name to a table or column. It is also used to identify an ambiguous column which is present in more than one table.

<u>Why aliases are required from performance point of view?</u>

> Reduce parse time as oracle engine will not check all the tables and their columns listed in the FROM clause, It will <u>check only the specific table</u> corresponding to the aliased table/column.

> Prevent syntax error occurring when ambiguous column names are added.
  For example

```
SELECT a.empno,
   tax_no,
   b.company_code
FROM emp a,
   company b
WHERE a.comp_code=b.company_code;
```

Now suppose "tax_no" column is added to table COMPANY then the above query will fail.
However if we aliased the above query by using a.tax_no then you will never encounter the error.

> Aliases make the query more compact and easy to debug and maintain.

Impact of choosing wrong data type:
The below example demonstrate how you will get wrong result because of choosing inappropriate datatype in the table design

```
CREATE TABLE Value_check_tab
  (sys_id VARCHAR2(10),sys_name VARCHAR2(30)
  );
```

```
INSERT INTO Value_check_tab VALUES
  (11111,'area office A'
  );
INSERT INTO Value_check_tab VALUES
  (222,'area office B'
  );
INSERT INTO Value_check_tab VALUES
  (876567,'area office C'
  );
INSERT INTO Value_check_tab VALUES
  (78901234,'area office D'
  );
INSERT INTO Value_check_tab VALUES
  (9988,'area office E'
  );
INSERT INTO Value_check_tab VALUES
  (654321,'area office F'
  );
INSERT INTO Value_check_tab VALUES
  (812345,'area office G'
  );
INSERT INTO Value_check_tab VALUES
  (687890,'area office H'
  );
```

Now if you try to compare sys_id based on inequality i.e. if the sys_id is greater than or less than the previous value it will give incorrect result.

Simply run the below query and it will order the data incorrectly.

```
SELECT * FROM Value_check_tab ORDER BY 1 DESC;
```

The output is displayed as below:

SYS_ID	SYS_NAME
9988	area office E
876567	area office C
812345	area office G
78901234	area office D
687890	area office H
654321	area office F
222	area office B
11111	area office A

The reson for displaying the data in wrong order is because the datatype for "SYS_ID" column is Varchar2 and in a string "9" come after "1" and hence 9988 is considered greater than 876567 and displayed accordingly.

In order to resolve this we have 2 solution:

Solution 1:

Alter the table structure to make the column "SYS_ID" as NUMBER instead of VARCHAR2

Solution 2:

Convert sys_id from varchar2 to number and run the query as below:

```
SELECT * FROM Value_check_tab ORDER BY to_number(sys_id) DESC;
```

Output is ordered correctly as below:

SYS_ID	SYS_NAME
78901234	area office D
876567	area office C
812345	area office G
687890	area office H
654321	area office F
11111	area office A
9988	area office E
222	area office B

Tips 16: Minimize number of table look up and improve response time

Here we will discuss how to reduce table I/O by refactoring a query.

I/O is the most important component of response time because oracle has to access the data block from the physical disk. By means of re-sequencing/reorganizing table data you can reduce the disk I/O to a large extent.
There is another way to reduce the disk I/O by means of reducing the number of table lookups. By minimizing the table lookups you can reduce the physical data block access and hence improve the response time of database operation for "select" or "update" as shown below.

Here is one example:

Reducing lookup in SELECT:
Instead of using
```
 SELECT *
FROM some_table
WHERE column1 IN
  (SELECT column1 FROM tab1
  )
AND column2 IN
  (SELECT column2 FROM tab1
  );
```

Use the below which will access the table "tab1" only once:
```
SELECT *
FROM some_table
WHERE (column1,column2) IN
  (SELECT column1,column2 FROM tab1
  );
```

Reducing lookup in UPDATE:

Instead of using this:

```
UPDATE some_table set column1= (SELECT column1 FROM tab1 where val=12)
, column2 =(SELECT column2 FROM tab1 where val=12)
WHERE id=3001;
```

Use the below:

```
UPDATE some_table set (column1,column2)
= (SELECT column1,column2 FROM tab1 where val=12)
WHERE id=3001;
```

This will reduce the disk I/O to a large extent.

Tips 17: Un-interrupted database testing using SET TRANSACTION

Here we will discuss mechanism as to how tester can do DB testing without being interrupted by transaction committed by other sessions.

Oracle support multi-versioning i.e. it provides more than one version of data to different concurrent users. Isolation is one of the oracle ACID property. It means transaction cannot be visible until the transaction is committed. By default oracle isolation level is **read committed** i.e. any changes committed by other session will be reflected in the query result.

Sometime Oracle database tester wants to do some functionality test without being affected by any Transaction (**DML+COMMIT**) done by any other sessions. Oracle provides a solution to achieve that:

Session 1
=======
```
SET transaction ISOLATION level serializable;
```

From this time in **session 1** any kind of query you make against any tables will be consistent and same and not affected/modified by transaction committed by **other sessions** on any tables. So tester can safely test any scenario uninterrupted.

Once the testing is done if you want to test based on the changes done by other sessions then simply do this from **session 1**
"COMMIT"
 Or
"ROLLBACK"
This will end the transaction for **session 1** and the **session 1** will work as per oracle default isolation level and hence do holistic testing based on as of now data.

Note: using **"SERIALIZABLE"** isolation level user in **session 1** can do update/insert/delete also but the **session 1** should not commit/rollback the changes as this will end the transaction setting. So using this isolation level tester can do the **functionality test** on the data inserted by himself in **session 1**.

If the tester does not want to do any DML operation for his testing then he/she can use isolation level "**READ ONLY**"

215

```
SET TRANSACTION READ ONLY NAME 'session readonly data';
```

Note: using "READ ONLY" isolation level user in **session 1 cannot do update/insert/delete.**

So using isolation level "SERIALIZABLE" and "READ ONLY" tester can do specific testing in isolation.

Tips 18: Connection to sqlplus from command line and example of multiversioning and read consistency.

Here we will discuss ways to connect to sqlplus without tnsnames configured and will discuss how you can see data which is no more existing in the database table.

You can connect to sqlplus without going via tnsnames.ora
E.g. you can connect to database in SQLDEVELOPER which does not go via tnsnames
Sometime you must connect to sqlplus to run certain steps which may fail in **sqldeveloper** because of limitation of the tool. Here is one example which shows how oracle shows the same data when the data was first read no matter if the data is deleted/committed subsequently.

Connect to sqlplus using command line:
User name: **u1**
Password: **u1**
Service_name:**dev.io.uk**
Hostname: **ags1**
Port: **1521**

```
SQL>
SQL> sqlplus u1/u1@(DESCRIPTION=(ADDRESS_LIST=(ADDRESS=(PROTOCOL=TCP)(HOST=ags1)(PORT=1521)))(CONNECT_DATA=(SERVICE_NAME=dev.io.uk)))
```

```
SQL> VAR X REFCURSOR
SQL> BEGIN
  2   OPEN :X FOR SELECT * FROM EMP_ADD WHERE ID=1;
  3   END;
  4   /

PL/SQL procedure successfully completed.

SQL> DELETE FROM EMP_ADD WHERE ID=1;

1 row deleted.

SQL> COMMIT;

Commit complete.

SQL> SET SERVEROUTPUT ON
SQL> DECLARE
  2   A EMP_ADD%ROWTYPE;
  3   BEGIN
  4   LOOP
  5    FETCH :X INTO A;
  6     EXIT WHEN :X%NOTFOUND;
  7     DBMS_OUTPUT.PUT_LINE('VAL IS:'||A.ID);
  8    END LOOP;
  9   END;
 10   /
VAL IS:1

PL/SQL procedure successfully completed.
```

You can see clearly in **EMP_ADD table for id=1 there is no data as this record is deleted** and commited however the PL/SQL block still return that id=1.
This is because of **oracle multiversioning capability** with the ability to read consistent data.

When you delete from the table the data is stored in rollback segment and when you fetch the data from the cursor it reads from that rollback segment and display.

The same is the case when you fire a complex **"select"** query which takes 30 minutes or more to return the result. Within the same 30 minutes period from other sessions all the data might have been deleted and committed but you will still see all the data at the end of 30 minutes. This is possible because of oracle's ability to maintain different versions of the data and display the data based on which particular point of time you need the data.

Different version of data retrieval using flashback has been discussed extensively in Chapter 4: **Flashback setup and data transfer**

Note: In sqldeveloper if you run the above code it fails with error because of the limitation of the SQLDEVELOPER tool:
```
ORA-01001: invalid cursor
```

Tips 19: Danger of using "NOT IN" clause

The simple innocuous "NOT IN" clause has potential to disrupt the business function by breaking your code. You know "NOT IN" clause is used extensively by programmer in their application. Here we will take a simple example to demonstrate how "NOT IN" clause gives incorrect data and disturb the business functionality if not used properly.
Example:

```
CREATE TABLE parcel
  (
    id        NUMBER PRIMARY KEY,
    track_no  NUMBER,
    colour    VARCHAR2(10)
  );
INSERT INTO parcel VALUES(1,1001,'Red');
INSERT INTO parcel VALUES(2,1002,null);
INSERT INTO parcel VALUES(3,1004,'Blue');
INSERT INTO parcel VALUES(4,1006,null);
INSERT INTO parcel VALUES(5,1007,null);
INSERT INTO parcel VALUES(6,1011,'Green');
INSERT INTO parcel VALUES(7,1091,null);
COMMIT;
```

Problem:
Now you have requirement to get the parcel which are not "Red" and "Blue"
So here is the query:
```
SELECT * FROM parcel WHERE colour NOT IN('Red','Blue');
```

The output is:

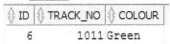

ID	TRACK_NO	COLOUR
6	1011	Green

As you can see the result is wrong. This all happen because "Colour" can contain "null" value and as per Oracle NULL is not comparable with any other value and hence evaluate to False which causes missing data.

So the solution is:
```
SELECT * FROM parcel WHERE NVL(colour,'NO COLOUR') NOT IN('Red','Blue');
```
Alternatively you can use:
```
SELECT * FROM parcel WHERE colour NOT IN('Red','Blue') OR colour IS NULL;
```

The output is correct now:

ID	TRACK_NO	COLOUR
2	1002	(null)
4	1006	(null)
5	1007	(null)
6	1011	Green
7	1091	(null)

Note: When you use "NOT IN" clause make sure the column you are referring is "NOT NULL" column in database, However if it is "NULLABLE" then you must handle NVL for that column to get correct result.
Also remember when you use NOT IN the index is not used as mentioned in Chapter 6, Tips 5: Oracle NOT IN or MINUS or JOIN or NOT EXISTS clause.

Chapter 8: Generic know how on Oracle PL/SQL for developer (34 Pages)

In database development knowing how a feature can be implemented in different versions of the database is a matter of necessity.

When I started using oracle versions 10g, 11g and 12c in parallel in multiple projects I found it extremely difficult to navigate between different versions of Oracle releases.

There are a lot of additional features in Oracle 12c which require an alternative approach to derive similar functionality in database versions prior to 12c.

In this chapter we will cover **PL/SQL** tips not covered in previous chapters so that you will know the different approaches employed in different releases of database to achieve the same functionality.

Tips 1: Sensitive data masking using REDACTION

Tips 2: Define view to act like invoker right programmer unit in 12c

Tips 3: PL/SQL code optimization by "inlining" in 11g

Tips 4: Implementation restriction in "FORALL" clause, solution prior to 11g and in 11g?

Tips 5: Sequence fetching enhancement in 11g?

Tips 6: Continue statement in 11g?

Tips 7: Performance improvement using Native compilation enhancement in 11g?

Tips 8: Restructuring error stack in 12c?

Tips 9: Restructuring backtrace in 12c?

Tips 10: PL/SQL only data type support in "native dynamic SQL", "SELECT call" and "as a bind variable" in 12c?

Tips 11: White listing and accessible by clause in 12c?

Tips 12: Invoker right code with Result_cache in 12c?

Tips 13: Returning implicit statement result set in 12c?

Tips 14: Improvement in conditional compilation in 12c?

Tips 15: Improve performance using Oracle package initialization?

Tips 16: How to match two input string for exact match with any combination?

Tips 17: Improve performance by incorporating one parse and multiple execute, use of BIND variable?

Tips 18: BULK OPERATION hinders performance and the solution?

Here we will discuss how to anonymize or mask sensitive data in 12c and prior to 12c in order to protect data from unwanted exposure.

Prior to 12c you could anonymize or mask sensitive data using FGAC/VPD or by using procedural approach of masking data by implementing some rules and then de-masking the data using the reverse rule. However in 12c using data redaction policy you can on the fly mask any sensitive data of a table. Oracle 12c Redaction is the extension to the FGAC/VPD used for masking in 10g.
Oracle Data Masking is available only with Enterprise Edition and it requires licensing of Advanced Security.

Prior to 12c (in 10g) solution:

Connect to sys:

```
GRANT EXECUTE ON dbms_rls TO U1;
```

Connect to U1:

```
create table dc_cust(ID number,bank_acc number(10),bank_name varchar2(30));

insert into dc_cust values(1,1234567898,'ABC bank');
insert into dc_cust values(2,1234566897,'ABC bank');
insert into dc_cust values(3,1234565896,'ABC bank');
insert into dc_cust values(4,1234564895,'ABC bank');
insert into dc_cust values(5,1234563894,'ABC bank');
insert into dc_cust values(6,1234562893,'ABC bank');
commit;


CREATE OR REPLACE FUNCTION dc_bank_f (v_owner IN VARCHAR2, v_tab IN VARCHAR2)
RETURN VARCHAR2 AS
  v_rule VARCHAR2 (200);
BEGIN
  v_rule := 'id >0';
  RETURN (v_rule);
END dc_bank_f;
/
```

This function set the rule as to which records the masking will be implemented
So if you give ID between 10 and 30 then the masking of bank_acc will happen only for those ID, Other ID will have full bank_acc displayed.

```
BEGIN
  DBMS_RLS.ADD_POLICY (object_schema       => 'U1',
                       object_name         => 'dc_cust',
                       policy_name         => 'mask_bank_acc',
                       function_schema     => 'U1',
                       policy_function     => 'dc_bank_f',
                       sec_relevant_cols   => 'bank_acc',
                       sec_relevant_cols_opt => DBMS_RLS.ALL_ROWS);
END;
/
```

Name of the table on which you will mask the sensitive columns

This will state list of columns (separated by commas) will be masked

This allows to display all the row of the table
But mask only the value as per function dc_bank_f

Now when you run

```
select id,bank_acc,bank_name from dc_cust;
```

The bank_acc value will be masked:

ID	BANK_ACC	BANK_NAME
1		ABC bank
2		ABC bank
3		ABC bank
4		ABC bank
5		ABC bank
6		ABC bank

In order to de-mask or remove the masking use this:

```
BEGIN
  DBMS_RLS.DROP_POLICY (object_schema    => 'U1',
                        object_name      => 'dc_cust',
                        policy_name      => 'mask_bank_acc');
END;
/
```

Oracle 12c (and also backported to 11.2.0.4) has introduced DBMS_REDACT package to define redaction policy for masking sensitive data of tables and this provides greater level of control and protection of sensitive data and it is much easier to implement as shown below:

Data redaction is part of advanced security option. It does not change the actual data, it just hides the sensitive data from the unauthorized user.

12c solution for full masking:

Connect to sys:

```
GRANT EXECUTE ON sys.dbms_redact TO U1;
```

Connect to U1:

```
BEGIN
  DBMS_REDACT.add_policy(
    object_schema => 'U1',
    object_name   => 'dc_cust',
    column_name   => 'bank_acc',        This will state list of columns
                                        (separated by commas) will be masked
    policy_name   => 'redact_mask_bank_acc',
    function_type => DBMS_REDACT.full,  Function_type state what kind of masking will take
                                        Place like if it is full or some part of the string of the
    expression    => '1=1'              sensitive column will be masked
  );
END;
/         This means redaction will always take place
```

Expression=>'1=1' means masking will happen for all users. However if you want to implement the masking for a set of users or not to mask for a set of users then use the following expression instead of "1=1"

```
expression      => 'SYS_CONTEXT(''USERENV'',''SESSION_USER'') != ''U2'''
```

This means redaction/masking will not take place for schema "U2" and hence from schema u2 if you run "select * from U1.dc_cust;" you will see actually original value (not the masked value of bank_acc.

Now when you run from user U1

```
select id,bank_acc,bank_name from dc_cust;
```

You will get bank_acc value masked to 0:

ID	BANK_ACC	BANK_NAME
1	0	ABC bank
2	0	ABC bank
3	0	ABC bank
4	0	ABC bank
5	0	ABC bank
6	0	ABC bank

12c solution for using substituted value:

If you want to display the substituted value instead of original value you can do that by adding additional parameter [FUNCTION_PARAMETRS] in add_policy or alter_policy function as shown below:

```
BEGIN
    DBMS_REDACT.alter_policy (
        object_schema       => 'U1',
        object_name         => 'dc_cust',
        policy_name         => 'redact_mask_bank_acc',
        action              => DBMS_REDACT.modify_column,
        column_name         => 'bank_acc',
        function_type       => DBMS_REDACT.partial,  <---
        function_parameters => '9,1,6'
    );
END;
/
```

Function_type state what kind of masking will take Place like if it is partial then some part of the string of the sensitive column will be masked as per function_parameters

This state how the redaction will be masked.
1st parameter 9: value to be masked to
2nd parameter 1: start point of the string to be masked
3rd parameter 6: end point of the string to be masked

So here 1st to 6th character of bank_acc column value will be replaced by 9

If the data type of **column** (Intended to be masked) is other than **number** then function_parameters will accordingly use different type of values/arguments.

Now when you run

```
select id,bank_acc,bank_name from dc_cust;
```

You will get bank_acc 1 to 6th character values masked to 9:

ID	BANK_ACC	BANK_NAME
1	9999997898	ABC bank
2	9999996897	ABC bank
3	9999995896	ABC bank
4	9999994895	ABC bank
5	9999993894	ABC bank
6	9999992893	ABC bank

From SQLDEVELOPER you can do this by selecting Add Redaction policy and subsequently adding a policy function.

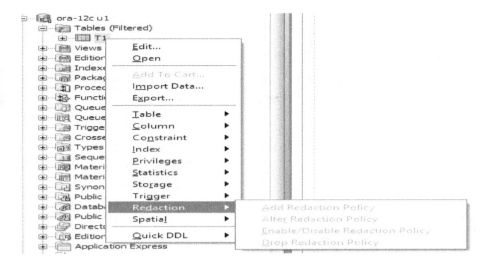

In order to de-mask (disable redaction) or remove the masking use this in oracle 12c:

```
BEGIN
  DBMS_REDACT.drop_policy (
    object_schema => 'U1',
    object_name   => 'dc_cust',
    policy_name   => 'redact_mask_bank_acc'
  );
END;
/
```

Note: Redaction policy is not applicable for Sys user because SYS has "EXEMPT REDACTION POLICY" and hence if you run the following from SYS user:

```
SELECT id,bank_acc,bank_name FROM u1.dc_cust;
```

It will show bank_acc without any kind of masking.

Tips 2: Define view to act like invoker right programmer unit in 12c?

Invoker right function behaves like invoker right even if it is called from view which is definer right, intriguing? Here we will discuss how it is done in 12c using BEQUEATH clause in a view. Prior to 12c an invoker right function behaves like definer right when it is called from view (View is definer right).

Prior to 12c when a view is executing/calling a function then the function is executed under the privilege of the view owner as per the rule below:
When an "**invoker right code**" is called by "**definer right code**" then the "**invoker right code**" is executed under the authority of "**definer right code**".
So if you have a "**invoker right function**" and it is called by a view (default of view is definer right)
Then the function will act as if it is definer right and will give result as per the owner of definer (**view owner**).

Often the expectation is that whoever invokes the function the result should be in accordance to that because the function is invoker right code.

Let us take one example:
Prior to 12c this is how it works:

```
connect U1

CREATE TABLE app
(
   app_id      INTEGER,
   dept_id   INTEGER,
   app_name       VARCHAR2 (50)
);

   INSERT INTO app VALUES (1, 10, 'CG');
   INSERT INTO app VALUES (2, 20, 'LLK');
   INSERT INTO app VALUES (3, 30, 'SUB');
   COMMIT;

CREATE OR REPLACE
  FUNCTION app_cnt(
     dept_id_in IN NUMBER)
   RETURN NUMBER AUTHID CURRENT_USER
 IS
   v_cnt NUMBER;
 BEGIN
   SELECT COUNT (*) INTO v_cnt FROM app WHERE dept_id = dept_id_in;
   RETURN v_cnt;
 END app_cnt;
 /
CREATE OR REPLACE VIEW app_cnts_view
AS
   SELECT dept_id,
          app_cnt (dept_id)
          count_of_app
     FROM app;
/


GRANT SELECT ON app_cnts_view TO U2
/
```

Now connect to U2 and create same "APP" table with different data as below:

```
connect U2

CREATE TABLE app
(
   app_id      INTEGER,
   dept_id   INTEGER,
   app_name       VARCHAR2 (50)
);

   INSERT INTO app VALUES (4, 10, 'CG_L1');
   INSERT INTO app VALUES (5, 10, 'CG_L2');
   INSERT INTO app VALUES (6, 10, 'CG_L3');
   INSERT INTO app VALUES (7, 40, 'LLK1');
   INSERT INTO app VALUES (8, 50, 'SUB2');
   COMMIT;
```

Two approaches to execute the function
Approach 1(Via view)
Now if you run as below from the view (**which will internally execute the function**):

224

```
connect U2
select * from U1.app_cnts_view;
```
You will get following result:

	DEPT_ID	COUNT_OF_APP	
This come view → Based on U1.app	10	1	← This come from function call based on u1.app
	20	1	
	30	1	

This result COUNT_OF_APP is derived based on the function app_cnt executed from user u1 even if the function is invoker right code and expected to invoke as per the authority of user U2.

Approach 2 (via direct function call)
However if you run the function directly by giving require execute privilege and grant to U2 it will give the result as below, note COUNT_OF_APP is derived based on U2.app as expected because function is invoker right code.
```
connect U2
select dept_id,U1.app_cnt(dept_id) count_of_app from U1.app;
```

	DEPT_ID	COUNT_OF_APP	
This come view → Based on U1.app	10	3	← This come from function call based on u2.app
	20	0	
	30	0	

So the result set COUNT_OF_APP of calling the function from "a view" and "executing independently from a sql" are entirely different. However expectation is that, the invoker right function should return exactly same way from both the **approaches** and the result should be as given in **approach 2**.

Prior to 12c it was not possible to get the result look like **approach 2** when the invoker right function is called from a view which can **only** be definer right.

In 12c, oracle has introduced **BEQUEATH** clause for view so it will not convert an invoker right function to definer right. In other words by using this clause, VIEW will keep the function in its purest form and intention.
So solution in 12c
Just add the BEQUEATH clause in the view definition as below:

```
connect U1

CREATE OR REPLACE VIEW app_cnts_view
BEQUEATH CURRENT_USER
AS
    SELECT dept_id,
           app_cnt (dept_id)
           count_of_app
      FROM app;
/

GRANT SELECT ON app_cnts_view TO U2
/
```

```
connect U2
select * from U1.app_cnts_view;
```

This come view   ⟶ | DEPT_ID | COUNT_OF_APP | ⟵   This come from function

Based on U1.app

DEPT_ID	COUNT_OF_APP
10	3
20	0
30	0

call based on U2.app

So in 12c you can see the function **app_cnt** is executed as invoker right (**here U2 is the invoker**) even if it is called by a VIEW because you can see under user U2 you have **3** applications in **dept_id=10** and **0** application count in department **20, 30**.

Note: The view "u1.app_cnts_view" itself is not invoker right code even if you use

```
BEQUEATH CURRENT_USER
```

It is evident by the result because it returns the dept_id from **U1 schema** which is the owner of the view not from user **U2** who invokes the view.

Tips 3: PL/SQL code optimization by "inlining" in 11g?

Here we will explore different ways to inline/rearrange the subprogram by the PL/SQL compiler during compilation time to get better performance.

Subprogram inlining is the process by which oracle internally replaces the stored program code in the calling program **during compilation**. Since the stored code (procedure/function) is in the main code (INLINE) the extra time and context switching for calling the program from oracle server is eliminated and this in turn improve performance for oracle PL/SQL code execution.

Inlining can be **done in 2 ways:**

1) By using PRAGMA INLINE compiler directive

```
create or replace function normal_f(name varchar2)
Return varchar2
Is
a varchar2(100);
begin
a :=upper(name);
return a;
END normal_f;
/
```

Now call "normal_f" function by making this function inline using pragma inside procedure "inline_demo_step"

226

```
Create or replace procedure inline_demo_step
Is
B varchar2(100);
BEGIN
PRAGMA INLINE (normal_f, 'YES ');
For I in (select name from EMP) LOOP
 B := normal_f(i.name);
END LOOP;
END;
/
```

So by using this Pragma, the optimizer will internally substitute the function code for inline_f and eliminate the overhead of extra call to server and enhance performance.
Please note we can use this pragma from Oracle 11g onward.

2) By setting PLSQL_OPTIMIZE_LEVEL parameter to value 3 as below in a session
```
ALTER SESSION SET PLSQL_OPTIMIZE_LEVEL = 3;
```

So when we set it to 3 oracle will automatically try and inline/rearrange the subprogram at compile time, however sometimes oracle prefers not to inline the subprogram even if it is set to 3 because it believes it is undesirable. The default value of this parameter is 2.

When you have **PLSQL_OPTIMIZE_LEVEL=3** and still you want to avoid inlining for some specific subprogram, then you can use
PRAGMA INLINE (subprogram_name,'NO') to achieve that.

You can see the current optimization setting for procedure:
```
SELECT name,plsql_optimize_level
FROM USER_PLSQL_OBJECT_SETTINGS
WHERE upper(name)='PROC_FLEXIBLE_COMMIT';
```

Output:

NAME	PLSQL_OPTIMIZE_LEVEL
PROC_FLEXIBLE_COMMIT	2

Note: **PLSQL_OPTIMIZE_LEVEL=3** was introduced in 11g, however optimization level 0, 1, 2 was there in pre-11g. For function/procedure inlining **without** the use of **Pragma INLINE** refer to Chapter 5, Tips 3 "**WITH Clause improvement in 12c**" and Tips 5 "**PRAGMA UDF to improve function call from SQL in 12c**"

Tips 4: Implementation restriction in "FORALL" clause, solution prior to 11g and in 11g?

Here we will see accessing the full PL/SQL table in a "FORALL" clause throws error prior to 11g. We will explore the solution pre-11g and how it works in 11g.

Prior to 11g you cannot access a specific attribute of a PL/SQL table inside "FORALL" clause.
You can access the full PL/SQL table but not specific attributes as shown below:

227

```
DECLARE
TYPE dc_cust_t
IS
  TABLE OF dc_cust%ROWTYPE INDEX BY PLS_INTEGER;
  dc_cust_tp dc_cust_t;
BEGIN
  SELECT * BULK COLLECT INTO dc_cust_tp FROM dc_cust;
  FORALL i IN 1 .. dc_cust_tp.COUNT
  UPDATE dc_cust
  SET online_flag = dc_cust_tp(i).online_flag+1
  WHERE id        = dc_cust_tp(i).id;
END;
/
```

Accessing attribute "id" and "online_flag"

You will get an error if you run this prior to 11g

PLS-00436: implementation restriction: cannot reference fields of BULK In-BIND table of records

This is **resolved in 11g** and you **will not get an error** when you **run the above code**.

To resolve this prior to 11g you need to create multiple PL/SQL tables as below:

```
DECLARE
TYPE dc_cust_id_t
IS
  TABLE OF dc_cust.id%TYPE INDEX BY PLS_INTEGER;
  dc_cust_id_tp dc_cust_id_t;
TYPE online_flag_t
IS
  TABLE OF dc_cust.online_flag%TYPE INDEX BY PLS_INTEGER;
  online_flag_tp online_flag_t;
BEGIN
  SELECT brn,
    online_flag BULK COLLECT
  INTO dc_cust_id_tp,
    online_flag_tp
  FROM dc_cust;
  FORALL i   IN 1 .. dc_cust_brn_tp.COUNT
  UPDATE dc_cust
  SET online_flag = online_flag_tp(i)+1
  WHERE brn       = dc_cust_id_tp(i);      It access the full associative array, not any specific array
END;
/
```

This will work fine prior to 11g as you do not access any specific element, but the full array.

Tips 5: Sequence fetching enhancement in 11g?

Prior to 11g **currval** and **nextval** attribute of a sequence can be accessed in PL/SQL through queries only.
Oracle 11g has introduced sequence fetching as an expression in a PL/SQL block which is easy to read and maintain.
Prior to 11g solution

```
declare
a number;
begin
select test_seq.nextval into a from dual;
end;
/
```
This runs successfully prior to and in 11g.

11g solution
```
declare
a number;
begin
a :=test_seq.nextval;
end;
/
```
If you run this prior to 11g it will fail, but in 11g it works fine.

Note: NEXTVAL and CURRVAL cannot be used in query/view as column in SELECT statement with DISTINCT, INTERSECT, UNION, MINUS, ORDER BY, GROUP BY and HAVING clause.

So the solution is: First **form an inline view** using the above clauses and then select from the inline view and add the attribute seq_name.nextval in the query as below:
```
SELECT seq_name.nextval,
       a,
       b
FROM
     (SELECT DISTINCT a,b FROM table_name ORDER BY 1
     );
```

Tips 6: Continue statement in 11g?

Here we will discuss how to terminate the current iteration of a loop and pass the control to the start of next cycle of the loop.

Oracle 11g has introduced "CONTINUE" statement which controls the loop iteration. It terminates the current iteration of a loop and passes the control to the start of the next cycle of the loop.

Example
```
SET serveroutput ON
BEGIN
  FOR i IN 1 .. 6
  LOOP
    IF i IN (3,5) THEN
      CONTINUE;
    END IF;
    DBMS_OUTPUT.PUT_LINE('current ieration is: ' || TO_CHAR(i));
  END LOOP;
END;
/
```

The output will be:

```
anonymous block completed
current ieration is: 1
current ieration is: 2
current ieration is: 4
current ieration is: 6
```

Iteration 3,5 are skipped using continue statement

Prior to 11g this will fail as invalid statement.

Instead of "CONTINUE" if you use "EXIT" then the output will be:

```
anonymous block completed
current ieration is: 1
current ieration is: 2
```

So the difference between the two is that "EXIT" transfer the control out of LOOP whereas "CONTINUE" terminates the current iteration and transfer the control to the start of the LOOP.

Tips 7: Performance improvement using Native compilation, enhancement in 11g?

Here we will see how to compile a code natively for enhanced performance of computation intensive codes.

PL/SQL Native compilation compiles the PL/SQL code as native code instead of interpreted 'P-Code' and stored in system tablespace of the database.

Prior to 11g, the PL/SQL native compiler translated the PL/SQL code into C code and then external C compiler translated the C code into the native code. So in a nutshell you need to have the following to compile PL/SQL code natively prior to oracle 11g.

> C compiler in the server
> PLSQL_NATIVE_LIBRARY_DIR parameter must be set and point to the os directory
> PLSQL_CODE_TYPE needs to be set to 'NATIVE'

However in 11g PL/SQL native compiler can generate native code directly.
You need to just do this, so simple:

> PLSQL_CODE_TYPE needs to be set to 'NATIVE'

Example how it works in 11g:

```
create or replace procedure native_test_proc
is
BEGIN
  FOR i IN 1 .. 6
  LOOP
    IF i IN (3,5) THEN
      CONTINUE;
    END IF;
    DBMS_OUTPUT.PUT_LINE('current ieration is: ' || TO_CHAR(i));
  END LOOP;
END native_test_proc;
/
```

In order to natively compile this normal PL/SQL code do this:

```
ALTER PROCEDURE native_test_proc COMPILE PLSQL_CODE_TYPE = NATIVE;
```

You can control the setting in session and system level:

```
ALTER session SET PLSQL_CODE_TYPE='NATIVE';
ALTER PROCEDURE native_test_proc COMPILE;
```
```
ALTER SYSTEM SET PLSQL_CODE_TYPE='NATIVE';
ALTER PROCEDURE native_test_proc COMPILE;
```

You can see the setting using this:
```
SELECT name, type, plsql_code_type
   FROM  user_plsql_object_settings
   WHERE  name = 'NATIVE_TEST_PROC';
```
Output:

NAME	TYPE	PLSQL_CODE_TYPE
NATIVE_TEST_PROC	PROCEDURE	NATIVE

In order to set it to interpreted level just do this:
```
ALTER PROCEDURE native_test_proc COMPILE PLSQL_CODE_TYPE = INTERPRETED;
```

When you have computation intensive code in your PL/SQL code then it is advisable to compile NATIVELY, using just 1 liner setup to set it to 'NATIVE', as this will give significant performance enhancement. However if you compile code (default mode INTERPRETED) normally then the code is stored in an intermediate form and needs to be interpreted at runtime and hence performs slower than NATIVELY compiled code.

Tips 8: Restructuring error stack in 12c?

Here we will demonstrate how to display the contents of error stack to find the root cause of an issue in 12c.

Prior to Oracle 12c using DBMS_UTILITY.FORMAT_ERROR_STACK we could display all the errors of an oracle application. However the output of the error is much unstructured and to determine the root cause of an issue is tedious. In 12c Oracle has introduced UTL_CALL_STACK package to display the content of the error stack in proper format. It has 3 API ERROR_DEPTH, ERROR_MSG, and ERROR_NUMBER.

The below API using **utl_call_stack** need to be created one time in your database and can be called by any code in your oracle PL/SQL application:
```
CREATE OR REPLACE
PROCEDURE show_error_stack
AS
  v_depth NUMBER;
BEGIN
  v_depth := UTL_CALL_STACK.error_depth;
  DBMS_OUTPUT.PUT_LINE('Depth       Err code     Error message');
  DBMS_OUTPUT.PUT_LINE('----------  -----------  --------------------');
  FOR i IN 1 .. v_depth
  LOOP
    DBMS_OUTPUT.PUT_LINE( RPAD(i, 12) || RPAD('ORA-' ||
    LPAD(UTL_CALL_STACK.error_number(i), 5, '0'), 12) ||
    UTL_CALL_STACK.error_msg(i) );
  END LOOP;
END show_error_stack;
/
```

231

Now you can call this API in any of your PL/SQL code
E.g. Here in the anonymous block we use error handling API "show_error_stack". "test_code" is any of your PL/SQL procedure.

```
DECLARE
a number;
BEGIN
test_code;
EXCEPTION
WHEN OTHERS THEN
  show_error_stack;
END;
/
```

Tips 9: Restructuring backtrace in 12c?

Here we will demonstrate how to display the line number and program details to find where is the root cause.

Prior to Oracle 12c using DBMS_UTILITY.FORMAT_ERROR_BACKTRACE we could display all the line numbers where an exception was raised. However the output of the backtrace information regarding the block and the line number of the error propagated is much unstructured.
In 12c Oracle has introduced UTL_CALL_STACK package to display the content of the backtrace in proper format. It has 3 API BACKTRACE_DEPTH, BACKTRACE_LINE, and BACKTRACE_UNIT.

The below api using utl_call_stack need to be created one time in your database and can be called by any code in your oracle PL/SQL application to backtrace the line number and responsible subprogram:

```
CREATE OR REPLACE
PROCEDURE show_backtrace_stack
AS
  v_depth NUMBER;
BEGIN
  v_depth := UTL_CALL_STACK.backtrace_depth;
  DBMS_OUTPUT.PUT_LINE('Depth      Line no      Unit');
  DBMS_OUTPUT.PUT_LINE('----------  -----------  ----------------------');
  FOR i IN 1 .. v_depth
  LOOP
    DBMS_OUTPUT.put_line( RPAD(i, 12) ||
    RPAD(TO_CHAR(UTL_CALL_STACK.backtrace_line(i),'99'), 12) ||
    UTL_CALL_STACK.backtrace_unit(i) );
  END LOOP;
END show_backtrace_stack;
/
```

Now you can call this API in any of your PL/SQL code
E.g. Here in the anonymous block we use error handling API "show_error_stack" to get backtrace information. "test_code" is any of your PL/SQL procedure.

```
DECLARE
a number;
BEGIN
test_code;
EXCEPTION
WHEN OTHERS THEN
  show_backtrace_stack;
END;
/
```

Tips 10: PL/SQL only data type support in "native dynamic SQL", "SELECT call" and "as a bind variable" in 12c?

Here we will discuss the usage of PL/SQL only datatype like BOOLEAN, associative array in **"SQL select"**, **"TABLE operator"** and **"native dynamic sql"** from PL/SQL in 12c.

Prior to Oracle 12c you could not bind **PL/SQL only specific datatype** (e.g. Boolean, associative array which do not exist in SQL but exists in PL/SQL) in dynamic SQL and also they cannot be used in "SQL SELECT" statements.
However, 12c improves the usability of PL/SQL and hence "SQL unsupported data type" can be used in native dynamic SQL and SQL select statement in PL/SQL anonymous block.

Simple example to demonstrate how it works in 12c and fails in 11g
Common step:
Create the function containing Boolean data type
```
CREATE TABLE t2 AS
SELECT * FROM all_objects WHERE rownum<20;

CREATE OR REPLACE FUNCTION f_object_name (
   object_id_in    IN t2.object_id%TYPE,
   v_upper_req         IN BOOLEAN)
   RETURN t2.object_name%TYPE
IS
   v_return    t2.object_name%TYPE;
BEGIN
   SELECT object_name
     INTO v_return
     FROM t2
    WHERE object_id = object_id_in;


   RETURN CASE WHEN v_upper_req THEN UPPER (v_return) ELSE LOWER(v_return) END;
END;
/
```

This function is created fine both in 11g and 12c database. This function returns the object name in upper case when Boolean value (v_upper_req) is TRUE, otherwise object name is returned in lower case.

Call from anonymous block using function call:
Call this from anonymous block using function call

233

```
set serveroutput on
declare
v_obj_name t2.object_name%TYPE;
v_upper_req BOOLEAN :=TRUE;
Begin
v_obj_name :=f_object_name(365,v_upper_req);
dbms_output.put_line(v_obj_name);
end;
/
```

→This works fine both in 11g and 12c as this is the basic functionality

Call from anonymous block using SQL select:

When the following code is called from SQL "**select**" statement inside an anonymous block it **fails in 11g** and run **fine in 12c**:

```
SET serveroutput ON
DECLARE
  v_upper_req BOOLEAN :=TRUE;
BEGIN
  FOR i IN
  (SELECT f_object_name(object_id,v_upper_req) obj_name
  FROM t2
  WHERE object_id=365
  )
  LOOP
    dbms_output.put_line(i.obj_name);
  END LOOP;
END;
/
```

→Prior to 12c it fails with error wrong number of argument because "v_upper_req" is Boolean
→In Oracle 12c onward it is successful as Boolean which a PL/SQL only data type is
   Supported now in "SELECT call in PL/SQL".

Dynamic SQL using bind variable:

```
SET serveroutput ON
DECLARE
  v_upper_req BOOLEAN :=TRUE;
BEGIN
  EXECUTE immediate 'BEGIN dbms_output.put_line
  (f_object_name(365,:bind)); END;' USING v_upper_req;
END;
/
```

→Prior to 12c it fails with error
```
PLS-00457: expressions have to be of SQL types
```
→In Oracle 12c onward it is successful.

Associative array call in SELECT and as TABLE operator

Prior to 12c you could not use associative array in "SQL select" and as "Table operator" or as bind variable, you can only use this in PL/SQL expression as below:

Example

```
CREATE OR REPLACE PACKAGE pkg
AS
    TYPE t1
    IS TABLE OF VARCHAR2 (30)
        INDEX BY BINARY_INTEGER;

    PROCEDURE show_name (
        names    IN t1);
END pkg;
/



CREATE OR REPLACE PACKAGE BODY pkg
AS
    PROCEDURE show_name (
        names    IN t1)
    IS
    BEGIN
        FOR i IN 1 .. names.COUNT LOOP
            DBMS_OUTPUT.put_line ( 'The name is:'||names(i));
        END LOOP;
    END;
END pkg;
/
```

Run the following both in 11g and 12c to test the effect of using bind variable for associative array in dynamic sql:

```
SET serveroutput ON
DECLARE
  v_names pkg.t1;
BEGIN
  v_names(1) :='scott';
  v_names(2) :='Stephen';
  v_names(3) :='Asim';
  EXECUTE immediate 'begin pkg.show_name(:names); end;' USING v_names;
END;
/
```

Error in 11g:

```
PLS-00457: expressions have to be of SQL types
```

The error is displayed because associative array (v_names is PL/SQL only data type) is not supported as bind variable prior to 12c

Output in 12c:
```
anonymous block completed
name is:scott
name is:Stephen
name is:Asim
```

Run the following both in 11g and 12c to test the effect of TABLE operator:

```
SET serveroutput ON
DECLARE
  v_names pkg.tl;
BEGIN
  v_names(1) :='scott';
  v_names(2) :='Stephen';
  v_names(3) :='Asim';
  FOR j IN
  (SELECT * FROM TABLE(v_names)
  )
  LOOP
    dbms_output.put_line(j.column_value);
  END LOOP;
END;
/
```

Error in 11g:
```
PL/SQL: ORA-22905: cannot access rows from a non-nested table item
```
The error is displayed because you could not use associative array in TABLE operator prior to 12c

Output in 12c:
```
anonymous block completed
scott
Stephen
Asim
```

Solution prior to 12c:
The only way you can call this in 11g, is to avoid bind variable/table operator as shown below:

```
set serveroutput on
DECLARE
    v_names   pkg.tl;
BEGIN
    v_names (1) := 'scott';
    v_names (2) := 'Stephen';
    v_names (3) := 'Asim';
pkg.show_name(v_names);
END;
/
```

Other way to make this works prior to 12c is to change the package to use nested table instead of associative array.

However in 12c as shown, PL/SQL developer has the flexibility to execute the function/package in many different ways even if they use associative array in the application.

236

Note: BOOLEAN, ASSOCIATIVE ARRAY **are only available** in PL/SQL but **not available** in SQL.
However other data type like VARCHAR2, CHAR are present both in SQL and PL/SQL.
Both CHAR and VARCHAR2 are used to store string values. The only difference between the 2 is: CHAR is fixed length variable and hence if you declared a variable as **CHAR (10)** and try to store value "ASIM" then remaining 6 character will be stored as 6 spaces whereas **VARCHAR2 (10)** is varying length **variable/data type** and hence if you store "ASIM" remaining 6 character will not be padded with space and hence these 6 bytes will be available for others to use.

Tips 11: White listing and accessible by clause in 12c?

Here we will explore how to prevent a user from executing a sensitive sub-program even if he has execute privilege. This is one more layer of security which ensure that the sensitive program is accessible by authorized set of package/procedure/functions.

Using "**grant** execute on package/procedure" you can grant privilege to execute certain package or procedure to a specific user. PL/SQL cannot prevent a user from executing a subprogram to which he has been granted execute authority. However using **white listing** by means of "accessible by" clause Oracle 12c enhances security by restricting the right to execute a specific subprogram to the users/procedures/package/functions which are in the white list.
E.g. to demonstrate the usage of accessible by clause

```
CREATE OR REPLACE
PACKAGE white_pkg
IS
PROCEDURE p1;
END;
/

CREATE OR REPLACE
PACKAGE protected_pkg ACCESSIBLE BY(white_pkg)
IS
PROCEDURE protected_p1;
PROCEDURE protected_p2;
END;
/
```

Note **protected_pkg** can only be accessed by **white_pkg** from a session as "**white_pkg**" is in the accessible by clause. You can give any number of users/package/procedure in the accessible by clause and separate them by comma e.g. (white_pkg1, white_pkg2, white_pkg3, procudre1).

Now let us create the package body for both the above packages.

```
CREATE OR REPLACE PACKAGE body white_pkg
IS
    PROCEDURE p1 is
    BEGIN
    protected_pkg.protected_p1;
    protected_pkg.protected_p2;
    END;
END;
/


CREATE OR REPLACE PACKAGE BODY protected_pkg
IS
    PROCEDURE protected_p1 IS
    BEGIN
    dbms_output.put_line('inside protected_p1');
    END;

    PROCEDURE protected_p2 IS
    BEGIN
    dbms_output.put_line('inside protected_p2');
    END;
END;
/
```

Now you can execute the protected_pkg as below (via white_pkg):

```
begin
white_pkg.p1;
end;
/
```

This will give output as below:
```
inside protected_p1
inside protected_p2
```

However if you try to execute the package independently it will fail as below:

```
set serveroutput on
begin
protected_pkg.protected_p1;
protected_pkg.protected_p2;
end;
/
PLS-00904: insufficient privilege to
access object PROTECTED_PKG
```

Also try to call the protected_pkg procedure from other program, it will fail as below:

```
CREATE OR REPLACE PROCEDURE test_proc
IS
BEGIN
  protected_pkg.protected_p1;
END;
/
```

238

```
PLS-00904: insufficient privilege to
access object PROTECTED_PKG
```

So now you can see using white listing "protected_pkg" can be referred/called only by the program mentioned in ACCESSIBLE BY clause of "protected_pkg" package.

Tips 12: Invoker right code with Result_cache in 12c?

Here we will see how **result_cache** work for invoker right code.

Oracle 11g has introduced function result cache however you cannot combine RESULT_CACHE for invoker right code. In **Oracle 12c** this restriction is lifted.
Here is one example

```
CREATE OR REPLACE
  FUNCTION f_object_name(
      object_id_in IN t2.object_id%TYPE)
    RETURN t2.object_name%TYPE AUTHID CURRENT_USER RESULT_CACHE
  IS
    v_return t2.object_name%TYPE;
  BEGIN
    SELECT object_name INTO v_return FROM t2 WHERE object_id = object_id_in;
    RETURN v_return;
  END;
  /
```

So in Oracle 11g if you run this it will fail with error:

```
PLS-00999: implementation restriction (may be temporary) RESULT_CACHE is disallowed on subprograms in Invoker-Rights modules
```

However the above is successful in Oracle 12c because oracle will pass the current_user as hidden parameter along with the argument value passed to the result cache function. So you will get performance benefit of result cache if the **same current user** executes the same function with same argument value. However normal result cache with definer right code gets the benefit of results cached by function calls done by **any users.**

Tips 13: Returning implicit statement result set in 12c?

Here we will demonstrate how to return the resultset implicitly to client applications.

Prior to 12c Oracle returns the result-set from stored subprogram to client (like sql*plus, Java, oci or any other client application) by defining explicitly REF CURSOR as OUT parameter.
And in the call to the stored procedure from sql*plus, JAVA or any other client application you need to
Fetch from the REF CURSOR, store the result-set and loop through each result-set to display the value in client application.

So here are the steps **prior to 12c**

```
CREATE OR REPLACE
PROCEDURE show_object_name(
    object_type_in IN all_objects.object_type%TYPE,
    v_cur OUT SYS_REFCURSOR)
IS
BEGIN
  OPEN v_cur FOR SELECT object_name FROM all_objects
  WHERE object_type=object_type_in AND rownum<10;
END;
/
```

Prior to 12c you can return the **result set** **explicitly** to the client application as below:

```
SET serveroutput ON
DECLARE
  v_cur SYS_REFCURSOR;              ←———————— Step 1
type obj_tl
IS
  TABLE OF VARCHAR2(30) INDEX BY binary_integer;
  v_obj_tl obj_tl;                  ←———— Step 2
BEGIN
  show_object_name('SYNONYM',v_cur);
  FETCH v_cur bulk collect INTO v_obj_tl;  ←——— Step 3
  FOR i IN 1..v_obj_tl.count         ←———— Step 4
  LOOP
    dbms_output.put_line(v_obj_tl(i));  ←——— Step 5
  END LOOP;
END;
/
```

However in 12c you can return the **result set** **implicitly** to the client application as below:

```
CREATE OR REPLACE
PROCEDURE show_object_name(
    object_type_in IN all_objects.object_type%TYPE )
IS
 v_cur SYS_REFCURSOR;
BEGIN
  OPEN v_cur FOR SELECT object_name FROM all_objects
  WHERE object_type=object_type_in AND rownum<10;
  DBMS_SQL.return_result (v_cur);
END;
/
EXEC show_object_name('SYNONYM');
```

So you can see in 12c it is so simple to return the result set **implicitly** to client application.

Tips 14: Improvement in conditional compilation in 12c?

Here we will show the new predefined inquiry directives which are introduced in 12c

$$PLSQL_UNIT_OWNER Owner of the PL/SQL unit

$$PLSQL_UNIT_TYPE: Type of PL/SQL unit like procedure/function/package etc.

You can display the value as below:

```
Dbms_output.put_line('Owner of the unit:'||$$PLSQL_UNIT||'          Introduced in 10g
                          is:'||$$PLSQL_UNIT_OWNER||'
            And the type of the unit is:'||$$PLSQL_UNIT_TYPE
                      );
                                                        Introduced in 12c
```

Tips 15: Improve performance using Oracle package initialization

Here we will explore how to instantiate a package so that during compilation the code is loaded into memory.

Generally, the package initialization concept is not very well known, here I give a brief explanation of the concept and show the performance gain using package initialization.
A package is loaded in the PGA from DISK when we refer to it for the first time in any session, so subsequent access will be faster. To make package access faster even for first time in any session we have to include one INITIALIZATION section at the end of the package. By incorporating the initialization section, data will be taken from memory which gives better performance.

This is how we incorporate the initiation section:
```
CREATE OR REPLACE PROCEDURE proc_test
IS
  y NUMBER;
BEGIN
  Dbms_output.put_line('inside proc test procedure');
END;
/

CREATE OR REPLACE
PACKAGE pack_test
IS
  L_initiation NUMBER; -- This line is added for package initiation
PROCEDURE proc_test;
PROCEDURE proc_testl;
END;
/
```

241

```
CREATE OR REPLACE
PACKAGE body pack_test
IS

PROCEDURE proc_test
IS
  y NUMBER;
BEGIN
  Dbms_output.put_line('inside proc test procedure in a package');
END;

PROCEDURE proc_testl
IS
BEGIN
  EXECUTE immediate 'Begin pack_test.proc_test; END;';
  EXECUTE immediate 'Begin Proc_test;END;';
END;
-- Initiation section is added for this purpose
BEGIN
  L_initiation :=1;
END;
/
```

Now when you execute the procedure PROC_TEST1 you will get the **output**:

```
SET serveroutput ON
BEGIN
  pack_test.proc_testl;
END;
/

anonymous block completed
inside proc test procedure in a package
inside proc test procedure
```

We have one application where we have debug functionality implemented which shows which function, procedure, subprogram the application is processing. There are many different versions of code, so we do not know which version of code is giving the error. The new requirement is to change the architecture of debug to append the version number from version string to the debug message.

To implement this we have to have a good understanding of package initialization.

Data structure which is there inside the package is loaded in the PGA when we refer the package for the first time in the session.
To implement the new requirement, add the following two lines in the package

```
          c_version_string CONSTANT VARCHAR2(255) := '@(#) $RCSfile: mdmregldr_cans.sql,v $ $Revision: 1.197 $';
```
specification: `c_version_digit varchar2(20);`

In package body add the following two lines just before the end of the package (package initialization

```
BEGIN
    c_version_digit :='('||SUBSTR(c_version_string,instr(c_version_string,':',1,2)+2,
    (LENGTH(c_version_string)-instr(c_version_string,':',1,2)-3)) ||')';
```

section): `END;`   So

whenever this package is called from other program the value of c_version_digit will be available instantly.

By computing the value of c_version_digit inside the calling package oracle improves the performance of the application as the computation is <u>done only once</u> but passes the value 1000s of times. If you do the computation inside the debug package then application will do the same computation 1000s of times and degrade performance.

Tips 16: How to match two input string for exact match with any combination?

Here we will discuss how to match 2 sets of concatenated string for any possible permutation and combination for an exact match.

Suppose we have a ref data table say ref_data_table and the structure is

CODE number
DESCRIPTION varchar2 (200);

And the data is as below

CODE	DESCRIPTION
1	Office, pond, road, tree, house, temple, lake
2	Office, temple, lake
3	Office, pond, road, tree
4	Office, road, tree, house, lake

Now if we have an input string then we must take the corresponding ref data CODE, irrespective of the order of the component parts.

So for example if the input string is
Office, pond, road, tree, house, lake, temple the code should be 1
Office, pond, road, tree, house, temple, lake the code should be 1
Office, pond, road, tree, temple, house, lake the code should be 1
Pond, road, tree, house, temple, lake, office the code should be 1
House, office, pond, road, tree, temple, lake the code should be 1
Office, temple, lake   the code should be 2
Lake, office, temple   the code should be 2

Etc.....

Here are the steps to providing the solution:

```
CREATE TABLE ref_data_table_mapping
  (
    CODE            NUMBER,
    src_code        NUMBER(38,0) NOT NULL ENABLE,
    map_desc VARCHAR2(100 BYTE) NOT NULL ENABLE,
    src_desc VARCHAR2(100 BYTE) NOT NULL ENABLE
  );

CREATE OR REPLACE
  FUNCTION f_no_of_occ_cnt(
      p_string    IN CLOB,
      p_substring IN VARCHAR2)
    RETURN NUMBER
  IS
    l_occurrences NUMBER;
  BEGIN
    IF ( p_string   IS NOT NULL AND p_substring IS NOT NULL ) THEN
      l_occurrences := ( LENGTH(p_string) - ( NVL(LENGTH(REPLACE(p_string, p_substring)), 0) ) ) / LENGTH(p_substring) ;
    END IF;
    RETURN ( l_occurrences );
  END f_no_of_occ_cnt;
  /
```

```sql
CREATE OR REPLACE PROCEDURE P_obj_typ_mapping
IS
  type t1 IS TABLE OF VARCHAR2(100) INDEX BY binary_integer;
  a_t1 t1;
  dyn_string VARCHAR2(2000);
  l_cnt NUMBER;
  l_code          NUMBER;
  l_src_code      NUMBER;
  l_map_desc VARCHAR2(100);
  ft_cnt          NUMBER;
  l_is_insert     NUMBER :=1;
BEGIN
DELETE FROM ref_data_table_mapping;
INSERT INTO ref_data_table_mapping(CODE,src_code,map_desc,src_desc) select rownum ,code,description,description from ref_data_table;
  FOR i IN
  (SELECT distinct lower(ife_feature_types) ft FROM source_table--This table contain obj_type with combination of "tree, house, lake, temple" in any order
  )
  LOOP
    SELECT COUNT(0)
    INTO ft_cnt
    FROM ref_data_table_mapping
    WHERE lower(src_desc)=i.ft;
    IF ft_cnt=0 THEN
      SELECT regexp_substr(i.ft,'[^,]+', 1, level) bulk collect
      INTO a_t1
      FROM dual
        CONNECT BY regexp_substr(i.ft, '[^,]+', 1, level) IS NOT NULL;
      l_cnt                               :=a_t1.count;

      if l_cnt                     =4 THEN
        dyn_string                                := 'select code,src_code,map_desc from ref_data_table_mapping where lower(map_desc) like '||''''%'||a_t1(1)||'%'''||'
        and   lower(map_desc) like '||''''%'||a_t1(2)||'%'''||' and   lower(map_desc) like '||''''%'||a_t1(3)||'%'''||'
        and   lower(map_desc) like '||''''%'||a_t1(4)||'%'''||' and f_no_of_occ_cnt(map_desc,'||''','''||')=3';
      elsif l_cnt                  =3 THEN
        dyn_string                                := 'select code,src_code,map_desc from ref_data_table_mapping where lower(map_desc) like '||''''%'||a_t1(1)||'%'''||'
        and   lower(map_desc) like '||''''%'||a_t1(2)||'%'''||' and   lower(map_desc) like '||''''%'||a_t1(3)||'%'''||'
        and f_no_of_occ_cnt(map_desc,'||''','''||')=2';
      elsif l_cnt                  =2 THEN
        dyn_string                                := 'select code,src_code,map_desc from ref_data_table_mapping where lower(map_desc) like '||''''%'||a_t1(1)||'%'''||'
        and   lower(map_desc) like '||''''%'||a_t1(2)||'%'''||' and f_no_of_occ_cnt(map_desc,'||''','''||')=1';
      END IF;
```

245

```
BEGIN
    EXECUTE immediate dyn_string INTO l_code,l_src_code,l_map_desc;
EXCEPTION
WHEN OTHERS THEN
    l_is_insert :=SQL%ROWCOUNT;
END;
IF l_is_insert =1 THEN
    INSERT
    INTO ref_data_table_mapping VALUES
      (
        l_code+1,
        l_src_code,
        l_map_desc,
        i.ft
      );
    END IF;
  END IF;
  l_is_insert :=1;
END LOOP;
COMMIT;
END P_obj_typ_mapping;
/
```

Once you execute the procedure you will see in the intermediate table ref_data_table_mapping the correct code for the input string is updated, no matter whichever combination the input string has arrived into your system.

To clarify further:
In your ref data table you have
2   Office, temple, lake
Now even if the input string in source_table is
"temple, lake, office"
OR
"temple, office, lake"
OR
"lake, temple, office"
In any combination of the above string always the code will be "2" which you can find in the intermediate table ref_data_table_mapping once the procedure is executed.

Tips 17: Improve performance by incorporating one parse and multiple execute, use of BIND variable

Here we will discuss how to parse a code once and execute multiple times to improve performance.

When dynamically we want to process each record from any table then we must design the code to have "one parse and multiple executes" instead of "multiple parse and multiple executes".

Performance improves from 5 hours to 10 minutes by using this strategy when we have more than 90000 records in 1 table.

In this example all the tables are queried dynamically based on their primary key (which are also formed dynamically).

See the code snippets

```
BEGIN
--This will get SCN number for the date from which we would like to process data
SELECT Timestamp_to_scn(sync_from_date) INTO fr_scn FROM dual;
--This will get SCN number for the date to which we would like to process data
SELECT Timestamp_to_scn(sync_to_date) INTO to_scn FROM dual;
--This LOOP contains list of table to be migrated
FOR i IN (SELECT table_name FROM MAPPING_TABLE) LOOP

    --This is the LOOP which get primary key column for a table
    FOR m_data IN (SELECT column_position, ai.column_name
      FROM all_ind_columns ai, all_constraints ac
      WHERE ai.table_name    =ac.table_name
      AND ai.table_name      =i.table_name
      AND ai.table_owner     ='user_nm'
      AND ac.owner           = 'user_nm'
      AND ac.constraint_type ='P'
      AND ac.constraint_name =ai.index_name   order by 1) LOOP

        IF m_data.column_position =1 THEN
          sel_stmt    :='select '||m_data.column_name||' as pkey_value1';
          pkey_name1 :=m_data.column_name;
          pkey_count :=1;
        elsif m_data.column_position=2 THEN
          sel_stmt      :=sel_stmt||','||m_data.column_name||' as pkey_value2';
          pkey_name2    :=m_data.column_name;
          pkey_count    :=2;
        elsif m_data.column_position=3 THEN
          --as above(here the table contain primary key with three columns)
        END IF;
      END LOOP; --This is the END LOOP which derived all the primary key column for a table


--This below sel_stmt will form the select statement to extract the version date between 2 scn numbers
sel_stmt :=sel_stmt||',versions_starttime,versions_startscn,versions_operation from '||'user_nm'||'.'||i.table_name||' '  ||'VERSIONS
BETWEEN  SCN '||fr_scn ||' and '|| to_scn ||' WHERE VERSIONS_OPERATION is NOT NULL AND versions_startscn>='||fr_scn ||' AND versions_startscn<'||
to_scn ||' order by versions_startscn,versions_operation';
--This will bulk collect primary key value, version starttime and version operation for a table.
EXECUTE immediate sel_stmt bulk collect INTO v_pkey_1_idx_tab,v_ver_starttime_tab,v_ver_startscn_tab,v_ver_operation_tab;

  FOR each_tab_rec IN 1..v_pkey_1_idx_tab.count LOOP --This will update,delete each records in a table between 2 SCNs
    IF v_ver_operation_tab(each_tab_rec) ='U' THEN
      EXECUTE immediate 'update '||i.table_name||' set m_END_DATE=v_ver_starttime_tab(each_tab_rec)'||',m_UPDATE_DATE=systimestamp where '||
      pkey_name1||'='v_pkey_1_idx_tab(each_tab_rec)'||' and m_END_DATE is NULL
      and m_DELETE_DATE is NULL AND m_START_DATE <v_ver_starttime_tab(each_tab_rec)';
      END IF;
  END LOOP;--End loop for update and delete of records in a table between 2 SCNs
END LOOP;   --end of main loop which works for each table present in MAPPING_TABLE
END;
/
```

Do you find any issue in the above code?

If you closely observe you can see the dynamic query is formed for each record of each table. So if in 1 table you have 1 million records then the dynamic query will be formed 1 million times and will kill the performance.

SOLUTION:

The way out is to form the dynamic query for each table for only one time and execute the query using bind variables provided through USING clause.

Note that you cannot use bind variables in your dynamic query for Oracle identifiers (e.g. Table name and column name [**pkey_name**1]) and hence we used normal variable to form the query and not bit it by bind variable.

```
DECLARE
--declare all variables......
BEGIN
--This will get SCN number for the date from which we would like to process data
SELECT Timestamp_to_scn(sync_from_date) INTO fr_scn FROM dual;
--This will get SCN number for the date to which we would like to process data
SELECT Timestamp_to_scn(sync_to_date) INTO to_scn FROM dual;
--This LOOP contains list of table to be migrated
FOR i IN (SELECT table_name FROM MAPPING_TABLE) LOOP

    --This is the LOOP which get primary key column for a table
    FOR m_data IN (SELECT column_position, ai.column_name
      FROM all_ind_columns ai, all_constraints ac
      WHERE ai.table_name     =ac.table_name
      AND ai.table_name       =i.table_name
      AND ai.table_owner      = 'user_nm'
      AND ac.owner            = 'user_nm'
      AND ac.constraint_type ='P'
      AND ac.constraint_name =ai.index_name  order by 1) LOOP

        IF m_data.column_position =1 THEN
          sel_stmt    :='select '||m_data.column_name||' as pkey_value1';
          pkey_name1 :=m_data.column_name;
          pkey_count :=1;
        elsif m_data.column_position=2 THEN
          sel_stmt      :=sel_stmt||','||m_data.column_name||' as pkey_value2';
          pkey_name2   :=m_data.column_name;
          pkey_count   :=2;
        elsif m_data.column_position=3 THEN
          --as above(here the table contain primary key with three columns)
        END IF;
      END LOOP; --This is the END LOOP which derived all the primary key column for a table
--This below sel_stmt will form the select statement to extract the version date between 2 scn numbers
sel_stmt :=sel_stmt||',versions_starttime,versions_startscn,versions_operation from '||'user_nm'||i.table_name||' '||'VERSIONS
BETWEEN SCN '||fr_scn ||' and '||to_scn ||' WHERE VERSIONS_OPERATION is NOT NULL AND versions_startscn>='||fr_scn ||' AND versions_startscn<'||
to_scn ||' order by versions_startscn,versions_operation';
--This will bulk collect primary key value, version starttime and version operation for a table.
EXECUTE immediate sel_stmt bulk collect INTO v_pkey_1_idx_tab,v_ver_starttime_tab,v_ver_startscn_tab,v_ver_operation_tab;
--This will form (only one time for each table)the dynamic update statement with bind variable.
    u_update_stmt :='update '||i.table_name||' set m_END_DATE=:1'||',m_UPDATE_DATE=systimestamp where '||pkey_name1||'=:2'|| ' and m_END_DATE is NULL
        and m_DELETE_DATE is NULL AND m_START_DATE <:3';

    FOR each_tab_rec IN 1..v_pkey_1_idx_tab.count LOOP --This will update,delete each records in a table between 2 SCNs
      IF v_ver_operation_tab(each_tab_rec) ='U' THEN
        EXECUTE immediate u_update_stmt USING v_ver_starttime_tab(each_tab_rec),v_pkey_1_idx_tab(each_tab_rec),v_ver_starttime_tab(each_tab_rec);
        END IF;
      END LOOP;--End loop for update and delete of records in a table between 2 SCNs
  END LOOP;   --end of main loop which works for each table present in MAPPING_TABLE
END;
/
```

The difference between two approaches are:

> First one was not using **bind variables** whereas second one **uses** them.
> First one forms the string for each record inside "FOR each_tab_rec IN 1..." Loop however second one forms the string only once before the LOOP.
> First one undergoes **many parses** and **many executes** whereas second one uses **one parse many executes** as it uses **bind variables** which result into improved performance. This behaviour is because oracle checks if the exact full statement is there in library cache by calculating hash value of the sql string. So if you do not use bind variable and use literal then each time the hash value of sql string will be different and hence for every **new** hash value of the string there will be hard parse. However if you use bind variable then the hash value of the SQL string is same and hence there will be one parse instead of millions of parse.

Another advantage of using **bind variable** is that it prevents SQL INJECTION attacks. When PL/SQL user provides input (let us say some password to validate the login credential) to online program it may form dynamic sql statement by replacing the variable with the user input (because **bind variable** is not used in the code) and thus exposing the details for malicious program to access the password. But using bind variable stops any kind of malicious database attacks as the bind variable values are not exposed/replaced by user input.

"SQL INJECTION" is an unintended database intrusion by a malicious program (by hackers) to steal data and to gain unintended access to the database. To minimize "SQL INJECTION" attack you can use bind variables in your code and make the code as per "invoker right model" and thus not exposing all the privileges to invoking users and also not exposing details to malicious programs. Another way to prevent SQL INJECTION attacks is to use DBMS_ASSERT package which will identify possible attack and abort the attempt. Details of how to use this package to prevent INJECTION attack is out of scope of this book.

Bulk operation process multiple rows at a time and reduce the context switching between SQL and PL/SQL engines. However there are scenario where BULK operation hinder performance. Here we will see how to resolve the use BULK operation without any hindrance to performance.

BULK COLLECT: In a single fetch retrieve multiple rows. SELECT statement uses this clause.
FORALL: Change multiple rows quickly by sending all the DML to SQL engine from PL/SQL engine with just one context switch.

Bulk operation improve performance however there are scenarios where they will **hinder performance of the system:**

Suppose you fetch millions of rows in a collection variable which will consume a huge amount of memory in PGA for that session and similarly another 100 users also call the same program and consume a huge amount of PGA memory. This will result in performance degradation for other application running in the system because of excessive PGA swapping.

Again via network when you update millions of rows using bulk binding it may cause network slowness because all the rows you bulk fetched into a collection may not be accommodated in the PGA and hence slow down the performance because of excessive swapping which slam the network.

If you fetch a single row at a time it is too slow and takes a long time to process millions of rows so bulk fetch is essential but not at the cost of jamming the network by causing performance degradation across the system.

So for effective performance improvement using BULK COLLECT there should be a trade-off between bulk operation and huge PGA memory consumption.

Solution:

You can control the amount of PGA memory consumption by bulk collect using **"LIMIT"** clause
This way you get the benefit of BULK COLLECT and not allowing the PGA memory swapping to happen.

```
DECLARE
  CURSOR C1 IS SELECT * FROM employee;
  TYPE t1 IS TABLE OF C1%ROWTYPE INDEX BY BINARY_INTEGER;
  v_emp t1;
BEGIN
  OPEN C1;
  LOOP
    FETCH C1 BULK COLLECT INTO v_emp LIMIT 10000;
    EXIT WHEN v_emp.COUNT=0;
    FORALL i IN 1 .. v_emp.COUNT
    UPDATE employee SET salary =salary*1.5 WHERE emp_id=v_emp(i).emp_id;
  END LOOP;
  CLOSE C1;
END;
/
```

So using **"LIMIT"** clause you bulk fetch **10000** rows at a time instead on 1 million rows and hence this consume considerably less amount of PGA memory but process all the rows like a nice steady stream of data.

Note: Instead of the below one(This one is correct and must be used as shown above)

```
EXIT WHEN v_emp.COUNT=0;
```

Do not use the following one

```
EXIT WHEN C1%NOTFOUND;
```

(Which many of the developer <u>are in the habit</u> of using and hence mentioning here)

Because if you use **C1%NOTFOUND** it will exit the LOOP when you have some fraction of **10000** records (Let us say you have **10012**) and hence for remaining **12** records the UPDATE statement will not be executed because in 2nd loop after you fetch the remaining 12 records **C1%NOTFOUND** will evaluate to true and hence exit the LOOP.

However if you still would like to use **C1%NOTFOUND** them use the EXIT just before the **"END LOOP"** (<u>not immediately after the "FETCH"</u>) **as shown below:**

```
EXIT WHEN C1%NOTFOUND;
END LOOP;
CLOSE C1;
```

Chapter 9: Generic know how on oracle administration for developer and dba (32 Pages)

In database development knowing how a feature can be implemented in different versions of the database is a matter of necessity.

When I started using oracle versions 10g, 11g and 12c in parallel in multiple projects I found it extremely difficult to navigate between different versions of Oracle releases.

There are a lot of additional features in Oracle 12c which require an alternative approach to derive similar functionality in database versions prior to 12c.

In this chapter we will cover **SQL, PL/SQL (for developer and dba)** tips not covered in previous chapters so that you will know the different approaches employed in different releases of database to achieve the same functionality.

Tips 1: Read only user can lock a system on a transaction, resolution in 12c?
Tips 2: How to find the value of bind variable while running the application?
Tips 3: Granting a Role to PL/SQL subprogram instead of USER in 12c?
Tips 4: Adaptive query optimization and online stats gathering in 12c?
Tips 5: Faster online table column addition in 12c?
Tips 6: DDL LOGGING and ONLINE DDL in 12c?
Tips 7: Foreign key is ignored in database?
Tips 8: How to enhance performance by adjusting Oracle clustering Factor
Tips 9: Oracle table Interval Partitioning
Tips 10: Adding multiple new Partition in 12c
Tips 11: Global temporary table enhancement
Tips 12: How to forecast performance of Oracle system
Tips 13: Throughput and response time concept
Tips 14: FGAC / VPD in Oracle with simple example
Tips 15: How to know all the dependent tables (parent and child) of any specific tables
Tips 16: Blocking session and blocked session and top running queries
Tips 17: Long running Oracle query predict the finish time
Tips 18: Selectivity/Cardinality/histograms and its importance in performance tuning
Tips 19: Find the OS of the server where oracle is running
Tips 20: Find SQL in your application without bind variable
Tips 21: Stats gathering improvement in 12c
Tips 22: SQL TRACE and TKPROF formatting?
Tips 23: Fundamental of HEAT MAP in 12c
Tips 24: Case insensitive unique constraint for a table column
Tips 25: understanding ORA_ROWSCN and block number for table rows
Tips 26: Primary key with non-unique value, possible?
Tips 27: Multitenant container database with Pluggable database option in 12c

Tips 1: Read only user can lock a system on a transaction, resolution in 12c?

Here we will demonstrate how a user having read only access to a schema can lock the system and will discuss possible solution in 12c and prior to 12c.

In oracle you can give "grant select" on a table to a read only user using
"**Grant select on table_name to read_only_user**" and then **read_only_user** can run the below select from his read only session:

```
SELECT *
FROM    Prod.ref_data
FOR UPDATE;
```

However this statement will lock the table and prevent any DML operation by any user (not even the owner of the table i.e. prod) who has insert/update/delete privileges.

This is really serious situation. Prior to 12c there are two possible resolutions:
1. DBA need to kill the read only session to release the lock or
2. The read only user need to give commit or exit the session.

In 12c the situation can be avoided by giving "grant **read**" **instead** of "grant **select**" on the table to the read only user:

```
grant read on Prod.ref_data to read_user;
```

This means the read only user will not have sufficient privilege to run the SELECT FOR UPDATE statement.

Note: Prior to Oracle 11g you cannot make a table read only in a tablespace where other tables are read write. However 11g onward you can make a table read only and read write in the same tablespace using command:

```
ALTER TABLE <TABLE NAME> READ ONLY;
```

You can convert it into read write using

```
ALTER TABLE <TABLE NAME> READ WRITE;
```

Tips 2: How to find the value of bind variable while running the application?

Here we will discuss a way to find how far your PL/SQL code has been executed by extracting the value of bind variable at particular point of time.

We have seen it is sometimes important to know how far your code has been executed as it runs.
Currently when a top level query is running, the log will record when each subquery starts and finishes but when a subquery using a bind variable is running, the current value of the bind variable is not shown. In order to know the bind variable value whilst the subquery is running, use the following query:

```
SELECT DISTINCT Sq.Sql_Text,
  Spc.Name,
  SUBSTR(Spc.Value_String,1,15) bind_value
FROM V$Sql_Bind_Capture Spc,
  V$Session S,
  V$Sql Sq
WHERE S.Sql_Hash_Value =Spc.Hash_Value
AND S.Sql_Address       = Spc.Address
AND Sq.Sql_Id           =S.Sql_Id
AND spc.was_captured    ='YES';
```

Tips 3: Granting a Role to PL/SQL subprogram instead of USER in 12c?

Here we will discuss how to provide role to a subprogram instead of granting role to a schema and avoid a big security threat.

By default subprograms are created based on definer right.
Execute privilege on the subprogram must be granted to the invoking schema by the definer schema in order to call the subprogram from a different schema
From the invoking schema you can execute the subprogram even if you do not have access to underlying structure (i.e. you cannot **select/insert/delete** from the table mentioned in the subprogram from SQL but can access through subprogram). This is fine in **definer right** subprogram as you do not expose the underlying structure to the invoking schema.

However when you use **invoker right** subprogram which executes under the authority of invoker you need to provide grant (**on the underlying objects**) to the calling user via role/explicit privilege and thus exposing the owner's table completely to the invoking schema. So before 12c each and every subprogram which is called from another schema has same privilege on the owner's tables and hence you expose the schema owner's tables completely to the invoking user.

However in 12c each subprogram when called from another schema could have different privileges on the owner table.

Just to simplify in oracle 12c you can have **function** func1, func2 and **procedure** proc1, proc2 in **schema u1** and each subprogram referring to a table (say t1) from same schema **u1**
But in the calling schema (say **schema u2**) each and every subprogram will have different privilege on the table from **schema u1**. So for example
Func1 may have select privilege on u1.t1
Func2 may have insert privilege on u1.t1
Proc1 may have update privilege on u1.t1
Proc2 may have delete privilege on u1.t1
And schema u2 has no privilege at all and hence schema owner u2 cannot do any operation independently (like select, insert, update or delete from sqlplus). [**Prior to 12c all the privileges percolates to calling user u2 always which could cause security issue as the privileges are exposed completely to the user.**]

Let us take one example how the code based access control works.

```
ALTER session SET "_ORACLE_SCRIPT"=true;
DROP USER u1 CASCADE;
DROP USER u2 CASCADE;
CREATE USER u1 IDENTIFIED BY u1 QUOTA UNLIMITED ON USERS;
CREATE USER u2 IDENTIFIED BY u2 QUOTA UNLIMITED ON USERS;

GRANT CREATE SESSION,CREATE TABLE, CREATE PROCEDURE TO u1,u2;
CONNECT TO u1

CREATE TABLE t1
    (a NUMBER,b VARCHAR2(30)
    );

  INSERT INTO t1 VALUES
    (1,'test'
    );
  COMMIT;
CREATE OR REPLACE
PROCEDURE proc_invoker AUTHID CURRENT_USER
IS
  x VARCHAR2(30);
BEGIN
  SELECT b INTO x FROM u1.t1;
  dbms_output.put_line('the value of x is:'||x);
END proc_invoker;
/

GRANT EXECUTE ON proc_invoker TO u2;

CONNECT TO u2

SELECT * FROM u1.t1;

SET serveroutput ON
EXEC u1.proc_invoker;
```

Both the "SELECT statement" and "procedure proc_invoker execution" will fail with error
```
ORA-00942: TABLE OR VIEW does NOT exist
```

To resolve this prior to 12c here is the step:
```
CONNECT TO SYS

CREATE role r1;
GRANT r1 TO u1,u2;
GRANT SELECT ON u1.t1 TO r1;

CONNECT TO u2
SELECT * FROM u1.t1;
SET serveroutput ON
EXEC u1.proc_invoker;
```

Now both the "SELECT statement" and "procedure execution" will succeed.
But the problem is now u1.t1 is exposed completely to user u2

255

In 12c we can have code based access control so that u1.t1 is not exposed to user but can have different privileges on different subprogram as per your requirement.

So 12c solution is:

```
CONNECT TO SYS
REVOKE r1 FROM u2;
GRANT r1 TO PROCEDURE u1.proc_invoker;
```

If you want to grant UPDATE privilege to the procedure u1.proc_invoker then run this:

```
[
CONNECT TO SYS
CREATE role r2;
GRANT r2 TO u1;
GRANT UPDATE ON u1.t1 TO r2;
GRANT r2 TO PROCEDURE u1.proc_invoker;
]
```

Similarly sys user can give some other privilege to other subprogram of your schema. (**Note you do not provide any privilege to the invoking user, you only provide privilege to the program unit**)

So now if you run

```
CONNECT TO u2
SELECT * FROM u1.t1;
```

It will fail as expected because **schema u2** does not have the privilege.
But the procedure will run fine as the role has been granted to the procedure only.

```
CONNECT TO u2
SET serveroutput ON
EXEC u1.proc_invoker;
```

Tips 4: Adaptive query optimization and online stats gathering in 12c?

Here we will discuss improvement in accuracy of execution plan and enhancement in online statistics gathering in 12c.

Adaptive query optimization is the **new feature** in 12c which helps the optimizer to improve the accuracy of an execution plan.

The purpose of oracle optimizer is to determine the best execution plan for a SQL statement. It makes the decision based on the statistics available and the optimizer used and execution features available in the Oracle release.
If no statistics are available then using dynamic sampling it generates some sample statistics and decides the execution plan.
Please note fixed object statistics (pre 12c approach) do not always give sufficient information to find the most accurate and best execution plan.

In Oracle 12c Oracle has introduced **adaptive query optimization**. This consist of **2 aspects**:

Adaptive plan: This enables the optimizer to delay the final execution plan until the execution of the query is completed. This is done by making adjustments at run-time using dynamic sampling and cardinality feedback. As the query runs, information is collected from and passed between each part of the execution plan, allowing the adaptive plan to switch between the HASH and NESTED LOOP join methods as required.

Adaptive statistics: This provides additional information to improve subsequent execution of the query.

256

In oracle 12c dynamic sampling has been enhanced to have online stats gathering (known as dynamic statistics). The dynamic stats improve the existing statistics by getting more accurate cardinality estimates for tables, Join clause, group clause etc. Initialization parameter OPTIMIZER_DYNAMIC_SAMPLING value "11" enables the optimizer to automatically collect dynamic statistics.

For example, because online stats gathering results are instantly available to the optimizer, we have seen substantial performance improvement when using CTAS (**Create table as select * from**) and IAS (**Insert into ...Select * from**).

Note: If optimizer is not using correct execution plan the query which is expected to finish in few minutes might take few hours due to incorrect cardinality estimates, absence of statistics or out of date statistics.

Tips 5: Faster online table column addition in 12c

Here we will demonstrate that addition of default nullable column in pre-12c, locks the system for a certain duration and generates huge undo and redo, however in 12c this issue is resolved.

In Oracle 11g if you need to add a default column which can be nullable it takes a significant amount of time. However if the default column is not nullable then it is instantaneous.

So the addition of a nullable default column performance issue is addressed in Oracle 12c

Here is one example
Run this in Oracle 11g:

```
CREATE TABLE t2 AS
SELECT * FROM all_objects;
```

Add a default column which is NOT NULL,

```
ALTER TABLE t2 ADD (c5 CHAR(100) DEFAULT 'yes' NOT NULL)
```

This takes 0.4 sec.

Add a default column which is NULLABLE,

```
ALTER TABLE t2 ADD (c6 CHAR(100) DEFAULT 'yes')
```

This takes **15-25 sec** and for this duration it will lock the entire table. Also this operation generates large amount of undo and redo.

However, when you run exactly same operations in **12c** both will take less than 0.4 sec and there is no locking.

To see the size growth of the table you can do as below in 11g and 12c:
Step 1:

```
ANALYZE TABLE T2 compute statistics;

SELECT AVG_ROW_LEN*NUM_ROWS/1024/1024
  ||' MB' size_of_table
FROM all_tables
WHERE owner   ='SCHEMA_NAME'
AND table_name='T2';
```

Step 2:
```
ALTER TABLE t2 ADD (c6 CHAR(100) DEFAULT 'yes')
```
Step 3:
```
ANALYZE TABLE T2 compute statistics;

SELECT AVG_ROW_LEN*NUM_ROWS/1024/1024
  ||' MB' size_of_table
FROM all_tables
WHERE owner    ='SCHEMA_NAME'
AND table_name='T2';
```

You can see there is significant growth in table size in oracle 11g, However in oracle 12c the growth is nominal.

Tips 6: DDL LOGGING and ONLINE DDL in 12c?

Here we will discuss how oracle write the DDL history in a dedicated log file and also understand how ONLINE DDL are performed.

Oracle 11g has introduced parameter **ENABLE_DDL_LOGGING** which will write DDL into alert log file
The alert log file is very large making it difficult to find the DDL versions.

However in Oracle 12c all the DDL is written into a dedicated log file located in "ADR Home"/log/DDL.

ADR Home can be found using below query:
```
SELECT name, value FROM v$diag_info WHERE name='ADR Home';
```

In order to log the DDL activity you need to enable the parameter
```
ALTER session SET enable_ddl_logging=true;
```

The DDL log records creation, alteration and drop of packages/procedures/function/Table/Trigger.
This is very useful when you need to know when a different version of a DDL statement was executed and by whom.

So now it is possible to reverse engineer the database as the log captures all versions and times of DDL execution.

ONLINE DDL:
ONLINE DDL signifies you can perform DML operations while doing alteration (DDL) of objects. In Oracle 12c you can perform few DDL operations ONLINE.
```
DROP INDEX EMP_IDX ONLINE FORCE;
ALTER TABLE EMP DROP CONSTRAINT CONS_NM ONLINE;
ALTER INDEX EMP_IDX VISIBLE;
ALTER INDEX EMP_IDX INVISIBLE;
ALTER INDEX EMP_IDX1 UNUSABLE ONLINE;
ALTER TABLE EMPLOYEES SET UNUSED (HIREDATE) ONLINE;
```

In Oracle 11g you can perform only index rebuild ONLINE
```
ALTER INDEX index_name REBUILD ONLINE PARALLEL;
```

That means if index rebuild command is running for 30 minutes, it will not hold lock on the table for 30 min. During 30 min period you can do any DML activities.

Tips 7: Foreign key is ignored in database?

Here we will see some scenarios where a foreign key is ignored.

In the following scenarios a foreign key in a child table is ignored and you will not get an error even if the parent record is not present in parent table. So the below error will not be

shown:
```
        SQL Error: ORA-02291: integrity constraint                    violated - parent key not found
02291. 00000 - "integrity constraint (%s.%s) violated - parent key not found"
```

Scenario 1
In the child table foreign key column is null
Scenario 2
Let us say column "a, b" combination is primary key in parent table. So in the child table (column "a" and "b") will refer to (column "a" and "b") of parent table.
In this case if any one column of the composite foreign key is null then foreign key check is not performed.
So if either Column "a" or Column "b" is null then oracle will not check if the parent record exists even if the other column has a value.

Tips 8: How to enhance performance by adjusting Oracle clustering Factor?

Here we will understand oracle clustering factor and the importance of organizing table data to improve query performance. Clustering factor is a measure of how data in a table is organized and sequenced so that an index scan can retrieve the data with the least effort by searching only a few data blocks instead of all data blocks.
A simple example to visualize this is as below:
You are asked to get 10 rows from a table and these 10 rows are located in 10 different data blocks rather than in a single data block.
A low clustering factor signifies that the data in a table is sequenced with respect to index whereas a high clustering factor signifies that the data in a table is out of sequence with the index and hence an index range scan will consume lots of IO.
So lower the clustering factor, the better the table is organized, and higher the clustering factor the more the table data is scattered.

```
SELECT index_name,
  clustering_factor,
  num_rows
FROM dba_indexes
WHERE table_name='<Table name>';
```

This provides information on how the table data is synchronized with the index.
If we have an index with a low clustering factor value then the optimizer will prefer to use an index scan, if we have an index with a high clustering factor value then the optimizer will prefer not to use an index scan and may choose a table scan.

So, as a rule, DBA will need to re-sequence the table rows in situations where, in your application, the majority of SQL refers to a column with high clustering factor value. Please note by reorganizing the table based on the column which is mostly used you can lower the clustering factor of that index column however the clustering factor of other columns will

be impacted. So there is a trade-off between performance gain by sequencing rows based on the column which is mostly used and performance penalty by disturbing the clustering factor of the other index columns which are not used widely.
So by reorganizing the table [by means of dbms_redefinition utility or by any other
Means like
-Recreating the table/or reinserting data with ORDER BY clause from temp table
-Recreating the table/or reinserting data using APPEND hint from temp table
The application as a whole performs with the best response time because both index and table become compact as can be seen by running the query:

After reorganizing table you need to collect statistics:
```
EXEC dbms_stats.gather_table_stats(ownname=>'SCHEMA NAME',tabname=>'TABLE_NAME')
```
Now you can see space used by table:
```
SELECT table_name,
   blocks, --amount of storage space of table
   num_rows
FROM all_tables
WHERE table_name='TABLE_NAME';
```

Now you can see space used by index:
```
SELECT index_name,
   leaf_blocks,--amount of storage space of index
   num_rows
FROM all_indexes
WHERE index_name='INDEX_NAME';
```

You can observe reorganization make both the table and index much compact in size which results in better performance.

Tips 9: Oracle table Interval Partitioning

Here we will see how automatic new partitions are created based on data.

One of the challenges in partitioning is the creation of new partitions to accommodate new records.
When using date-based range partitioning with each partition storing data for a particular month, you would need to create new partitions as new months arrive.
Removing the on-going maintenance activity to accommodate new data can be done by the help of Interval Partitioning
When you create an interval-partitioned table you use the new interval keyword in the create table statement to indicate the interval that you want each partition to represent.
Oracle Database 11g will automatically create new partitions in the table as the need arises.

Sample example:

```
CREATE TABLE mv_trans
  (
    id              NUMBER NOT NULL PRIMARY KEY,
    lebe_id_owner NUMBER,
    batch_id_in   NUMBER,
    date_inserted TIMESTAMP(9)
 WITH LOCAL TIME ZONE DEFAULT systimestamp NOT NULL, date_modified TIMESTAMP(9)
 WITH LOCAL TIME ZONE DEFAULT systimestamp NOT NULL,
  date_inserted_fresh DATE DEFAULT TRUNC(SYSDATE)
  )
  PARTITION BY RANGE
  (
  date_inserted_fresh
  )
  INTERVAL
  (
    NUMTOYMINTERVAL(1, 'MONTH')
  )
  (
  PARTITION trans_data_p2 VALUES LESS THAN (TO_DATE('17-6-2010', 'DD-MM-YYYY')),
  PARTITION trans_data_p3 VALUES LESS THAN (TO_DATE('17-7-2010', 'DD-MM-YYYY'))
  );
```

Partition names are system-generated names. So you can use the alter table rename partition command to rename these partition names if you like.

Here is an example:

First from oracle dictionary table user_part_tables, find out what the system generated partition name is, then run the command

```
ALTER TABLE mv_trans RENAME partition sys_p41 TO p_Jan_2007;
```

You can migrate existing range-partitioned tables to use interval partitioning.

Suppose you have a range-partitioned table where you create a new partition every month, in that case just run the Below:

```
ALTER TABLE (TABLE name) SET interval (numtoyminterval(1,'MONTH'));
```

Tips 10: Adding multiple new Partitions in 12c?

Here we will show how addition of more than one partition at a time in oracle 12c is done.

Before Oracle 12c it was not possible to add more than one new partition at a time. So to add new partitions you had to execute "alter table add partition" command multiple times. However in Oracle 12c R1 you can add multiple partitions using 1 command as below:

```
Alter table mv_trans add partition
Partition trans_data_p4  VALUES LESS THAN (TO_DATE('17-7-2010','DD-MM-YYYY')),
Partition trans_data_p5  VALUES LESS THAN (TO_DATE('17-8-2010','DD-MM-YYYY')),
Partition trans_data_p6  VALUES LESS THAN (TO_DATE ('17-9-2010','DD-MM-YYYY'));
```

Tips 11: Global temporary table enhancement in 12c?

Here we will find how to reduce redo generation for Global temporary tables in 12c.

Prior to 12c, Oracle global temporary tables generate huge redo because the <u>undo segment is stored in regular undo tablespace</u>.
However In 12c Oracle global temporary tables reduces redo generation substantially by <u>storing the undo segment in temporary tablespace</u> instead of undo tablespace and hence improve performance on creation of GTT. This is useful for reporting as report uses Global temporary table for achieving better performance.

Tips 12: How to forecast performance of Oracle system

Here we will explore forecasting of oracle performance in an oracle system and ways to improve response time.

Here are some basic steps to forecast the oracle system performance.
We need to know some basic concepts like user calls which you see in tkprof report

User calls: It is number of user calls such as login, parse, fetch, or execute

At a certain time to get the user calls we have below query:
```
SELECT name, value FROM v$sysstat WHERE name = 'user calls';
```

To know amount of user calls generated or to get total raw oracle workload data within certain period, we can run the query before and after a certain interval of time as below:

```
SELECT name, value FROM v$sysstat WHERE name = 'user calls';
```
The output is: user calls   5100
Then tell the system to sleep for 500 seconds
Exec sys.dbms_lock.sleep (500);
Run the user query again to get no of user calls
```
SELECT name, value FROM v$sysstat WHERE name = 'user calls';
```

The output: user   calls 9100

So the **arrival rate** of workload is
= (s1-s0)/T= (9100-5100)/500
=4000/500
 =8
To know what the CPU utilization is we need to run the following command from UNIX
 SAR -u 500 1

Linux 2.6.18-164.11.1.e	12/14/2015 04:33:15 PM	CPU e	%user	%nice	%system	%iowait	%steal %idle
04:34:55 PM all		15.99	0.00	9.01	0.08	0.00	74.5

So the **CPU utilization** = user time + system time
 =15.99+9.01=25%

Now to derive **service time** for each transaction (Considering it is **10 CPU mchine**) the formula is
svc time= (CPU utilization)*(no of CPU)/ (rate of arrival)

=.25*10/8
=0.3125 s

So if you increase no of CPU the svc time will reduce

Now to find the **response time** system formula
Response time= (svc time)/ (1- CPU utilization %)
=0.3125/ (1-0.25)
=0.4166

This way we can forecast the performance of any oracle database system and can take appropriate action like adding more CPU or adding faster CPU, increase CPU utilization etc. to have a better response time.

Note: For the R&D I refer the formula given by Mr. Dan to calculate service time and response time to forecast the oracle system performance

Tips 13: Throughput and response time concept

Here we will understand throughput/response time and ways to improve both.

Throughput is the measure of number of transactions per seconds.
Response time is the measure of average elapsed seconds per records retrieved.
When optimizer **goal** is best throughput you set optimizer_mode=all_rows.
When optimizer **goal** is best response time you set optimizer_mode=first_rows

So when you are working on a Decision Support System where you want to improve the performance of reporting application and at the same time need to have best throughput of the application then you check the top disk usage by top 5 query using the following step:

```
SELECT schema,
  sql_text,
  disk_reads,
  ROUND (cpu, 2)
FROM
  (SELECT s.parsing_schema_name schema,
    t.sql_id,
    t.sql_text,
    t.disk_reads,
    t.sorts,
    t.cpu_time / 1000000 cpu,
    t.rows_processed,
    t.elapsed_time
  FROM v$sqlstats t
  JOIN v$sql s
  ON (t.sql_id              = s.sql_id)
  WHERE parsing_schema_name = 'SCOTT'
  ORDER BY disk_reads DESC
  )
WHERE ROWNUM <= 5;
```

So the challenges are
1. Throughput of the DSS needs to be improved

2. Response time of the reporting application needs to be improved

Please note there are many ways to improve the throughput and response time of an application which you will find in this book. However in this Tips, I will throw light on the "direct path loading and compression perspective" of improving throughput and response time.

To improve the throughput:
Set the table's logging attribute to NOLOGGING thus redo generation for direct path operations is minimized (this feature has no effect on regular DML operations).

1. ALTER TABLE table_name NOLOGGING;
2. Use direct path loading
   Here are the few ways to improve this kind of operation
   a. INSERT /*+ APPEND */ INTO table name SELECT (sub query based on source tables joins)
   b. INSERT /*+ APPEND_VALUES */ INTO table_name VALUES (...........);
   c. DROP table table_name;
      CREATE TABLE table_name as select (sub query based on source tables joins)
3. Use parallel loading
   INSERT /*+ PARALLEL (table_name, 6) */ INTO table name SELECT (sub query based on source tables joins)

For the options **2 a), 2 b) and 3** you must make sure the data is committed immediately after executing the direct path insert, otherwise it will not allow you to "SELECT" the record from that table and the subsequent select will fail with oracle error ORA-12838.

The APPEND hints tell the database to find the last block and placed the newly inserted records at the end of the table's physical storage space (datafiles). This step will write the inserted data directly in the datafiles bypassing data block buffer cache.
Please note point 1 and point 2 combined make the DML very fast.

However if you can combine 1, 2 and 3 steps then it will work extremely fast.
Steps 2 and 3 can be combined to take advantage of APPEND and PARALLEL hints together as below:
   a. INSERT /*+ APPEND PARALLEL(table_name,6) */ INTO table name SELECT (sub query based on source tables joins)

Important thing to consider before using PARALLEL processing: It uses more I/O resource and more processing memory and hence you must make sure the system has enough CPUs. The more CPUs you have the higher the degree of parallelism you can employ in your query.
Total number of threads spawned when you set degree of parallelism to 6:
6*2+1=13 processes or threads generated for the parallel operation.
So a 13 CPU machine is required to run the parallel operation.
The degree of parallelism in a parallel query must be set based on how many CPUs are available.

To improve response time:
When you compress data as it is loaded the data will be compacted into fewer database blocks and thus will require less I/O for subsequent reads from the table and result in improved data retrieval performance.

```
CREATE TABLE t1 COMPRESS AS SELECT * FROM t2;
```
This will create a table with compress data and subsequent direct path load will load the data in compress mode.

To compress a table command is:

```
ALTER TABLE t1 compress;
```

To compress the existing data of the table and activate it for future data loads command is
```
ALTER TABLE t1 move compress;
```

Tips 14: FGAC / VPD in Oracle with simple example

Here we will explore how different user can see different data from same table.

Virtual Private Database (VPD) allows different user to access the same table but restricts the access and allows each user to see the relevant data only from the same table.
VPD is implemented using Oracle's Fine Grained Access Control (FGAC). It provides a row-level security mechanism based on dynamic predicates acquired at statement parse time, when the base table or view is referenced.
For example, if a user is supposed to see only accounts of account manager 'ADMIN', the FGAC setup automatically rewrites the query:
```
SELECT * FROM empl;
```
To:
```
SELECT * FROM EMP WHERE ENAME = 'ADMIN';
```
Let us take one example of how it works

Connect to sys and grant:
```
GRANT EXECUTE ON DBMS_RLS TO PUBLIC;
```

Conn scott/tiger
```
SELECT * FROM empl;
```

EMPNO	ENAME	MGR	SAL	DEPTNO
7876	ADAMS	7788	1100	20
7900	JAMES	7788	950	30
7788	FORD	7566	3000	20
7566	MILLER	7782	2300	10

```
Create user ADAMS identified by ADAMS;
Create user JAMES identified by JAMES;
Create user FORD identified by FORD;
Create user MILLER identified by MILLER;
Grant dba to ADAMS, JAMES, FORD, MILLER;
```

Create the policy function:

```
CREATE OR REPLACE
  FUNCTION rls_policy_fun(
      p_schema IN VARCHAR2,
      p_object IN VARCHAR2)
    RETURN VARCHAR2
  AS
  BEGIN
    IF (USER=p_schema) THEN
      RETURN '';
    ELSE
      RETURN 'ename=user';
    END IF;
  END;
  /
```

Add the policy:

```
Begin
dbms_rls.add_policy( object_schema => 'SCOTT',
   object_name => 'EMP1',
   policy_name => 'POLICE_FOR_EMP',
   function_schema => 'SCOTT',
   policy_function => 'RLS_POLICY_FUN',
   statement_types => 'SELECT,INSERT,UPDATE,DELETE',
   update_check => TRUE,
   enable        =>TRUE);
end;
/
```

Now you can see each user will get a different result and can do different DML activities:

Conn ADAMS/ADAMS

```
SELECT * FROM scott.emp1;
```

EMPNO	ENAME	MGR	SAL	DEPTNO
7876	ADAMS	7788	1100	20

```
UPDATE scott.emp1 SET sal=sal*1.1 WHERE ename='FORD';
```
0 rows updated.
Even if there is record for ename='FORD'

266

```
INSERT
INTO scott.empl
  (
    empno,
    ename,
    mgr,
    sal,
    deptno
  )
  VALUES
  (
    7777,
    'MILLER',
    7782,2200,10
  );
```
ERROR at line 1:
ORA-28115: policy with check option violation

```
DELETE FROM scott.empl WHERE ename='FORD';
```
0 rows deleted.

So using FGAC we are able to restrict the DML activity in the table also we are able to restrict the view on sensitive data!!!!

Please note:
1. FGAC is not applicable for sys user:
2. Referential key integrity may or may not work when there is parent child relationship.
3. If you use "statement_types => 'SELECT' " instead of "statement_types => 'SELECT,INSERT,UPDATE,DELETE' " in the add_policy, then the policy is applicable for select only and hence the user will not be able to delete/insert/update the records associated to them, they will only be able to view the records associated to them.

Example:

Conn FORD/FORD

```
SELECT * FROM scott.empl;
```

EMPNO	ENAME	MGR	SAL	DEPTNO
7788	FORD	7566	3000	20

Conn scott/tiger
```
SELECT * FROM scott.empl;
```

EMPNO	ENAME	MGR	SAL	DEPTNO
7876	ADAMS	7788	1100	20
7900	JAMES	7788	950	30
7788	FORD	7566	3000	20
7566	MILLER	7782	2300	10

Enter password: ***
Connected.

```
SELECT * FROM scott.empl;
```

EMPNO	ENAME	MGR	SAL	DEPTNO
7876	ADAMS	7788	1100	20
7900	JAMES	7788	950	30
7788	FORD	7566	3000	20
7566	MILLER	7782	2300	10

Note that for sys (and the table owner) the policy check does not apply.

Tips 15: How to know all the dependent tables (parent and child) of any specific tables

Here we will find dependent tables of any table
The following query returns all the associated dependent tables of table "XXX"

```
SELECT a.table_name,
    a.constraint_type
FROM all_constraints a,
    all_constraints b
WHERE b.constraint_type ='R'
AND a.constraint_name    = b.r_constraint_name
AND b.table_name         = 'XXX'
UNION ALL
SELECT table_name,
    constraint_type
FROM all_constraints
WHERE r_constraint_name IN
    (SELECT constraint_name FROM all_constraints
    WHERE table_name = 'XXX'
    );
```

Result:

Table_name	Constraint_type
X1	P
Y1	R
Z1	R

P- Primary key constraint
R- Referential integrity constraint

Tips 16: Blocking session and blocked session and top running queries

Here we will find the session that is blocked by some other sessions, and the reason for wait. Also will find the top queries based on I/O, run time.

Here are some frequently used queries which help to find out bottleneck of any oracle issue.

Find blocking session and all the blocked sessions:

```
SELECT sess1.username
    || '@'
    || sess1.machine         <---- Blocking session details
    || ' ( SID='
    || sess1.sid
    || ' ) is blocking '
    || sess2.username
    || '@'
    || sess2.machine         <---- Blocked session details
    || ' ( SID='
    || sess2.sid
    || ' ) ' AS block_status
FROM v$lock lock1,
    v$session sess1,
    v$lock lock2,
    v$session sess2
WHERE sess1.sid    =lock1.sid
AND sess2.sid      =lock2.sid
AND lock1.BLOCK    =1
AND lock2.request > 0
AND lock1.id1      = lock2.id1
AND lock1.id2      = lock2.id2 ;
```

Find blocked object using v$LOCKED_OBJECT:

```
SELECT l.oracle_username ,
    o.owner,
    o.object_name,
    o.object_type
FROM v$locked_object l,
    dba_objects o
WHERE l.object_id = o.object_id
```

Find top 5 query for max I/O:

```
SELECT sql_text,
    disk_reads
FROM
    (SELECT sql_text,
        buffer_gets,
        disk_reads,
        sorts,
        cpu_time/1000000 cpu,
        rows_processed,
        elapsed_time
    FROM v$sqlstats
    ORDER BY disk_reads DESC
    )
WHERE rownum <= 5;
```

269

Find top 5 query for max elapsed/runtime:

```sql
SELECT sql_text,
   elapsed_time
FROM
   (SELECT sql_text,
      buffer_gets,
      disk_reads,
      sorts,
      cpu_time/1000000 cpu,
      rows_processed,
      elapsed_time
   FROM v$sqlstats
   ORDER BY elapsed_time DESC
   )
WHERE rownum <= 5;
```

Get the reason for wait:

```sql
SELECT username,
   sid,
   event,
   state,
   wait_time,
   seconds_in_wait
FROM v$session
WHERE state    ='WAITING'
AND event NOT IN ('SQL*Net message to client', 'SQL*Net message from client','rdbms ipc message')
AND username   ='SYS';
```

Tips 17: Long running Oracle query predict the finish time?

Here we will explore how to find how far your SQL query has been executed and how much time left to finish execution.

We have seen many times that oracle takes a long time to execute a single query or set of queries.
Here are the steps to find out how long a query will take to complete its execution:

First of all run the following query which will give the top queries and corresponding SID, based on latest run.

```sql
SELECT s.username,
   s.sid,
   s.status,
   t.sql_text
FROM v$sqltext t,
   v$session s
WHERE t.address  = s.sql_address
AND t.hash_value = s.sql_hash_value
AND s.username    = '<provide the user name>'
ORDER BY s.sid,t.piece;
```

270

The query can be written as below if you do not have access to v$sqltext

```
SELECT a.sid,
  a.serial#,
  b.sql_text
FROM v$session a,
  v$sqlarea b
WHERE a.sql_address=b.address
AND a.username      ='Provide user name'
ORDER BY a.sid;
```

From the output of the above query you can identify the query you want to know the execution time of and note down the corresponding SID.

To find how much more time the query will take to finish its execution run this:

```
SELECT username,
  target,
  sofar blocks_read_sofar,
  totalwork total_blocks_to_read,
  ROUND(time_remaining/60) minutes
FROM v$session_longops
WHERE sofar    <> totalwork
AND username   = '<Provide the user name>'
AND SID            =<provide the sid value FROM earlier step>;
```

Tips 18: Selectivity/Cardinality/histograms and their importance in performance tuning?

Here we will discuss performance related terminology like selectivity, cardinality and histograms.

Cardinality is the measure of unique number of specific value in a table column.
Selectivity is the measure of variety of the column value in relation to total number of rows in that table.
To derive **selectivity** the formula is:

Selectivity of column1= (Cardinality of column1) * 100 / (Number of rows in the table)

So if we have Table EMP which has 10000 records with columns gender, age, emp_id.
The age can be between 20 and 40

The **cardinality** of gender column is: 2 (male or female)
The **selectivity** of gender column is: 2*100/10000=0.02%

The **cardinality** of age column is: 20 (approx.)
The **selectivity** of age column is: 20*100/10000=0.2%

The **cardinality** of emp_id column is: 10000 (as this is primary key)
The **selectivity** of emp_id column is: 10000*100/10000=100%

Query optimizer uses the selectivity of a column to decide if it is worth to use the index or not to find a certain row in a table.

271

When data in a certain column is not distributed evenly then it is difficult to predict the **cardinality** or **selectivity** of the column.

The **selectivity of query/index** is derived based on (**Number of indexed rows fetched for certain query*100/Total number of rows**) and hence if the data distribution is skewed you cannot use the generic "**selectivity or cardinality**" formula as this will give wrong result. So for this kind of scenario Oracle provides **Histograms** which predict cardinality.

Histogram is a special type of column statistics which provide detail information about data distribution which are skewed/uneven in nature.

A new feature of the dbms_stats package has the ability to look for columns that should have histograms, and then automatically create the histograms.

By using the below steps Oracle will automatically find the columns which have uneven data distribution and create histograms for them. When you use "Method_opt" as "skewonly" as shown below oracle looks for data distribution of each column and creates histograms only for the columns which have uneven data distribution.

Exec dbms_stats.gather_table_stats ('HR','EMPLOYEES', method_opt=> 'for all columns size skewonly');
HR   -> is name of the Schema
EMPLOYEES -> name of table

To check which tables and which columns have **histogram statistics** just run this:
```
SELECT column_name,table_name,histogram
FROM DBA_TAB_COLUMNS
WHERE table_name='EMPLOYEES';
```

Tips 19: Find the OS of the server where oracle is running?

Here we will find how to get the operating system of your oracle server.

In order to find the OS of the server the database is running on, here is the code:

```
SET serveroutput ON
BEGIN
  dbms_output.put_line (dbms_utility.port_string);
END;
/
```

Output:
```
PL/SQL procedure successfully completed.

x86_64/Linux 2.4.xx
```

Tips 20: Find SQL in your application without bind variable?

Here we will find how to identify the queries in your application which do not use bind variables.

As you know using bind variable will reduce the hard parse substantially and improve performance however there is still lots of SQL used in an application where bind variables are not used.
In order to find and identify these SQLs here is the code:

```
WITH no_bind AS
        (SELECT force_matching_signature,
                COUNT( * )  matche_count,
                MAX(sql_id || child_number) max_sql_child,
                DENSE_RANK() OVER (ORDER BY COUNT( * ) DESC) AS ranking
        FROM v$sql
        WHERE force_matching_signature <> 0
          AND parsing_schema_name = '<SCHEMA_NAME>'
        GROUP BY force_matching_signature
        HAVING COUNT( * ) > 5)
  SELECT sql_id,matche_count, parsing_schema_name, sql_text
    FROM        v$sql JOIN no_bind
      ON (sql_id || child_number = max_sql_child)
  WHERE ranking <= 10
  ORDER BY matche_count DESC;
```

This will provide us with SQL used in an application which does not use bind variables, is present in the cache with different literals and the same sql occurs more than 5 times with different literals.
In cases where bind variables are used then there would have been only one entry in the cache instead of 6 or more entries for each SQL.

This is very useful to find SQLs which will potentially cause performance problems. How you can use bind variable, you can refer to Chapter 8: Tips 17: **Improve performance by incorporating one parse and multiple execute**

Note: If the application is not using bind variables then there will be an increase in hard parsing which cause performance penalty. So it is advisable to modify the application to use bind variables. However when it is not possible to modify the application, you can still avoid hard parse to some extent using the "**CURSOR_SHARING**" parameter as below:

```
ALTER session SET cursor_sharing=force; --session level
ALTER system SET cursor_sharing=force;  --system level
```

The parameter "FORCE" lets the database replace the literal values by system generated bind variables which in turn improve performance by reducing number of hard parse considerably. There are some implication when you use this setting, so you must be careful before you set the parameter in SYSTEM level.
To get the system statistics related with amount of hard parse and total parse, just use dynamic performance view V$SYSSTAT

```
SELECT * FROM V$SYSSTAT WHERE NAME LIKE 'parse%';
```

The output:

STATISTIC#	NAME	CLASS	VALUE	STAT_ID
622	parse time cpu	64	259008	206905303
623	parse time elapsed	64	868538	1431595225
624	parse count (total)	64	56326820	63887964
625	parse count (hard)	64	704647	143509059
626	parse count (failures)	64	45726	1118776443
627	parse count (describe)	64	1724	469016317

You can see no of hard parse: 704647 out of total parse: 56326820. Percentage of hard parse=704647*100/56326820 %

In case you see percentage of hard parse is more than 5-10% you must take action to reduce the hard parsing by finding all the SQL which does not use bind variable using query given in this tips.

V$SYSSTAT dynamic view is very handy to get amount of **table scan** happening in the system by using the predicate: 'NAME LIKE 'table scan%'' in the above query

Tips 21: Stats gathering improvement in 12c?

Here we will demonstrate, in 12c how you can gather statistics of multiple objects in parallel

Oracle optimizer decides the best way of retrieving data from a database based on execution plan. The execution plan is generated based on statistics present in the database. Oracle stats contain
Object statistical information like
  ➢ number of rows,
  ➢ number of distinct values,
  ➢ smallest and largest value,
  ➢ presence of NULL,
  ➢ column histogram ,
  ➢ clustering factor ,
  ➢ Index tree depth etc.

These stats are important information used by the optimizer to estimate the selectivity of WHERE clause predicate and subsequently generate the best execution plan.
Prior to 12c oracle used to gather stats one table at a time. You could parallelize the stats gathering if the table was big enough.
So when you run this **prior to 12c**

```
EXEC DBMS_STATS.GATHER_SCHEMA_STATS('SCOTT');
```

It will gather stats for the whole schema but one object at a time.

12c solution:
In 12c you can gather stats of multiple tables, partitions concurrently.
Here is the setup for achieving this:

```
ALTER SYSTEM SET RESOURCE_MANAGER_PLAN='DEFAULT_MAIN';
ALTER SYSTEM SET JOB_QUEUE_PROCESSES  =4;
EXEC DBMS_STATS.SET_GLOBAL_PREFS('CONCURRENT', 'ALL');
```

Now you can gather stats concurrently for a schema

```
EXEC DBMS_STATS.GATHER_SCHEMA_STATS('SCOTT');
```

Tips 22: SQL TRACE and TKPROF formatting?

Here we will show how to set SQL TRACE and generate human readable trace file using TKPROF utility.

To diagnose a performance issue in an application we trace the SQL activity and then using TKPROF utility we can format the trace file into readable format. Here are the steps:

Connect to user "U1" and run the below steps:

Step 1: start tracing

```
ALTER SESSION SET SQL_TRACE=TRUE;
```

Step 2: Run some SQL queries and also execute some procedure from your application which you would like to trace

Step 3: Get the name of generated trace file using below query. Here p.tracefile will give name and location of trace file.

```
SELECT s.sid,
    s.machine,
    s.username,
    s.port,
    s.terminal,
    s.program,
    s.sql_id,
    sa.sql_fulltext,
    s.serial#,
    s.process,
    p.spid,
    p.tracefile
FROM v$session s,
    v$process p,
    v$sqlarea sa
WHERE s.sid =userenv('sid')--sys_context('userenv','sid')
AND s.paddr = p.addr
AND s.sql_id=sa.sql_id;
```

The output of above query contains tracefile:

```
/oracle/app/oracle/diag/rdbms/pd/trace/db_ora_12566.trc
```

Note: If the above query fails **connect** to **sys** and provide grant and then rerun the above query:

```
GRANT SELECT ON v_$session TO U1;
GRANT SELECT ON v_$process TO U1;
GRANT SELECT ON v_$sqlarea TO U1;
```

Step 4: Run the TKPROF utility (from SQL PROMPT) to convert the tracefile into human readable txt file format

SQL PROMPT>

```
ho TKPROF /oracle/app/oracle/diag/rdbms/pd/trace/db_ora_12566.trc h:\output.txt
```

Now you can open the output.txt file and do your analysis it.

If you want to see the execution plan of each query in the output.txt use this instead:

```
ho TKPROF /oracle/app/oracle/diag/rdbms/pd/trace/db_ora_12566.trc h:\output.txt
EXPLAIN=U1/U1 SYS=NO SORT=EXEELA
```

Here **U1** is username and password, SORT=EXEELA means sorting the SQL in the output.txt based on Elapsed time spent executing.

275

You can use different value for **SORT** parameter e.g.

EXEELA Elapsed time spent executing
PRSELA Elapsed time spent parsing
PRSDSK Number of physical reads from disk during parse
EXECNT Number of executes
FCHCNT Number of fetches

Tips 23: Fundamental of HEAT MAP in 12c

Prior to 12c Information Lifecycle Management (ILM) assistant performs archival of data from high performance storage to low cost storage.

Oracle 12c (under ILM) has introduced "heat map" and "automatic data optimization (ADO)" to improve data storage and compression.
Using heat map oracle internally either compress data or move data to low cost storage tablespace. It tracks when data is being accessed at table level and row level. Heat map provide specific information about the age of data based on hot, warm or cold as explained below:

Hot: It means data is accessed/modified frequently and last accessed/modified date is less than 2 days.
Warm: It means data is accessed/modified not so frequently and last accessed/modified date is greater than 5 days but less than 60 days.
Cold: It means data is accessed/modified rarely and last accessed/modified date is greater than 60 days.

Note: In one single table you can have all these three sets of data.

Implementation of heat map:
The "HEAT_MAP" initialization parameter is used to enable or disable heat map as well as Automatic Data Optimization (ADO). By default it is disabled (OFF).

```
ALTER session SET HEAT_MAP=ON;--session level
ALTER system SET HEAT_MAP =ON;--system level
```

Once enabled all the table and data will be tracked.
Heat map captures details (e.g. read, write, full scan, index lookup etc.) using dictionary view V$HEAT_MAP_SEGMENT and user views USER_HEAT_MAP_SEGMENT, USER_HEAT_MAP_SEQ_HISTOGRAM, USER_HEATMAP_TOP_OBJECTS.

Using heat map, oracle automates policy-driven data movement and compression. To do that DBA has to create multiple policies which compress the set of data (**hot**) in "OLTP" mode, **warm** data can be compressed using "compress for query" mode, and **cold** data can be compressed using "compress for archive" mode. Also DBA can create one more policy to move the **cold** data to low cost storage space.
These policies once created by DBA, are invoked automatically when age criteria for the data is satisfied.

You have a table with unique column ename. The requirement is that ename column should not accept same name no matter whichever case you enter the details.
E.g. ename column you cannot insert both "Asim" and "asim". If you try that it should fail with unique constraint violated error.

```
CREATE TABLE emp_case_in
  (
    empid NUMBER PRIMARY KEY,
    ename VARCHAR2(30) UNIQUE,
    sal   NUMBER(10,3)
  );


INSERT INTO emp_case_in values(1,'Asim',1234);
INSERT INTO emp_case_in values(2,'asim',1234);
```

The above insert statement executed successfully. So the current UNIQUE constraint has not implemented the case insensitive unique constraint.

In order to implement that there are 2 solutions:

Solution 1: Using Virtual column

```
DROP TABLE emp_case_in;

CREATE TABLE emp_case_in
  (
    empid NUMBER PRIMARY KEY,
    ename VARCHAR2(30) UNIQUE,
    sal   NUMBER(10,3)
  );

ALTER TABLE emp_case_in ADD ename_lower VARCHAR2(30) AS (LOWER(ename)) VIRTUAL UNIQUE;
```

Now if you try to run the below INSERT:

```
INSERT INTO emp_case_in(empid,ename,sal) values(1,'Asim',1234);
INSERT INTO emp_case_in(empid,ename,sal) values(2,'asim',1234);
```

It fails with error:

```
SQL Error: ORA-00001: unique constraint (U1.SYS_C0010690) violated
```

Solution 2: Using function based index

```
DROP TABLE emp_case_in;

CREATE TABLE emp_case_in
  (
    empid NUMBER PRIMARY KEY,
    ename VARCHAR2(30) UNIQUE,
    sal   NUMBER(10,3)
  );
CREATE UNIQUE INDEX emp_case_in_idx ON emp_case_in(LOWER(ename));
```

Now if you try to run the below INSERT:

```
INSERT INTO emp_case_in(empid,ename,sal) values(1,'Asim',1234);
INSERT INTO emp_case_in(empid,ename,sal) values(2,'asim',1234);
```

It fails with error:

```
SQL Error: ORA-00001: unique constraint (U1.EMP_CASE_IN_IDX) violated
```

Tips 25: understanding ORA_ROWSCN and block number for table rows

ORA_ROWSCN denotes the **System Change Number (SCN)** <u>for a row</u> in a table. **SCN** is the indicator of committed version of a database.
By default ORA_ROWSCN is stored at block level. That means when any row in a block is modified then all the rows associated with that block will have same new ORA_ROWSCN.

However if you want to get the ORA_ROWSCN at **<u>row level</u>** then the table need to be created with "rowdependencies" enabled. That means when a row is modified then the specific row only will have new ora_rowscn. All the remaining rows associated with the block will have different ORA_ROWSCN.

Example:
Block level (default):

```
CREATE TABLE ora_rowscn_test_blocklevel_tab
  (
   id   NUMBER,
   name VARCHAR2(30)
  );

INSERT INTO ora_rowscn_test_blocklevel_tab VALUES(1,'This is 1st test');
INSERT INTO ora_rowscn_test_blocklevel_tab VALUES(2,'This is 2nd test');
COMMIT;

INSERT INTO ora_rowscn_test_blocklevel_tab VALUES(3,'This is 3rd test');
INSERT INTO ora_rowscn_test_blocklevel_tab VALUES(4,'This is 4th test');
COMMIT;
```

Now if you run the below query:

```
SELECT rowid,
   dbms_rowid.rowid_block_number(rowid)block_number,
   id,
   name,
   ora_rowscn
FROM ora_rowscn_test_blocklevel_tab;
```

ROWID	BLOCK_NUMBER	ID	NAME	ORA_ROWSCN
AF4hyQAAcAAAPRjAAA	62563	1	This is 1st test	69334926763
AF4hyQAAcAAAPRjAAB	62563	2	This is 2nd test	69334926763
AF4hyQAAcAAAPRjAAC	62563	3	This is 3rd test	69334926763
AF4hyQAAcAAAPRjAAD	62563	4	This is 4th test	69334926763

All the 4 rows have same ora_rowscn
As they belong to same block: **62563**

Row level:

```
CREATE TABLE ora_rowscn_test_rowlevel_tab
  (
    id    NUMBER,
    name VARCHAR2(30)
  )
  rowdependencies;
INSERT INTO ora_rowscn_test_rowlevel_tab VALUES(1,'This is 1st test');
INSERT INTO ora_rowscn_test_rowlevel_tab VALUES(2,'This is 2nd test');
COMMIT;

INSERT INTO ora_rowscn_test_rowlevel_tab VALUES(3,'This is 3rd test');
INSERT INTO ora_rowscn_test_rowlevel_tab VALUES(4,'This is 4th test');
COMMIT;
```

Now if you run the below query:

```
SELECT rowid,
  dbms_rowid.rowid_block_number(rowid)block_number,
  id,
  name,
  ora_rowscn
FROM ora_rowscn_test_rowlevel_tab;
```

ROWID	BLOCK_NUMBER	ID	NAME	ORA_ROWSCN
AF4iYEAAcAAAPRrAAA	62571	1	This is 1st test	69335104435
AF4iYEAAcAAAPRrAAB	62571	2	This is 2nd test	69335104435
AF4iYEAAcAAAPRrAAC	62571	3	This is 3rd test	69335106793
AF4iYEAAcAAAPRrAAD	62571	4	This is 4th test	69335106793

This 2 rows have same ora_rowscn

This 2 rows have same ora_rowscn

All rows have different ora_rowscn based on modification even if they belong to same block: 62571

Note: If you have flashback enabled for your table then you can use version query and get the SCN number of a row using VERSIONS_STARTSCN column. (VERSIONS_STARTSCN analogious to ORA_ROWSCN provided you have **rowdependencies** set for the table). How to use version query to derive VERSIONS_STARTSCN refer to Chapter 4: **Flashback** setup and data transfer to warehouse

Getting number of blocks occupied by a table:

```
SELECT COUNT(DISTINCT dbms_rowid.rowid_block_number(rowid))
FROM ora_rowscn_test_blocklevel_tab;
```

Getting number of rows associated with a block:

```
SELECT dbms_rowid.rowid_block_number(rowid) block_number,
  COUNT(*) no_of_rows_in_a_block
FROM ora_rowscn_test_blocklevel_tab
GROUP BY dbms_rowid.rowid_block_number(rowid);
```

Output:

BLOCK_NUMBER	NO_OF_ROWS_IN_A_BLOCK
62563	4

Getting all the rows associated with a block:

```
SELECT *
FROM ora_rowscn_test_blocklevel_tab
WHERE dbms_rowid.rowid_block_number(rowid)=62563;
```

Output:

ID	NAME
1	This is 1st test
2	This is 2nd test
3	This is 3rd test
4	This is 4th test

Note: Remember it is easy for database to derive the result of sql operation when rows are located in same **block** number. So if you have prior knowledge as to which rows are coexisted in same **block** it will help you design your query more efficiently. Always organizing data plays an important role in terms of response time of your application. This query will let you know how the data is physically organized in the disk by letting you know which are the rows present in a block.

Use of ORA_ROWSCN on lost update:

We use "**FOR UPDATE**" clause to resolve lost updates scenarios. Normal use of "**FOR UPDATE**" reduces lost update issues as it will hold the lock on the records while the program update the records. This is good.

However consider a scenario where a record has been updated by **session 1** but not committed, so for this kind of scenario in **session 2,** FOR UPDATE clause will wait for the "COMMIT" from **session 1** and once "COMMIT" is provided by **session 1**, the **session 2** will perform the update by overwriting the update done by earlier COMMIT from **session 1**. This results in LOST UPDATE.

To resolve this "LOST UPDATE" issue here is the fullproof solution using ORA_ROWSCN and "FOR UPDATE" clause:

Session 1

```
UPDATE ora_rowscn_test_rowlevel_tab SET name='This is 444ttth test' ;
```

Session 2

```
DECLARE
  CURSOR c1 IS SELECT ora_rowscn,a.* FROM ora_rowscn_test_rowlevel_tab a FOR UPDATE;
BEGIN
  FOR i IN c1 LOOP
    UPDATE ora_rowscn_test_rowlevel_tab
    SET name       ='This is 44th test'
    WHERE id        =i.id
    AND ora_rowscn=i.ora_rowscn;
  END LOOP;
  COMMIT;
END;
/
```

Here **session 2** will wait for **session 1** to COMMIT and then the PL/SQL block in **session 2** will be executed but will not perform the update because the SCN number of the record when the PL/SQL block started is different from current ORA_ROWSCN. This way you avoid "LOSTUPDATE" performed by **session 1**.

Now if you select you can see that the COMMIT done by **session 1** is not lost.

```
SELECT * FROM ora_rowscn_test_rowlevel_tab;
```

```
  ID   NAME
   1 This is 444ttth test
   2 This is 444ttth test
   3 This is 444ttth test
   4 This is 444ttth test
```

Tips 26: Primary key with non-unique value, possible?

As discussed in Chapter 2, Tips 12: Primary key with UNIQUE index or NON-UNIQUE index
When we create a primary key, automatically oracle will create one unique index.
However it is possible to decouple index creation and primary key.

Here we will show how you can have non unique value in a primary key column.
```
CREATE TABLE test_pri_key_non_uni(a NUMBER);
INSERT INTO test_pri_key_non_uni VALUES(1);
INSERT INTO test_pri_key_non_uni VALUES(1);
INSERT INTO test_pri_key_non_uni VALUES(2);
COMMIT;
```

Now if you want to skip the check on the existing data and want to implement the primary key constraint you will most likely use "NOVALIDATE" clause as below:
```
ALTER TABLE test_pri_key_non_uni ADD CONSTRAINT test_pri_key_contraint
PRIMARY KEY (a) ENABLE NOVALIDATE;
```
However this will fail with error:
```
02437. 00000 -  "cannot validate (%s.%s) - primary key violated"
*Cause:    attempted to validate a primary key with duplicate values or null
           values.
*Action:   remove the duplicates and null values before enabling a primary
           key.
```
So here are the steps if you would like to skip the check on existing data and want to implement primary key constraint on future data:

Step 1:
Create one non unique index on the key column
```
CREATE INDEX test_pri_key_non_uni_idx ON test_pri_key_non_uni(a);
```

Step 2:
Create primary key with "NOVALIDATE" clause
```
ALTER TABLE test_pri_key_non_uni ADD CONSTRAINT test_pri_key_contraint
PRIMARY KEY (a) ENABLE NOVALIDATE;
```

Now you can see the non-unique data (i.e. a=1, a=1 in the table) as part of primary key however any future data will undergo the primary key constraint check.

Tips 27: Multitenant container database with Pluggable database option in 12c

Oracle 12c multitenant container database is based on the architecture for next generation cloud.

In this architecture there is a container database which hold many pluggable databases. All the pluggable databases share the same memory and background process of the container database.

Consider the scenario where in your organization you have a database with set of schema say HR, SALES, GIS, FIN and different group say "DEVELOPER", "TESTER", "DESIGNER" and "DBA" want to use the same framework to do certain work uninterrupted.

In order to achieve that you have to create 4 physical database which means you have to maintain 4 instances.

However in Oracle 12c by virtue of multitenant architecture you can create many pluggable databases which will share the same instance. Now same framework can be independently used by "DEVELOPER", "TESTER", "DESIGNER" and "DBA" By simply creating 4 pluggable databases.

Here are the setup:
Connect to **sys as sysdba** and run all the commands.

To see if 12c database has been created as CDB (container database) just run:

```
SELECT cdb FROM v$database;
```

This will return "YES" or "NO"

To see how many pluggable database are present
```
SELECT con_id, dbid, name FROM v$pdbs;
```
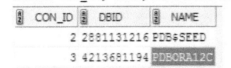

To drop a pluggable database:

```
ALTER pluggable DATABASE PDBORA12C CLOSE immediate;
DROP pluggable DATABASE PDBORA12C including datafiles;
```

Now you see how many pluggable database are present because one is dropped.
```
SELECT con_id, dbid, name FROM v$pdbs;
```
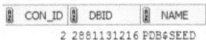

To create a pluggable database:

```
SELECT file_name FROM dba_data_files;
```

FILE_NAME
C:\APP\ASIM.A\ORADATA\ORA12C\USERS01.DBF
C:\APP\ASIM.A\ORADATA\ORA12C\UNDOTBS01.DBF
C:\APP\ASIM.A\ORADATA\ORA12C\SYSTEM01.DBF

```
CREATE pluggable DATABASE pdb_test admin USER dbaclass IDENTIFIED BY dbaclass
FILE_NAME_CONVERT=('C:\APP\ASIM.A\ORADATA\ORA12C\PDBSEED\',
'C:\APP\ASIM.A\ORADATA\ORA12C\pdb_test\');

ALTER pluggable DATABASE pdb_test OPEN;
```

You see how many pluggable database are present:

```
SELECT con_id, dbid, name FROM v$pdbs;
```

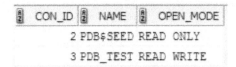

CON_ID	NAME	OPEN_MODE
2	PDB$SEED	READ ONLY
3	PDB_TEST	READ WRITE

"DEVELOPER" can use this pluggable database by running the following command:
```
ALTER session SET container=pdb_test;
```
Now he can use the common framework with set of schemas and work independently.

Similarly you can create another 3 pluggable databases for "DESIGNER", "TESTER" and "DBA"

This way each and every user can use the same framework in terms of object, schema, synonyms etc without any hindrance by other users.

This is truly a boon for database administrator.

INDEX PAGE

Query used to generate the index page:

```
SELECT upper(rpad(idx,30,'-'))
  ||page_number "Index Page"
FROM
  ( SELECT DISTINCT idx,
    listagg(page_no,',') within GROUP(
  ORDER BY page_no) over(partition BY idx) page_number
  FROM test_a
  ORDER BY 1
  )
ORDER BY 1;
```

E

F

G

H

I

J

K

L

M

N

O

P

R

S

291

V

W

X